# Herb Cooley:
# The Law Enforcement
# Legacy of My Father

## Zach Cooley

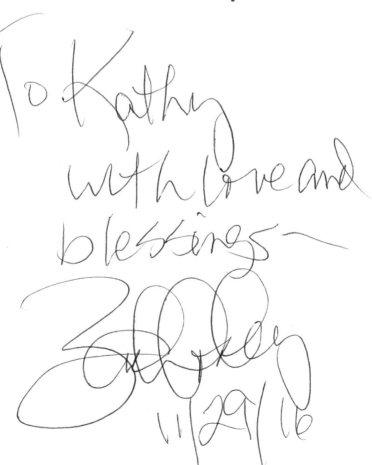

To Kathy
with love and
blessings —

11/29/16

Photos are courtesy of the private collection of Herb Cooley unless otherwise noted.

Information other than personal interviews is courtesy of the following:

Chapter 1-4: *High Point Enterprise* 1966-1974 via newspapers.com subscription

Chapter 5-12: *Southwest VA Enterprise* 1980-1994 via Kegley Library Archives

Chapters 13-19: *Southwest Times* 1994-2000 via online archive of Pulaski County Library.

All quoted or transcribed material was used with permission.

## Acknowledgements

First and foremost, I thank God for allowing me to complete this project, which has been the both the most difficult but gratifying of my career. The fact that He allowed me to share it with my father is one of the greatest privileges of my life. The fact that it also serves as the launching pad for my own company, named in honor of my wife and daughter, makes it even more poignant.

The officers of EmBell Publishing, LLC are the most trusted and reliable people of my life. To my vice president, caregiver and right arm, Jodi Shirk, I have no words to express my gratitude for sacrificing your life so that I may have on. For this project, you have been my number one assistant and cheerleader, combing with me through thousands of newspapers and countless hours of interviews to provide the best story possible. To Marcella Taylor, editor in chief, for your invaluable advice, expertise and support, I am eternally grateful. To my neighbor and partner, transcription specialist Edie Van Marter, you have my eternal friendship for so carefully transcribing all those interviews so meticulously.

Thanks to communications director Sarah Combs for her PR expertise and to art director Diann Lilly for designing my company logo, which honors the memory of my great-grandmother Rose, I am blessed with a decade and counting of partnership. To my assistant and dearest friend Trevor Malchano, for helping me every step of the way, I appreciate you more than you know.

In High Point, thank you to Wayne Pike, Bill Collins, Tommy Bryant, David Armstrong, Stewart Hartley, Van McSwain and Benjamin Collins. In Wythe County, thank you to my Uncle Doug Cooley, former and current sheriffs Wayne Pike, Kermit Osborne, Doug King and Keith Dunagan as well as our dear friend Teny Underwood. I offer a huge thank you to the archive department of Pulaski County Public Library and Wytheville Community

College, especially Mr. William Allen Veslick for his generosity and invaluable resources. In Vinton, thank you to Andy Corbin, Jimmy Houff, Sharon Poff, Kip Vickers and everyone else who participated in any way that I may have forgotten in this brief space. I love you all and thank you from the bottom of my heart!

This is especially for one person. Dad, thank you for the sacrifices you made it your job for your family and your country. Your accomplishments are unprecedented and to express my love and pride for you in this way is a gift beyond measure.

For Dad

## Introduction

When my Dad retired in July 2011, I was amazed when I tried to comprehend the career he was leaving behind. I was obviously aware that my father had been a successful police officer as the leader of two town departments in the final 17 years of his career and second in command of my native county Sherriff's Office 15 years before that. However, to me, he has always been just my Dad.

I knew that he had been the first Chief of Police to ever achieve state accreditation status for the Town of Vinton's department, which had been virtually disgraced before he came into office. It wasn't until attending my father's retirement banquet that I realized that this was only the tip of the iceberg concerning achievements in my father's illustrious 45 years in law enforcement. I never knew that each holiday or birthday my father missed was spent changing the face of how I and my fellow citizens were being protected for the better. Hearing the respected colleagues of my dad and fellow law enforcement leaders from all over Virginia and North Carolina, where Dad started his police career with the High Point Police Department in 1966, praising my father with one accomplishment after another was overwhelming to say the least.

By the time the evening was finished, there wasn't a dry eye in the house. I had an opportunity to interview my dad as a columnist for my hometown newspaper after the retirement banquet. Hearing him discuss his career with me was one of the biggest thrills of my own career. We were both working together as professionals in our respective fields. Moreover, I was given a glimpse of a side of my father I had never known and I wanted to be better acquainted with that side. My father was more than Herb Cooley, my dad. He was Chief Herb Cooley, a respected leader in law enforcement and community service statewide.

The result of my research into this side of my father is the book you now hold in your hands. It is a gift to him, to honor him as best I know how, for his admirable work and sacrifice. It is a gift to my daughter, currently nine months old, so that she will know of her grandfather's impressive professional legacy. It is a gift to me as I intimately acquaint myself with my father's professional side in addition to the terrific opportunity this project has been for me. I pray it will be of equal reward to those who paved the way for him as well as those for whom he paved the way. Most of all, I hope my Dad is as pleased to read it as I have been to write it.

## Chapter 1
## A Quiet Night

My Dad's history as a police officer is very deeply rooted. In 1842, one hundred years before my Dad, Herb Cooley, was born, Benjamin Cooley, his great-great-great grandfather, was appointed the first sheriff of Carroll County, VA. Nearly 170 years later, law enforcement still thrives in our family. My Dad's uncle, Jack Higgins, was Chief of Police in Galax during the 1930s and 1940s. Dad has three first cousins who were Virginia State Troopers. His brother, Doug, who now directs the Southwest Virginia Criminal Justice Training Academy in Bristol, also served as Chief Deputy for the Wythe County Sheriff's Office. He took over this position in 1994, when my Dad left it to become Chief of Police in Pulaski.

"I guess police work does seem to run in the family," Dad agreed. "My brother, Mike, is the smart one and chose a career outside law enforcement."

I have never known my Dad to be anything but a policeman. Some of my happiest memories of my father and I growing up include going to work with him at the Wythe County Sheriff's Office where everyone treated me like family. It seems almost surreal to me that, as of July 1, 2011, my Dad officially retired after an illustrious 45 years in law enforcement.

"Being a police officer requires an even temperament, compassion, and an understanding of human nature," my father told me. "You have to be tough but with a sense of honesty and fairness."

Dad says he's always seemed to fit that role and has done his best to treat fellow officers as he would want a member of his family to be treated.

"If I weren't a police officer, I would have loved to have been an archeologist, anthropologist or a cosmologist," he added. "Those fields really intrigue me, but I'm just not sure that I had the attention span or brains for all the required education."

Throughout his 45 years career, my father has faced a variety of challenges including constantly dealing with members of the public who do anything but respect him.

"You are cursed, assaulted, and threatened on a regular basis," he remarked. "You have to make split second decisions that courts and politicians have months and even years to second guess."

I could relate to some of the challenges Dad mentioned very well.

"You miss birthdays, holidays, and weekends," he recalled. "You routinely see gruesome sights that others only see in horror films."

However, as has always customary for my dad, he has remained tough, something he says everyone in his position must be.

"Police officers have to remain tough without becoming hardened," he said. "It can be physically and psychologically draining."

Of course, along with the tough times, being a police officer comes with its share of rewards including the satisfaction of doing your best to maximize protection of a community as well as putting a criminal behind bars after a grueling case and helping kids get off drugs and onto the right path. These are rewards that, for my Dad, are worth the challenges.

It was my Dad's lifelong friend and field training officer, Bill Collins, whose tearful speech at his retirement banquet choked us all up. Having got my Dad his first police job as a beat cop in 1966 in High Point, NC, they have been friends for more than 60 years.

"I've known him longer than anyone here," he said. "I've followed his career all the way and consider him a great man, a fine officer and a good friend."

When I interviewed Bill Collins, he couldn't recall the year that he first met my dad. However, we can assume it would have been in the fall of 1950. That would have been when my father would have been seven years old and would have been attending his inaugural day of first grade at Baywood Elementary School in Grayson County, Virginia. He had been born just up the road from that schoolhouse on October 25, 1942 to newlywed parents Herbert Wiley and Irene Higgins Cooley.

My grandparents were married by a Preacher Ball on December 13, 1941. They rented a house in the Baywood community and that's where my father, Herbert Gray Cooley would make his earthly debut ten months later. The happiness of the proud parents would be short lived, as Uncle Sam called my grandfather to serve in the U.S. Army during World War II when my dad was just a month old.

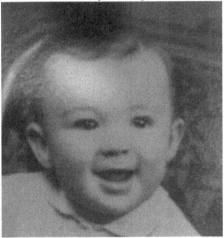

Dad arrived on the scene on October 25, 1942.
A month later, his father was off to war.

With her husband gone indefinitely, my Granny moved back across the road to her large family home that still housed her parents and most of her siblings. The Higgins home was nearly as old as the nation in which it was built. Somewhere within its confines are slave graves among countless other hidden mysteries of its centuries-old past.

"Two rooms were twenty square feet," my great-aunt Annie told me shortly before her death in 2013.

When I was around eight years old, my Dad took me see this old home place, which was also where he spent his childhood. He and my late grandfather showed me around what was left of the large structure, which he explained at the time was built nearly 200 years earlier. Though it was sad for me to see this home in decay, no doubt more so for my father and grandfather, I was fascinated to see what I could. I was especially thrilled to see some old furniture and snuff cans that my father knew belonged to his grandmother, whom he adored.

When Granny moved back home with Dad, her three sisters, Annie, Emma and June still lived at home. With Dad being the firstborn of his generation, he was the apple of each of their eyes. Granny and his three aunts spoiled Dad rotten and he still talks about his childhood with them in glowing terms.

Sadly, the house is now gone, along with all eighteen of my grandmother's siblings. Nevertheless, in 1942, it was overflowing with the love of family with Dad at its center. Meanwhile, my grandfather was halfway across the world risking his life for his country. He would receive the Purple Heart for being hit with shrapnel in his side while staving off the enemy. The lodged ammunition would remain inside my grandfather until his dying day. I can only imagine my grandmother's horror when she read the telegram telling her that her husband had been "slightly wounded" while in battle.

Papa Cooley came home from the war on my Dad's third birthday, October 25, 1945, a memory Dad recalls clearly over seven decades later.

"I remember watching him come over the hill and up onto the porch," he has told me several times. "Mama and I met him at the door and he looked at me with tears in his eyes."

Herbert Wiley Cooley (1921-1997), my
grandfather, spent three years in World War
II.  He received the Purple Heart and came
home on Dad's third birthday.

I can't imagine leaving your only child behind as a newborn only to find your next sighting of him as a three-year-old. However, unlike so many other war stories of the time, my grandfather's ended happily. He made it home. With him, he brought the Swastika patch of a dead Nazi soldier among several other trinkets that prove to be a stirring piece of history to this day.

After the war, my grandparents decided to stay at the Higgins home place that included a full scale farm. Milking cows and feeding chickens were a very small part of my father's every day duties on the farm. My father grew up very poor if you went by his parents' bank book. Their table, however, was always filled with ample portions of food for every meal, all homegrown and prepared by hand. The Cooley family would grow to include my uncles, Michael Lee Cooley, born on August 25, 1950, and Douglas Heath Cooley, born on June 18, 1958.

I didn't have my paternal grandparents in my life for nearly long enough. Granny died on May 17, 1992, when I was just seven. Papa died on August 15, 1997. Cancer claimed them both at ages 72 and 76 respectively. However, I had them both long enough to know that he was a master gardener and carpenter while she was the best cook I ever knew. In my mind, neither of them can be touched to this day at their crafts.

Even as a child, Dad marveled at his father's strength and endurance. He was a very diminutive man of average height and never weighing over 150 pounds for a day in his life. Nevertheless, my Dad can recall with vivid clarity seeing his Dad carrying a fifty pound sack of feed over each shoulder without a groan. Meanwhile, his mother, a tall and lanky beauty with dark hair and eyes, would be busy making from scratch her daily batch of cornbread and biscuits, which were consumed at every meal.

My Dad recalls the days of his childhood without one reflection of hardship or strife, but instead with an increasing sense of nostalgic longing as he grows older. I know his misses Herbert and Irene Cooley very much and so do I. But I do know without question that they raised him to be tough and self-sufficient, which quite possibly led to his career in law enforcement.

This brings me back to the point in which I began my story in which Bill Collins first saw my Dad on the school bus in 1950 on his first day of school. According to Bill, my Dad and his family lived down the Meadow Creek Road, which is now called Delhart Road. They lived up on top of the hill probably three quarters of a mile off that main highway.

"There was just a little road, a country road or driveway and his granddaddy walked him down to the road to meet the bus that morning," Bill told me. "There he was, six, seven years old standing there with his granddaddy and I was on the bus I saw him there on the inside road and that's the first time I ever saw the lad. I got to know him just as the kid that lived down the road and that was what I referred to him as, from that time on."

"I remember one morning we were going down the road in the school bus and there stood Herb with his granddaddy standing on the other side of the bridge but the water was going over the bridge and they couldn't get across the bridge to get to the road to catch the bus," Bill recalled. "We just looked at each other and went on down the road."

Dad and Bill went on to the school in Baywood, which is an old schoolhouse still in operation today. They were among the first students to walk its halls.

"I believe they had the building complete when he started school, but I don't know," Bill surmised. "He might have gone to the old building a little bit before the new one was built but this was in the early 50's."

He and Bill also participated in extracurricular activities within the school such as sports and Boy Scouts.

"I started out with the first original troop that they had there in Baywood," Bill told me. "I remember when they were having a Court of Honor for Herb when he got his tenderfoot there in the school auditorium."

According to the U.S. Scouting Service Project, Tenderfoot is the second rank. A Scout can work on the requirements for the Tenderfoot, Second Class, and First Class ranks at the same time, but each rank must be earned in sequence. The badge is awarded when the Scout completes requirements in the areas of craftsmanship, physical fitness, citizenship, personal growth and Scout spirit.

"This is very unusual," Bill noted. "The Principal we had at the school was Mr. Daniel Slaby and everywhere that old man went, he would start a scout troop. He started one there in Baywood and at one time, I guess there were probably 25 to 30 boys in that troop and the school wasn't sponsoring it, but that's where we met at the school in the evenings."

Bill said that he and Dad were just more or less an acquaintance that during the early years until he graduated in 1958 from Galax High School and went into the Marine Corps.

Dad graduated in 1961. The next year, he enlisted with the U.S. Coast Guard. He was based out of Norfolk, Virginia on a three hundred foot ship called the Absecon. Dad was picked for United States Coast Guard radio school and was sent to Connecticut for the school, at which he excelled. During Dad's period in the service, the Absecon had some interesting history herself.

She was damaged by heavy seas on March 7, 1962 while putting to sea from Norfolk to assist merchant ships during a storm. From July 20-23, 1963, *Absecon* stood by the disabled merchant ship *Seven Seas* in the mid-Atlantic and escorted the ship to St. John's, Newfoundland, Canada. On 13 September 1963, *Absecon* rescued the third engineer of the West German merchant ship *Freiberg* midway between Bermuda and the Azores after he had fallen overboard and remained in the water for 17 hours. In February 1966, *Absecon* stood by the disabled British merchant ship *Parthia* while waiting for a commercial tug. *Absecon* was reclassified as a high endurance cutter and designated as WHEC-374 on May 1, 1966.

Dad served in the North Atlantic for a long time and did cruise to the Caribbean a couple of times. His service in the North Atlantic is noted by one great historical note that amazes me to this day. Dad was the radio man on the ship and he took the message about the assassination of President John F. Kennedy on November 22, 1963. This came in Morse code, which he deciphered and wrote it out for the captain. Dad was the first man on the ship to know that President Kennedy had been killed. Morse code was the only means that they communicated with there in that area.

Serving in the North Atlantic was treacherous duty. Many great vessels have been lost there including the Titanic and the storms and waves are horrifying. Dad saw them come over the ship. Sometimes, the cutter would roll down in between the waves that were like mountains, towering above on both sides. He finished his naval career at Virginia Beach in what he would say was really good duty.

Dad in the Coast Guard, 1963.

"I pulled time in there and I knew Herb at some point in time had gone into the Coast Guard," Bill said. "After we had finished, I was going up to his old home place about 5 miles from where he lived then and saw him in the front yard with his whole family and so I stopped to talk with him."

"Do you know where I could find a job?" Dad asked him.

"I think I could probably get you a job at the High Point Police Department," Bill told him.

"I don't remember exactly how that did happen," Bill admitted. "He went down and met with the Chief, or whatever, when the boy got out of the Service. I know it seemed like he got out of the Coast Guard on a Friday and started working for the High Point Police Department and started rookie school on a Monday or just a very short time thereafter."

"I don't think it was a matter of more than three or four days out," Bill said in response to Dad's saying he went to work the very next day after being honorably discharged from the Coast Guard. "I don't know whether he went to work for the Police Department the next day or not but surely he had tested up."

Either way, Dad never had any particular desire to be a police officer. On March 9, 1963, he married Carolyn Joyce Bartlett and by September 25, he was a father to his firstborn son, Travis Gray Cooley. On May 28, 1965, their second son, John Eric Cooley, was born. In short, he had a family to support and needed a job as quickly as possible.

"He was just getting out of the Coast Guard and he'd had all he could stand of it," Bill added. "He was just looking to get out and go to work."

Bill had joined the police department in the summer of 1963, three years before Dad joined.

"It was during the race riots and everything when I went in and they almost hired me right off the street because they were in bad shape, wanting people to work at that time," he stated. "I remember I was on the Patrol Division and they went on to the Police Academy and then after he got out of the Police Academy, I had, I guess you could call it, a vested interest in the boy, but he asked around and got on my platoon and I was a training coach at that time."

With Bill's experience, he would become Dad's field training officer in addition to being his lifelong friend. He invited Dad to ride along with him for a shift on an autumn evening in 1966. This ride would be etched in the minds of both men forever.

"I believe," Bill began. "I'm not quite sure of this, but the first night that he worked with me. I know it was cold; it was the midnight shift that we worked that night and we were riding down Greene Street and we passed this car, there were four guys in the car. It was still freezing and cold. I was driving; he didn't know the town or anything at that time. So I saw these four guys in this car turn around and was looking at us so I hit my brakes and started turning around on them. Well, naturally, when I hit my brakes, they took off so I spun around in the road and took off after them. I believe we went down Main Street. So I went with my lights and siren on. I was talking on the radio and we ended up on the Interstate 85 and started toward Greensboro and it was cold and snowing and sleeting and it was all freezing on the highway. I was probably doing about 90 mph was about the highest we got but they couldn't go that fast but by the time I started to try get in front of them, I'd start slipping and sliding. At that time, the police car I had was an old Pontiac Catalina which is the worst police car I've ever been in my life, but that's what we were driving at that time. So, we were on the Interstate and heading toward Greensboro. I was on the radio with our dispatcher and they were relaying things back at the Sheriff's Department and they were coming on down the Interstate from the Greensboro Police Department waiting there at the city limits trying to help us. Every time I'd get in that inside lane to try and get in front of them, I'd start slipping and sliding and start seeing and sparks and sliding and have to fall back in behind them. In the meantime, they started throwing stuff out of the car. We didn't know what it was at first, but come to find out, later on, we figured out that what they were throwing out was ammunition and guns. Now, keep in mind that this was his first night that he worked on the record on patrol for the Police Department. Here we were sliding around at 80 and 90 mph on the Interstate. Greensboro was behind me and we moved down into the Industrial Park and then. Just over the top of that hill was a great big stop sign and they ran the stop sign and we couldn't stop. We ran the stop sign and run right down into that Industrial Park. So, we stepped out of the car. We finally got them to get stopped and there was the Greensboro Department and the Sheriff's Department and so we got everything straightened out and started back home."

Dad's first day as a police officer. High Point, NC. September 19, 1966

"Is it always like this?" Bill recalls Dad asking him.

"No," Bill said calmly. "This is a quiet night."

"I think he was about ready to go home," Bill laughed. "I guess it was one of the bigger things to happen back then. Back then, this was in the 60's and everybody had hot cars and usually with town officers like that, if you hit your brakes and start turning around, a lot of them would run."

"It wasn't unusual to have a chase problem, especially on third shift late at night," he said. "Everybody started out in the Patrol Division and then you go from there."

"I stayed in the Patrol Division for two maybe even three years and I transferred to Traffic Division in the Motorcycle Office so I was riding motorcycles for awhile while I was in the Traffic Division and he was in the Patrol Division," Bill added. "I had a real bad wreck in '68 and that about took me out completely. I had fractured both legs and both arms and had a lot of deteriorated skin."

Bill could recall Dad's promotion into the Traffic Division, where he eventually became a motorcycle cop. From routine ride along ventures in the early days to several years apart, Bill and Dad worked together in the Detective Division again some years later.

"We worked different shifts," he said. "We did work a couple of large cases together and I remember we broke up a theft ring, I don't know how many cases we cleared, maybe forty or fifty cases. Somewhere over $100,000 worth of merchandise was recovered."

Dad was pretty quick to catch the attention of his professional superiors. Bill remembers Dad being complimented by the Chief of Police very early on in his career.

"Can you go back up the mountain and find some more boys like Herb Cooley and bring them back here?"

the Chief asked Bill. "We need to find some more people like that."

"He was just a good, steady cop," Bill concurred. "He didn't have a whole lot to say, but was always there and you could always depend on him."

Bill left the High Point Police Department in 1972. Dad had transferred to the Public Defender's Office with another fellow motorcycle cop and Wythe County, Virginia native named Wayne Pike.

"I was out of law enforcement for about a year and I went to Nevada and worked security out there in the casino and when I came back I was living back in Grayson County," Bill said. "I then went to Hillsville as Chief of Police and Herb and Wayne were working together."

"I believe they were working for Erie Insurance as adjusters and so then Wayne was planning on running for Sheriff of Wythe County and Herb went with him as Chief Deputy," he added. "I remember when they came back. Your Dad was living over in Elk Creek; that was before Hilda and I married."

Bill followed Dad's career very closely after that, praising him almost to the point of reluctance.

"Your Dad ran the Wythe County Sheriff Department," he said bluntly. Wayne was the politician, shaking hands and everything like that and was in charge of the Sheriff's Department on a day-to-day basis, but your Dad didn't get the credit he should have gotten out of that position."

Therefore, it was no surprise to Bill that Dad went on to pursue positions as Chief of Police in the towns of Pulaski and Vinton.

"That was a natural progression for him," Bill remarked. "That was like breathing for him."

Serving in the U.S. Coast Guard, my Dad went to work, on his first day as a civilian, in 1966 as a rookie beat cop in downtown High Point, NC, where he was later promoted to Detective and Detective Sergeant. It was also in High Point that he served a short term as Narcotics Sergeant. In 1980, Dad became Chief Deputy for the Wythe County Sheriff's Office where he served until 1994 when he became Chief of Police in Pulaski and, finally, Vinton in 2000.

"Attending the FBI National Academy with officers from every state in the union and 11 foreign countries was one on the highlights of my career," Dad noted. "Being appointed Chief of Police in the Towns of Pulaski and Vinton certainly rate high among my memories."

Despite receiving a Bachelor's and Master's Degree and attending the FBINA, he has never stopped learning.

"I feel that you can learn something from everyone that you meet," my father stated. "Continuous training is a valuable key to a successful law enforcement career."

As diligent as my dad was in his work, he was never so timely otherwise.

"If I could have, I would have collected some good wages while I was waiting on Herb Cooley," he laughed. "I once waited on that dude 24 hours to go canoeing."

Then, there was my Dad's beloved runt pug, Buford, which he got just weeks after his birth in 1974.

"First time I ever saw Buford, my son and I went over to see Herb at his house in Elk Creek," Bill recollected. "I was just infatuated with Buford. Buford was one of a kind."

After more than 40 years, Buford stories are still the stuff of legend. He lived until he was hit by a car just shortly before I was born in 1985. My dad has been an avid pug lover ever since.

The two gentlemen have remained friends for more than a half century. At one point, their sons, John and Brett, hung out together. I'm ashamed to admit that my earliest memory of Bill is a bit embarrassing for me.

As a preschooler, whenever, I heard him speak of Bill, I misunderstood him to say "Phil Collins," my favorite singer. Having always misheard "Bill" as "Phil," you can imagine my excitement when my dad interrupted one of my MTV video sessions. I was probably watching "Sussudio."

"Bill Collins is outside," my dad told me.

"He is?" I asked with my face illuminated with excitement.

He carried me outside to meet some guy that was obviously not my hero. I don't remember what happened next, but given my parents' embarrassment to my obvious disappointment, I probably threw a tantrum on this poor, unsuspecting fellow.

"I lost touch for years but while he was doing midnight I went down to see him," Bill told me. "I don't have a lot of people I call my friends but Herb is definitely someone I'd call my friend and I've always kept up with him and his career."

## Chapter 2
## Military All the Way

Of all the key figures of Dad's career, none has been more pivotal than George Wayne Pike. A Wythe County native, Wayne had a keen desire to be a leader in the law enforcement world. He saw the same zeal in Dad. This sparked a friendship that would endure over the next half a century.

"I had gotten out of the United States Air Force and in a few days went to work at the High Point, North Carolina Police Department," Wayne told me via email. "This was in the mid-sixties and a sort of tumultuous time in the US with the Viet Nam war and racial tension going on."

According to research conducted by Kerry Robinson for the Global Nonviolent Action Database, on February 18, 1960, the High Point Biracial Committee was formed to ease racial tensions in High Point. As the group gained more legitimacy, more facilities desegregated thanks in part to negotiations between the committee and city officials. By 1963, nearly all government and public institutions were integrated. The remaining stronghold of segregation was privately-owned buildings such the town theaters.

The high school students who organized the High Point lunch counter sit-ins began picketing the local theater, The Paramount, once the lunch counters shut down. Their strategy was to attempt to purchase tickets in the white line and sit in the area reserved for whites. Once refused, the group would simply get back in line.

This campaign ended around the spring of 1961, partly due to older members of the group leaving for college. On November 30, 1962, the campaign restarted, this time with only Brenda Jean Fountain as the main organizer followed by members of the local Youth Council for the National Association for the Advancement of Colored People.

After a few months of picketing, the group decided to accelerate the demonstrations. In April 1963, they formed a human chain in front of the ticket booth and the theater door. In less than a week, after shoving and verbal attacks from white onlookers, the mayor ordered the arrest of the group.

Once released, Fountain, along with Edna Tomlin and chairman of CORE, D. Z. Mitchell, issued a lawsuit against the owner of the Paramount, Key Theaters Inc., for discrimination against blacks on city property. In July, members the Youth Council for the NAACP collaborated with the High Point NAACP chapter for a series of demonstrations in High Point and Thomasville, a nearby town. From approximately July 13-20, a growing number of High Point and Thomasville protesters demonstrated in at Thomasville's theater, Davidson Theater, each day with picketing and marches. The groups during the first two days numbered only about eight to twenty protesters and brought little attention.

On the night of the third day, Rev. W. E. Banks, chairman of Thomasville's NAACP led a large group of protesters to the theater to repeat the strategy in High Point of making a human chain and singing songs of freedom. After a while, a large crowd of whites gathered. Some white teenagers marched and sang against the protesters. In the commotion, the police arrested 28 protesters and a number of disorderly whites. Juveniles were released the next day, and non-minors faced 60-day suspended sentences for violating a fire ordinance.

The demonstrations came to climax on July 18, 1963, when a gunshot was fired into a church where protesters were meeting to discuss the segregation issue with the local biracial committee. No one was hurt, but the movement suspended demonstrations for the weekend. National Congress of Racial Equality (CORE) defense attorney Floyd McKissick worked for months to get the charges against the Thomasville demonstrators dismissed or reduced to fines; he eventually succeeded. Meanwhile, the injunction against Key Theaters Inc., the owner of the Paramount, in High Point slowly progressed.

On November 29, 1963, a pre-trial occurred, presenting the case that the owner leasing the Paramount could not discriminate, as he is leasing a publicly-owned building. The owner's attorney, James Lovelace, maintained that the refusal to integrate is a purely economic decision, despite the fact that due to extensive picketing and boycotts, few blacks attended the theater and the black section of the theater had been shut down for months. The case was thrown out in 1964 after the passing of the Civil Rights Act of 1964. The theater was then legally forced to abide by federal law and desegregate.

"I had just gotten out of the military and a high school friend named Roy Jones from Sheeptown was an officer there in HP and he came to my dad's house and asked me to come down and ride around with him in the city," Wayne recalled. "I took the civil service exam and they hired me while I was there on the visit. On major case in the civil unrest era was the gun battle with the members of the Black Panther Party. That is a whole story in its self. I became an instant friend of Herb because he was likable and he was from the same area I was. He was a pro and sharp and wanted to do the job just like I did. We were a team."

Sheeptown is a section of Austinville, Virginia in Wythe County. Wayne not only had ambitions to one day return to Wythe County, but he would be crucial in Dad becoming a part of the community as well. This is the reason, of course, why I can proudly call Wytheville my lifelong home.

"One challenging case was that of a huge number of burglary cases and thefts that could not be solved and Herb and I was asked to be on a special investigation to try to solve them," Wayne added. "Right away, we saw that they happened when a certain one of our platoon shifts were working the midnight shift. We became suspicious that police officers were involved. We focused on that, cleared hundreds of cases and 6 officers were charged. One officer named Jarrett was the ring leader. This was all heavily reported on in the newspaper."

"High Point was a factory and blue collar town with hundreds of textile and furniture and other related factories and production facilities from chemicals to all kind of accessories," he noted. "Twice a year, buyers and factory representatives from all over the world came to High Point for the big furniture market. Show rooms were large and beautiful."

According to Wikipedia, by 1959, North Carolina had become the state employing the most number of people in the furniture industry, beating out New York. In 1961, *The State* magazine declared that "High Point, in Guilford County, is the world's leading manufacturing center of wood furniture. It is also the location of one of the nation's principal furniture markets."

"People of all types came from all over to work in High Point," Wayne noted. "It was a big money city. There were a mixture of Native American, black people, white people and people from the sand hills and the mountains."

"Mainly blue collar jobs were always available as were office and other positions in the many factories in High Point," he added. "There was no unemployment in High Point, NC but there was a lot of activity that required the services of a very active police department. The city could be a rough place, especially on the weekends and there were many places for the factory workers to hang out and have a beer. There were many beer joints all over and often crime related to them. There were always fights, drunks and occasionally a homicide, robbery, burglary and/or some other incident that required the police. High Point was often called "Little Chicago"."

High Point's history with crime dates back to the early twentieth century. It earned its nickname due to its extremely large population in comparison to surrounding cities and the raucous nightlife that permeated throughout the town. By 1966, crime rates were at yet another peak and Dad's joining the police force could not have been a more welcome addition.

"I had been there about two years when a young man showed up named Herb Cooley," Wayne recalled. "I was excited because, like me, he was from the mountains of Southwest Virginia. Before long, we were friends and working together and having success in doing quality police work. This was recognized and we were both placed in the two-wheel motorcycle unit. This was a really sharp unit of professional men with military backgrounds."

Dad, Wayne and Bill Collins, who Wayne described as a tall, athletic mountain man, were in the motorcycle group together, all with a variety of military backgrounds. Dad was fresh out of the Coast Guard while Wayne was from the Air Force. Bill was a former marine. The three Southwest Virginia boys would remain friends to this day.

"There were others, all tall and sharp in leather jackets, shined tall boots and gleaming Harley Davidson Electra Glides were the steeds that we rode," Wayne remembered. "When one or more of us arrived on the scene, folks knew we were there to keep order, keep them safe and get the job done in a professional manner. There were no fat slobs in this unit. Aside from our regular work, we did celebrity escorts such as Miss North Carolina and the Richard Nixon family and put on precisions riding in parades."

Dad was promoted to the traffic division of the High Point
Police Department in 1968.

Dad with his oldest son Travis in 1969.  Both are in their gun-toting attire.

"Eventually Herb and I were promoted to detectives and we solved a lot of cases," Wayne recollected. "There is real documentation of a lot of this and we made a difference. In those days, we were given a clothing allowance to buy out suits and related apparel and we went to a local well-known and popular clothier named Wright Brothers Clothing. Using my allowance, I went during one season and got this pink sport coat and white pants and related tie, shirts and belt. Unknown to me, Herb had come in and got the same clothing. We showed up to work one day dressed alike, in pink and white and it was a big laugh. We later went on a burglary call.

"You two are the prettiest men I have ever seen," said and the man who owned the place.

"The pink outfits were a real joke from then on," Wayne said.

"Herb and I were always getting a lot of attention for the job we did as did others who were hard workers," he added. "After more promotions and awards and commendations, we were offered jobs by the state. We also attended college and got our degrees."

Dad made detective at High Point in 1971. Here he is in a 1972 department photo. Courtesy of David Armstrong.

Dad's academic excellence was well recognized within his community. On December 10, 1975, the *High Point Enterprise* reported that he was one of only two seniors at Guilford College in Greensboro whose name was published in the edition of *Who's Who Among Students in American Colleges and Universities*. He was a resident of Route 3 in Trinity, North Carolina at the time, majoring in administration of justice in the college's Urban Center. At that time, Dad was also employed by the state of North Carolina as a special investigator for the office of the public defender. He was also a member of the North Carolina Law Enforcement Officers Association and Lambda Alpha Epsilon, a criminal justice fraternity. Dad was also busy working with youthful criminal defenders through High Point Volunteers to the Court program, helping young criminal to create a better life for themselves.

* * * * * *

Dad became a detective in January 1971, after three years in the traffic division as a motorcycle cop. He remained a detective for three years before being promoted in February 1974 to the narcotics and vice department.

Vice officers investigate crimes related to prostitution, gambling and narcotics. In some jurisdictions, a vice squad may also be tasked with monitoring guns, alcohol, bookmaking, pornography and human trafficking. Although most of these items are legal when produced and sold in their regulated form, vice is concerned with immoral uses and activities. For example, selling guns and alcohol to adults is legal, but to traffic the items illegally is a criminal activity.

"My ambition was to run for sheriff in Wythe County someday and I was offered a job that centered in Southwest Virginia that paid what I was making and came with a company car," Wayne Pike told me. "I took the job and later convinced Herb to come with the same company."

This marked dad's return to Virginia. He lived in Elk Creek and worked in Wytheville at Erie Insurance with Wayne as an adjuster. This was also around the time Dad and his first wife, Joyce, divorced.

"I also began to run for sheriff and was successful," continued Wayne. "I hired Herb as Chief Deputy."

Wayne was elected as sheriff of Wythe County for five terms. He and Dad would remain partners for the next fourteen years until he took the position as police chief in Pulaski. After six years, Dad relocated to Vinton as the chief of police for the next eleven years, which would finish out his career.

"That agency was in a real situation at the time and Herb stabilized it and made it a real department," Wayne noted. "He was well liked by everyone. At the time, I was the United States Marshal over the Western District of Virginia. My main office was in Roanoke and I often saw Herb and saw the good work he did. By that time Herb had obtained his Masters degree and was well recognized for his administrative ability."

"Herb Cooley was and is an honest police office and administrator," Wayne commended Dad. "He is an honorable military veteran and has served his fellow man in many ways for so many years. He was a really good investigator and an all around good officer. He was a master on the motor cycle as an officer and was always sharp. He worked out and kept mentally and physically fit. You never saw him in uniform that he did not look like a real pro. He was military all the way. That was one thing that I always respected. He cared about how he reflected on the office he held."

"When Herb and I worked for the State of North Carolina, our boss and one of the superior court judges owned a large ocean fishing boat," Wayne recalled. "Sometimes, we went to the coast and we would operate the boat. I had taken a class on operation and Herb and I were out in the Gulf Stream on a trip and Herb became deathly ill. That is when I found out that Herb, the Coast Guard vet, was prone to sea sickness. I gave him a hard time over it and I told him I did not know how he completed his tour in the Coast Guard and got sea sickness. He said he toughed it out."

"From the beginning I knew that Herb was a very honest, clean, intelligent officer who had the tenacity and dedication to get the job done," Wayne said of my dad. "He was an excellent planner and organizer. Herb cleared many cases in High Point and he was also a great traffic officer when he started and was so dependable and sharp. Of course, his promotions reflect all that. He looked and acted professional. You have to understand that I say this because I do not accept slobbery and people who do not fit the image of a military man or a police officer. If you come to me and ask for a job and you are not clean and neat, then that is it. The military taught me that and I still make my bed in the same manner as I did in basic training. These are also the reason I made your dad the chief deputy."

Chapter 3
A Cool Cop

On February 10, 1971, my Dad along with the rest of
his fellow officers of the High Point Police Department
made national headlines when they participated in a
shootout with members of the Black Panther Party, a civil
rights socialist organization whose Winston Salem, North
Carolina chapter made its way through High Point on that
cold winter morning. My Dad's friends, officers Jim
Robbins and Tommy Bryant, recalled the day's events on a
local religious television show called *Extreme Passions*
hosted by Rex and Elaine Uhl in commemoration of the
shootout's 40th anniversary.

Dad's original HPPD patch

"We were working a third shift that morning under
Lt. Shaw Cooke," Robbins explained in 2011. "I hated third
shift and had been called in because I had taken the
previous night off."

It was on that shift that Robbins received the call that officers were needed to evict the Black Panthers, who had set up headquarters in a rented house on Hulda Street. Within minutes, he and his former training coach, Tommy Bryant, were standing in a cluster in front of the house along with fellow officers, George McDowell and Larry Miller, ready to performer their duty.

"Information had come to us that the Black Panthers had set up a home for training purposes as well as to feed free meals to hungry kids on the street," Tommy Bryant interjected on the television show. "Fearful people in the neighborhood had called us reporting sights of sandbags in the windows and heavy ammunition."

Parents were afraid of potential booby traps that might ensnare their children. As a result, Judge Byron Hayworth, who owned the home, immediately set forth an eviction notice. The High Point Police Department was then ordered to aid the Guilford County Sherriff's Office in serving the notice within the same day.

"We were told at assembly the night before that, as members of the fourth platoon, we could all be expected to be called in for a special mission in the early hours of the following morning," Bryant recalled. "A reserve force would be called in to cover our regular calls that day."

By 6 a.m., officers were at Hulda Street on a bitterly cold morning before sunrise. Officers were staked out in two houses on both sides of the street while Chief Laurie Pritchett and another officer went to the front door announcing the eviction and asking that the house be vacated. With no response, they retreated behind a police car and gave the order once more. After ten minutes of silence, Wayne Pike was given the orders to release the tear gas. His shot missed, ricocheting off the roof. The second shot enter the window.

"There was a crack of fire that started in the back of the house," Bryant recollected. "It reminded me of the crowd at a football game as the sound travelled in a wave around the house that Lt. Cooke had been shot."

"Has Cooke been hit or what?" Chief Pritchett asked in confusion.

"Are they shooting at us?" Jim Robbins heard someone say.

At that moment, a barrage of shots rang out from both sides. Jim Robbins could see nothing, but heard it all.

"Does anybody have any ammo left?" he hears an officer ask.

"I did because I didn't shoot," Robbins recalled. "Tommy went into the house and extracted the Four Panthers. I heard one of them had been hit, but I didn't know which one. We put them on the ground in the dirt on Hulda Street and I stood over them with a shotgun.

Still, Robbins remained modest about his role in the shootout.

"I was just a target," he told the TV moderators. "I didn't do anything."

"He was fogged up, as he usually is," Bryant joked. "It happens frequently."

After Lt. Cooke was confirmed shot, orders were given to fire. Bryant did so by emptying his round into the bottom window of the house. A projectile bullet that had ricocheted from Sgt. McDowell's nametag struck Bryant in the chest, hitting his bullet-proof vest, but knocking him about three feet backwards.

"Are you okay?" McDowell shouted, jerking him up by his vest.

"Yes," he muttered, emptying his rounds instinctively into the top and side windows, where he believed the bullet that hit him had been fired.

"They're giving up," Bryant heard another officer say.

With that, Bryant headed inside the house.

"It was eerie and smoky obviously," he recalled soberly. "There was a cardboard mannequin dressed in a police suit with a pig face and a bull's eye target on its heart. I saw the egg and vinegar solution in the fireplace that was presumably used to counteract tear gas and there were all kinds of literature. I could see why parents were afraid for their kids in that neighborhood."

Immediately after the shooting, Bryant visited Cooke in the hospital who told him of his near death experience.

Cooke told Bryant that he crawled about four feet before rolling over on his back and collapsing. Another lieutenant rushed to his side.

"He's gone," he announced to his fellow officers, seeing that his eyes were rolled back in his head.

Cooke, a General Patton sort of stoic, told Bryant that he saw the lieutenant standing over him and heard his announcement, after which he saw an immensely white light that was accompanied by an all-encompassing feeling of warmth.

"I knew all my sins had been forgiven," Cooke told Bryant. "I wanted to go."

Cooke only began to struggle when he felt himself becoming conscious again.

"I didn't want to come back," he said.

After multiple surgeries, the 47-year old officer did come back. He worked with the department another five years.

Following the events of that cold February day, Bryant and his wife took a brief vacation to Myrtle Beach, South Carolina.

As it ended, Bryant asked his wife to stay a few more days.

"Why?" she asked.

"I've got something I need to do and I don't know what it is yet," he told her. "I need a few more days to figure it out."

Within that time, Bryant had an epiphany. He knew that those young Black Panther teens wanted to be recognized for achievement. He knew they had the ability and determination to do so and he wanted to provide them with an opportunity to display those attributes in the right way.

Through a court referral system and the aid of local federal funds, Bryant set up an athletic league commissioned by the police department in which all underprivileged teens could participate. After he left the department, Bryant established Pro Teem Sports, which broadcast local games on television and radio stations area-wide to this day.

"Cooke was shot in the chest, losing part of his long, traveled through his side and up his arm and finally exiting his wrist," Bryant said. "Other officers thought he was dead and it's a miracle he survived at all."

On February 19, 2003, Bob Burchette's article in the *Greensboro News and Record* memorialized Cooke, who died the day prior.

\* \* \* \* \* \*

According to Tommy Bryant, when he joined the force in 1968, Dad had just been promoted to the Traffic Division.

"We never worked in the same position until the mid-seventies when we were detectives together," he told me in an interview. "As a rookie cop, I looked up to Herb."

Dad was regarded as a cool
cop from day one.
Courtesy: HPPD
Personnel

Bryant said that my father lived up to his name.

"He was a very cool cop," he recalled. "He dressed
nicely and presented himself with a bright smile that turned
the heads of many ladies."

Bryant shadowed Dad when he first joined the force
and really admired his skill with his motorcycle. Later, as
detectives, Dad assisted Bryant on a particular case in which
they hadn't originally been partners.

Bryant had received a call while on patrol from a
receptionist at the Highland Cadillac dealership had filed a
complaint about some stolen 8-track tapes. He met the lady

at her residence on the northern end of town during her lunch hour.

"Do you have any idea about who you think may have stolen your tapes?" Detective Bryant asked.

"I think a police officer stole them," she replied.

"Why do you think that?" he asked perplexingly.

"I saw a police car park near where my car was parked," she replied.

"Where was your car parked?" he inquired.

"In the bank parking lot across the street," she told him.

"About what time of day did you see the police car go by?" the detective probed further.

"Around nine or nine thirty this morning," the woman answered.

Bryant stopped in his tracks.

"Well, ma'am," he said humbly. "That was my car you saw."

"Well," the woman smugly concluded. "You must have been the one who stole my tapes."

"No, ma'am," Bryant assured her. "The bank had called in a complaint about a customer and I went out there to answer the call."

"No," she insisted. "I think you stole my tapes. I know why that police car was out there."

Bryant immediately radioed his commander, Lt. Shaw Cooke, and requested that a crime lab be sent to her house, after which he excused himself from the case.

Cooke immediately came to his detective's defense.

"Ma'am," he said. "I can assure you that Tommy Bryant didn't steal your tapes."

"Well, I know he did," she snapped back. "I know all about your theft rings and I think all you policemen are corrupt."

Dad was assigned to the case after this exchange, but after working on it, kept hitting a dead end. Cooke decided to call Bryant back in to work with Dad on finding the real culprit.

"I think we can find out who did this," Bryant told his lieutenant.

"Take all the time you need," he agreed. "Don't worry about taking any other calls."

Bryant then returned to the bank in an effort to pinpoint the exact location of his accuser's parked car at the time of the theft.

Through an interview with the back manager, Dad learned that the woman from the dealership had parked her car adjacent to one that had been repossessed that day by the bank. The former owner of the repossessed car had told the bank manager he wanted to get his own tapes out of the car. The bank manager unlocked the car and left the man alone. The man not only collected his own tapes but those from the neighboring car, which was unlocked, and fled the scene.

"Herb and I then tracked down the man who had formerly owned the repossessed car and he remained unwilling to confess," Bryant told me. "However, there was a younger guy that was with him, his 17-year old brother who was a student at Central High School."

They decided to pick the young boy up and bring him back to the police station. This proved to be the cooperative witness that Dad and Detective Bryant had hoped to run across.

The 17-year old boy confessed that the two of them had stolen the tapes. He then directed Dad and Bryant back to his home where the located and recovered the tapes.

"At the point, we brought the kid with us back to the dealership and made him give her back the tapes," Bryant said. "That way she would be absolutely sure that the police had nothing to do with the stealing of her tapes."

When the boy handed her the tapes with an apology, tears began to stream down her face.

"I think you owe these officers an apology," Sgt. Larry Miller prompted the woman.

"I apologize," the woman said tearfully. "If you hadn't caught this guy, I would have always thought the police had something to do with it."

"At that time, the climate was not good between the police department and the community," Bryant explained. "There had been a theft ring uncovered a couple of years before, which made some people think that the whole department was corrupt."

As it turns out, Dad was not present at the Black Panthers shootout in 1971. That was a special mission for all patrol division officers and Dad was well into his motorcycle days in the traffic division of the department by that time. However, when 16-year-old Larry Medley was shot, Dad was one of the officers assigned to guard his hospital room.

Having reached Tommy Bryant by the telephone number provided on the YouTube video in which he discussed the shootout on local TV with Jim Robbins and Larry Medley, the former Black Panther who became a minister, I felt sorry that I couldn't talk to Dad's good friend Jim Robbins during this project. I don't recall ever meeting Jim face to face, but I talked to him a couple of times over the telephone years ago when he would call our house to get in touch with Dad from time to time. He was always very friendly, kind and engaging. Sadly, he passed away on September 7, 2013. Just over two months later on November 18, Dad lost his brother Mike suddenly to pancreatic cancer. It was around this same time that Dad received a call from Jim's widow informing him of his passing.

Dad left HPPD in 1974 for the NC Public Defender's Office. Courtesy: HPPD personnel file.

Dad and Tommy Bryant have remained in contact over the years. In fact, he told me that he and Jim had gone to Myrtle Beach, South Carolina, to visit him shortly before Jim passed away. After Dad retired in July 2011, he and Mom relocated to Myrtle Beach the following April. I was so glad to hear that they had visited him because I knew Dad thought so highly of both of these men. He still talks about Jim and I know he misses him a great deal.

Apparently, for Bryant, the feelings are entirely mutual.

"If war broke out tomorrow, I would want Herb Cooley in my foxhole with me," Bryant stated. "He was a policeman's policeman."

He reiterated his earlier compliments of dad as a sharply dressed model officer, with whom working was a pleasure.

"He was a great guy with a wonderful sense of humor and bright smile that made him fun to be around," Bryant told me. "He, Wayne Pike and Bill Collins all knew how to do those special tricks on the motorcycles that really got the crowds stirred up during parades."

Chapter 4
Detective Dad

Thanks to Wayne Pike and Tommy Bryant, I have
been given exclusive information on a couple of the murder
cases on which Dad served as a detective. The first of such
cases is that of the murder of a 19-year-old girl named
Bonnie Lynn Gallimore, who was brutally raped and
murdered after completing her shift at a shoe store in the
mall, located on Westchester drive. The killer was 20-year-
old Darrell Lee Young, a serial rapist and murder, of whom
Gallimore was his first victim.

According to newspaper reports, Gallimore left her
job at Marilyn's Shoe Store at Westchester Mall shortly after
6 P.M. on November 4, 1972. She had told her mother that
she was going to a movie with a girlfriend that night.
Witnesses later said they saw Gallimore struggling with a
man at her car in the shopping center parking lot. The man
forced her in the backseat of her car and, taking the wheel,
sped off with her. Her body was found the next afternoon in
an isolated area in the southwestern end of the city beside
her car. She was naked and had been shot once in the chest
as well as brutally raped.

The kidnapping and murder spread fear and
concern throughout the city of High Point. Guards were
employed to patrol the parking lot of the shopping center.
Confidence in the police department was shaken yet again,
especially when Chief Laurie Pritchett terminated Capitan
Detective George Leverett from the case and placed Dad in
charge. Ironically, this would the same detective whose
secretary would name Dad in the testimony involving
Leverett's alleged office break-in.

Finally, on November 21, two weeks after the
murder, Chief Pritchett announced the arrest of Young, then
a resident of George Place, on charges of murder,
kidnapping and robbery. On New Year's Eve in 1972,

the *High Point Enterprise* reported that Young was undergoing diagnostic study at Cherry Hospital in Goldsboro, North Carolina before appearing at a court hearing of the charges against him.

On February 3, it was reported that the preliminary hearing was to continue that afternoon with a ruling on the admissibility of certain evidence. Presiding over the case was Judge Ed Washington, who called for a three day recess to study the testimony that had already been heard, would now make a ruling as to whether or not statements made by the defendant would be submitted into evidence. One of Young's defense attorneys submitted a motion that any statement made by Young subsequent to November 3, 1972 be suppressed from entering into evidence.

That February 3, 1973 ruling of District Court Judge Ed Washington resulted in the denial of the defense request to suppress any of Young's statement from being used as evidence, dating back to the day before the murder. Gallimore's body was found in a field off of Blandwood Circle, which runs off of Albertson Road on the southwestern end of High Point. Police reported that the 19-year-old victim died from a single gunshot wound to the chest from a small caliber pistol.

On January 26 and 29, testimony was taken and court reconvened on Friday, February 2.

After testimony was started in the regular preliminary hearing, a single witness was called. State Bureau of Investigations agent E.L. Sneed took the witness stand, testifying in regard to three individual statements made by Young. According to Sneed, Young admitted to killing Gallimore on November 20. Sneed also quoted Young's confession as to kidnapping her, stealing her car and revealing the location in which her body was disposed.

It was Dad who got the confession from Young.

"I got the girl's purse and ordered her out of the car," Young told Dad. "I had the pistol cocked and when I went to put my arm around her, she hit my other arm that was holding the gun and it went off."

The trial dragged on through the summer of 1973. At the urging of Capt. Leverett, Young entered a guilty plea of murder in the second degree, for which he was sentenced to 25 years in prison. Afterwards, Chief Pritchett slapped more than 1,000 merits against Leverett, who oversaw the Gallimore murder investigation, after testifying as a witness against him in the trial. This was the second time in a year that Leverett had been reprimanded by Pritchett, who had previously had an unblemished record. The resulting controversy spread through the community and enlisted the involvement of the City Council and Civil Service Commission. When the possibility of court action loomed, the issue was eased. Pritchett withdrew the demerits and reassigned Leverett to other duties within the police training academy. As a result, Leverett also withdrew his complaint to the Civil Service Commission against Pritchett.

Leverett later died in prison for murder, when Dad squeezed a confession out of him by saying that his son would be charged also if he did not confess.

What I want remembered from this chapter is that it was my Dad who got the confession from the young man who committed this crime. You won't find that in any of the newspaper reports or even in the detective magazines that shed a national spotlight on this case, but it was Dad who brought this grieving family some justice when her killer was revealed.

"Herb went and picked up Darrell Lee Young," Tommy Bryant told me. "It was Herb who cracked him and got the confession out of him."

Dad also pushed for a greater sentencing at the trial than a second degree 25-year prison term.

"He was convicted of only second degree murder in a plea bargain of the first murder case because of what the captain did," Wayne Pike added. "The case was saved because Herb and I raised the alarm of the real truth."

Wayne also informed me that Young escaped from prison in 1979, only to brutally rape another woman and steal her car. He was given two life sentences. Young's luck had finally run out.

The parents of Bonnie Lynn Gallimore sued Marilyn's Shoes, their daughter's employer for worker's compensation benefits in 1977, for which they were denied, as the court ruled that her death was not a direct result of her employment.

Wayne told me that Bonnie Lynn's parents literally grieved themselves to death and that father did not even make it through the civil case before he died.

"It makes me sad today when I think of this tragic case," Wayne said. "Young was a monster."

When Young requested a retrial in 1981, the court ruled that "the defendant was tried upon indictments, proper in form, with kidnapping, felonious larceny, second degree rape, and felonious escape. The jury found defendant guilty on each charge. From the trial, the court's judgment sentencing him to life imprisonment for second degree rape, ten years imprisonment for felonious larceny, one year imprisonment for felonious escape, and not less than fifty years nor more than life imprisonment for kidnapping. The state allowed defendant's motion to bypass the Court of Appeals on the offenses of kidnapping, felonious larceny, and felonious escape on November 5, 1980.

According to case notes, The State's evidence tended to show that on October 24, 1979, the defendant was an inmate at the Davidson County Prison Unit near Lexington, North Carolina, serving a prison sentence for felonious breaking and entering and second degree murder. At approximately 9 a.m. on that day, the defendant was working as a member of a road crew whose task was to repair road pavement. Defendant requested and obtained permission from his foreman to enter the woods nearby in order to relieve himself.

Prosecuting witness Mrs. Stella Ivey testified that her door bell rang a few minutes after 9 a.m. on October 24, 1979, and that upon opening the door she observed a man whom she identified at trial as the defendant. Mrs. Ivey stated that defendant jerked the screen door open and forced his way into the house, saying that he wished to use the telephone. He then put one hand over her mouth and the other around her throat, dragged her to a couch and raped her. Subsequently, defendant bound Mrs. Ivey's wrists, gagged her and took her billfold and car keys. He attempted to pull Mrs. Ivey out of the door and towards her Oldsmobile automobile, but she escaped and ran down the road toward the group of men working on the pavement. She reported the incident to the foreman of the work crew, and law enforcement officers were summoned.

The foreman of the work crew and another State Department of Transportation employee testified that approximately twenty minutes after defendant was given permission to relieve himself on the morning of October 24, 1979, they heard Mrs. Ivey scream for help and observed her running from her house toward the work crew. They saw an Oldsmobile automobile backing out of Mrs. Ivey's driveway and recognized defendant as the driver. Both witnesses stated that Mrs. Ivey's lip was bleeding and that her arms appeared to have friction burns on them. Mrs. Ivey's husband testified that he owned a 1978 Oldsmobile Cutlass automobile, with an approximate fair market value of $5,000, which was taken on that date without his permission or consent. The defendant presented no evidence in his behalf.

Another case with which Dad was involved a convicted murderer that turned into an eventual escapee. According to a 1998 Michael Grossman story in the *Greensboro News and Record*, Ronnie Gene Jackson had been incarcerated since he confessed to killing his wife and the credit manager of a furniture company in unrelated incidents in 1973. Jackson told police he had been having marital troubles with his wife, Edrie Ann Jackson, 20, and that he strangled her. Jackson said he beat 43-year-old William E. Thayer while the two men were drinking beer and talking in Thayer's home. Both victims were tossed down a well on Kivett Drive near Triangle Lake Road in High Point. Jackson led police to the bodies after he was caught breaking into Thayer's home. Jackson was sentenced in April 1974 to life plus 90 years after he pleaded guilty to two counts of second-degree murder, kidnapping, common-law robbery, automobile larceny and breaking and entering. He was 20-years-old when the murders were committed.

Jackson had been among the inmates who were least supervised in minimum-security prisons until January 1996, when he refused to take a routine drug test in the Caldwell Correctional Center in Hudson, according to Department of Correction records. Jackson was demoted then to the minimum-security classification that is the most supervised. After being turned down for parole for the twelfth time, he planned his escape on October 9, 1998 from Davidson County Jail by having an accomplice call a cab for him while he was mowing the prison lawn.

"It was my understanding that he had a female guard that helped him escape," Tommy Bryant told me. "They caught him several days later in the Smoky Mountains of Tennessee."

Along with every other detective on the force, Dad was on this case. When William E. Thayer went missing, there was a nationwide search out for this man. As best as Tommy Bryant can recall, Dad would have probably been involved in the arrest and capture of Jackson by the police.

I got in touch with David Armstrong who was on the High Point Police Department with Dad for five years.

"We never worked together," Armstrong explained. "But your dad was a good friend of mine and a really great guy."

Armstrong said that Dad was already a detective by the time he joined the department as a patrolmen, but he recalled him fondly as a model officer to whom everyone looked up.

"He was always on top of things," Dad's colleague recalled of him. "He was always sharply dressed and followed everything to the letter."

Still, it is Dad's friendship that Armstrong remembers most.

"We spent a lot of time working out together, laughing and cutting up," he told me. "He had a great smile and a great sense of humor."

Armstrong was also Dad's neighbor.

"When I lived in High Point, he lived just around the corner from me.

* * * * * *

The International Association of Chiefs of Police submitted its report on the investigation of the High Point Police Department in May 1974. The High Point City Council had contracted the agency to the tune of $18,600 in the wake of a theft ring within the department in 1972. In the report the IACP praised the department for its leadership and direction as well as its operational progress over the previous five years. However, the report criticized the department for having poor morale and excessive favoritism and that the investigation into the theft ring had been mismanaged.

"Herb was a really close friend," said retired Lt. Col. Stewart Hartley. "During that time, he showed his loyalty to the police department in each and every one of his professional actions."

A traffic inspection with Dad and his fellow officers under the direction of Capt. Van McSwain. *c. 1968.* Courtesy of Stewart Hartley

The first news report I could locate from the *High Point Enterprise* is dated December 1, 1972, which declared the reinstatement of Lt. L.J. Boyd, one of a dozen officers dismissed on May 28, 1972 in association with the theft ring by Chief Laurie Pritchett. The order, which was set to take place on December 5, stated that Boyd shall be reinstated without penalty or changing of pay or rank. Half of the dozen officers were charged with criminal offenses. The other half, which included Boyd, was accused of having knowledge of criminal activity within the department and failing to report it.

"This is the sickest day of my life," Chief Pritchett said when he held the press conference announcing the dismissal of the first five men on May 26.

Another traffic inspection photo featuring Dad from around 1968 courtesy of Lt. Col. Hartley.

The changing of the guard at High Point Police Department. November 5, 1998. Courtesy of Stewart Hartley. Dad is second from right on the back row.

Dad, first from left, at the HPPD Motorcycle Cop reunion. November 5, 1998. Courtesy of Stewart Hartley

Benjamin F. Collins joined the High Point Police Department in 1960. He and Dad were promoted to detective at the same time in 1971.

"I recall working with him very well," Collins said. "He was a likeable guy who did his work without showing any partiality."

That was obviously a rare thing within the department at that time, given the investigation of the theft ring within the department that was soon to follow.

"He was devoted to being a model police officer in every sense of the word," Collins told me. "He did every part of his job diligently and without any sort of manipulation whatsoever."

He also noted that Dad's dedication never went unrecognized.

"I never recall him being reprimanded by his superior officers for any reason," he stated. "He was very highly regarded by his supervisors, his colleagues and the general public as well."

Collins, like Dad, went from the police department to working as a special investigator for the office of the public defender in 1972. He remained there for nearly a quarter of a century before retiring in 1996 after 36 years of services. An African American, Collins can vividly recall the turmoil of the repercussions Civil Rights Movement as it made its way through High Point, North Carolina.

"There was a lot of uneasiness going on back then," Collins recollected. "With the marches and everything going on, the officers of the High Point Police Department had to be especially on their toes."

Collins credited Dad with being at the top of the list of those who orchestrated every occurrence with as much fairness and equality as possible while enforcing that every law was abided by all citizens to the letter.

"I would say 99 percent of the department handled themselves very well during this tumultuous time," Collins said. "Your father was a prime example of this."

A rule of thumb among the department at that time was to expect the unexpected.

"You had to be prepared for anything," he remembered. "Just when you had finished patrolling the entire town and everything looked clear, you would be called right back out to settle some disturbance."

"The worst times were at night," he added. "People would line the streets and even be on top of buildings."

Collins made mention of the Rev. W.E. Banks who headed up most of the Civil Rights protestors in the High Point area as the NAACP chapter leader in the neighboring city of Thomasville.

"I know your dad remembers that name," Collins said. "I know I will never forget it."

In summary, Ben Collins remembers my dad in pretty much the same way all of his colleagues recall him.

"He was a likeable guy who was always fun to be around and always gave a hundred percent to his job of protecting the people," he said in closing. "He knew what being a true police officer was all about and I enjoyed working with him."

## Chapter 5
## Becoming Chief Deputy

In 1979, Wayne Pike made a successful run for sheriff in his native home of Wythe County. He chose Dad as his chief deputy.

"As chief deputy, Herb was the second in command," Wayne told me. "He was my direct assistant and that meant he was in command of all operations as for as carrying out my policy and procedure."

According to Wayne, this was not an easy task. He and Dad arrived in Wythe County on December 31, 1979, to take office at the very moment the new decade rang in. From there, they hit the ground running, building the department up from scratch.

"You have to understand that when your dad and I and the other employees took office at midnight on January 1, 1980, we were taking over an agency in name only," Wayne told me. "There were no viable communications, no work schedules, no departmental structure or organization, no record system, no equipment and the employee's pay was horrible. Even before taking office we set out to fix as much as we could and the rest as soon as we could as we went along."

"There was no investigative system or forms or techniques," he went on. "It was horrible and actually no one had ever done anything to correct any of this. I am not being negative; it is just how it was. I have no reason at this juncture of my life to make up anything or try to enhance what we did. I need nothing nor do I need credit for anything. People who knew the before and after know the real truth. Not only did we fix all this, we started many new programs to help the citizens and many became a standard for other agencies to use."

According to Wayne, the work he and Dad did paid off quickly in a very big way.

"Almost immediately, we doubled and even in some cases quadrupled the pay of employees and got the best equipment," he recalled. "We set up programs and grants to pay our own way. We reduced crime and made the county a better place. The Wythe County Sheriff's Office became a model for many and your dad was a part of it."

It was interesting that Wayne noted the different management styles between him and my dad.

"Herb and I are different," he said. "I am harsh, aggressive and fixated on what I want to do and somewhat a perfectionist. Herb is an easier going, compassionate person and a better listener, prone to give a second chance to an employee. I do not give many second chances and none when someone does something deliberate. I say if you make a mistake of the brain then you can be forgiven but if you make one of the heart, then it is wrong and deliberate. In this way, Herb and I complimented each other because we could make a case for harshness or compassion."

Promoted to Captain, Dad was sworn in as second in command on Friday, January 1, 1980 to Pike's three-platoon system by Circuit Court Clerk Marie Flanagan. Held over from the administration of outgoing incumbent Buford Shockley were deputies Kent Vaughn, Nathan Lephew, Jackie Kitts, Bill May, Kermit Osborne and K.B. Shockley. New deputies were Kerry L. Hanks, Herman Ray Howell, Robert Lee Whitt, Jr., and William Jennings Bryan Jackson. Jailers were Ernest Horne, Don Crockett, Tom Kolis, Frank Plummer and Robert M. Burnette. Betty Vaught served as matron with Ann Ward, Faye Armbrister, Ora Dickenson and Steve Jackson serving as radio dispatchers.

Sheriff Pike addressed the Wythe County Board of Supervisors on Tuesday, January 16, 1980 expressing concerns in several areas within his department.

"I feel there is a duplication of work in certain areas, notably in the town and county dispatch centers," Pike told the board. "The two groups could pool our resources to have a top-notch communications center."

The Board of Supervisors voted to put the item on the agenda for their joint meeting on March 31 and deferred action until the February meeting Pike's request for an additional $1,000 in funding to purchase new uniforms for deputies and matrons. While some of the uniforms were salvageable, leather belts, shirts and hat badges were also needed. Of particular note, one deputy wore a size 18 ½ shirt, which was unavailable at the time. The new sheriff also reported that his staff had cleaned the jail and that all employees were paying for meals they consumed from the cafeteria on a daily basis in an effort to cut costs on food that was purchased locally for the jail.

Apparently, Dad was catching some flak for not living within the county line at the time he took office. The same thing happened when he became Chief of Police in Pulaski. At any rate, Dad had found a home within the county limits. However, it had not been vacated as of the board meeting. Wayne went to bat for him, assuring the board that he would be moving within the week. Dad's home at the time was in Elk Creek, one mile over the Grayson County line, which led to a number of complaints. The Board then went into executive session to discuss personnel with the sheriff.

As Wayne told me that no drug arrests had been implemented at the point, he, Dad and their team went right to work. On March 5, 1980, members of the Wythe County Sheriff's Office and Virginia State Police Investigators arrested a 41-year old resident of Max Meadows in the "Piney" community, confiscating a large quantity of drugs. Dad and Pike, along with State Investigators T.S. Svard and A.E. Crane, issued a warrant at the residence of Marvin Eugene Roberts near Fort Chiswell, who was charged with possession of marijuana and possession of a controlled substance with intent to distribute after their police raid netted some 10,000 capsules and tablets in addition to a large quantity of marijuana.

Roberts was incarcerated at the Wythe County Jail in lieu of a $10,000 cash bond or $20,000 property bond.

"We're pleased with cooperation of the State Police on recent cases," Pike told the *Southwest Virginia Enterprise* on the morning following the arrest. "We hope to accomplish even more when working with them in the future."

Three Wythe County men were also arrested by the Wythe County Sheriff's Office in connection with the January 31 and February 29, 1980 breaking and entering on a Sand Mountain residence. Paul Sutliff, 34, of Wytheville was charged with the break-ins following an investigation completed by Dad and Deputy Jackie Kitts. Sutliff was also charged with carrying a concealed weapon, a .25 caliber handgun, upon his arrest.

In the *Southwest Virginia Enterprise*, Dad was recognized as a newly ranked captain, filling the position of Wythe County's newest Chief Deputy. The Grayson County native was credited with having extensive training in law enforcement, erroneously stating he had 12 years of experience. He actually had 14, as a former Detective Sergeant and State Investigator. A graduate of Galax High School, Dad held AA and BS degrees in Criminal Justice from Guilford College in Greensboro, NC.

"I am proud to be associated with the Wythe County Sheriff's Office and the experienced personnel that make up the department," Dad said.

Admin Staff of Wythe County Sheriff's Office early 1980's. Left to right: The late Betty Vaught, Jail Supervisor; Kermit Osborne, Civil/Court Supervisor (later became Sheriff);Ray Howell, JB Jackson, Paul Bailey, and the late Jackie Kitts, Patrol Supervisors; Herb Cooley, Chief Deputy; and Wayne Pike, Sheriff.

His new Wytheville home was at 830 W. Spiller Street, were he lived with his former wife Joy and my two half-brothers, Travis and John, who were 16 and 14-year-old students of George Wythe High School at the time. It is ironic that Dad is noted as an attendee of the Wytheville Church of Christ, as some 30 years later, I would be baptized there on March 18, 2010, without ever knowing Dad had been there. My wife Emily and I were also married there on July 10, 2010.

Moving to Wythe County proved to have a greater impact on his life than just his career. Newly divorced, my 37-year-old father would meet my mother, 19-year-old Rhonda Lynne Arnold, who was fresh out of high school working for court services in the county courthouse just upstairs from the Sheriff's Office. A 1979 graduate of Fort

Chiswell High School, Mom was a tiny, shy and freckled face girl that immediately stopped my dad in his tracks at first.

"She was standing across the hall from the Sheriff's Office with the brightest smile," Dad recalled once of their first meeting. "She was the cutest little redhead I had ever seen."

My parents, shortly after meeting in 1980.

Some of Dad's earliest challenges at being Chief Deputy in Wythe County included helping to find good employees and getting to know people in a new place.

"Our goal was to build a law enforcement agency that was professional, effective and fair but tough," Wayne said. "He came here and even though he was from an adjoining county, he was an outsider and he fit in and got the job done."

"Herb left a legacy of honesty, organization and professional ethics in law enforcement," he said of Dad's mark on Wythe County. "You have to remember that we built a real agency that had not been seen in most areas at that time. It was the beginning of professionalism in sheriff's departments throughout the state."

Of course, along with the tough times, being a police officer comes with its share of rewards including the satisfaction of doing your best to maximize protection of a community as well as putting a criminal behind bars after a grueling case and helping kids get off drugs and onto the right path. These are rewards that, for my dad, are worth the challenges. He counts his work in Wythe County among some of his greatest rewards. Maintaining a home in Wythe County since 1980, Dad considers his tenure with the Sheriff's Office, as well as his interaction with the community, to be a high mark in his career. In addition to his law enforcement accomplishments, Dad has been involved in many community organizations including the Wytheville-Wythe-Bland Chamber of Commerce, Rural Retreat Lake Authority, Wythe County Transportation Safety Commissions, and American Cancer Society.

"I met my beautiful wife, Rhonda, in Wythe County and raised two fine children there of whom I am very proud," he said of my mom, sister and I. "My daughter, Tara, is off to college and doing well while my son, Zach, writes for the *Wytheville Enterprise*, has been married to the lovely Emily Krug Cooley for almost a year now and is doing great!"

Our family vacation to Disney World, 1999.

"No matter where I go," my Dad added. "Wythe County and Wytheville will remain dear to my heart."

Dad feels he has accomplished everything he has set out to do as a law enforcer, has no regrets and is ready for the next chapter in his life. Despite its many challenges, my Dad says he still feels that law enforcement is honorable, satisfying and the greatest career in the world.

"It has always been my goal to do the best job possible for the community I serve and to leave every place better than I found it," he stated. "I hope I have done that."

I am humbled by my Dad's kind words towards me, but can only say that I am just as proud of him. Few people in his field will achieve what he has. My Dad will always be remembered for his accomplishments locally and throughout the state of Virginia and I'm very proud of that. However, even more so, I am simply proudest of him, not for his many well-deserved achievements in law enforcement, but for being my Dad.

Since my Dad has retired, I have looked at him in a different light than ever before. First off, the realization that he is no longer a police officer has yet to sink in. All my life and over the last 30 years my mother has known him, that's what he's been. I imagine no one is more affected by the surrealism of this fact than my Dad himself, who has devoted two-thirds of his life to a successful career in law enforcement. Until I intended his lavish retirement banquet at the beautiful Vinton War Memorial on June 28, 2011, which honored his 45-year career, I never realized just how successful his career has been.

"Your dad was very likable," Wayne added. "He presented a professional image and had a lot of good and sensible input."

One of Wayne's most vivid recollections of his and Dad's earliest work involved the chase of a local drug dealer named Mike Otey.

"Otey was a local drug dealer and was well-known when we arrived but he had not been arrested," he explained. "We began working to get rid of a large number of dealers that had been operating with almost impunity. "The Wythe County Sheriff's Office, prior to our arrival, had never made charges against anyone for dealing in drugs. That was hard to believe. We had Otey under surveillance and when we tried to stop him, he fled and ultimately hit the Adkins Mill Road bridge.

Amazingly, Otey survived with the bridge collapsed with his car.

"Sgt. Ray Howell was the vehicle in front of me that first activated the lights to stop Otey," the sheriff added. Your dad did a lot of work on this matter also."

\* \* \* \* \* \* \*

Mom and Dad were married on August 11, 1984 and I came along on March 25, 1985, a full 15 weeks ahead of schedule. Diagnosed with cerebral palsy, I was confined to a wheelchair for life, having only been given a ten percent chance of survival. Born at two pounds and three ounces, I spent the first two months of my life in Roanoke Memorial Hospital. While I was still in the hospital, Dad was airlifted there after being in a serious car accident that threw him through the windshield.

"I knew I was going to the hospital where my son was," Dad recalled as he was being lifted into the helicopter. "But I didn't know his name."

Mom was notified by Cliff Dicker, the deputy who was tragically murdered by a 15-year old gunman on December 6, 1994. I believe he drove her to the hospital.

"Your dad was coming into town and was in front of where Burger King used to be and a woman veered over into his lane and hit him head on," Wayne said. "She died and Herb had some head injuries and other things, but he was lucky."

Wayne recalls being really scared for my dad, but we both survived. I went to work a lot with Dad and have very fond memories of everyone there at the Sheriff's Office.

"When your dad brought you around later, you were a cute, wide-eyed kid with a bright smile and everyone loved you," Wayne stated. "When you were born, you were not expected to live and I was really worried for your dad."

My most endearing memory of Wayne Pike began one morning when I woke up with a terrible stomach ache. As my mother fed me my cereal, she thought my complaints were just an attempt to get out of school. However, she knew something was wrong when I suddenly told her I couldn't see. I blacked out and fell backwards. I regained consciousness to the sight of my mother crying, something by which I was horrified, having never seen it before. I remember trying to assure her I was okay, but could barely muster the words. Dad was away at training in Bristol. Mom frantically dialed 911, who sent an ambulance, but when the Sheriff's Office heard the news, they arrived and took me to the hospital first. My sister was just an infant so she couldn't leave until the babysitter arrived. Wayne held me in his arms as a tall, skinny officer with a black mustache whose name I cannot recall, drove me to the hospital with sirens blaring and stayed with me until Mom arrived. I'll never forget that.

As it turned out, my condition was quite serious. As I wrote in my book, *Hazel's Little Bud*, this was a disease from which I had suffered since that age of seven called autonomic dysfunction, which involves a malfunction of the autonomic nervous system. Symptoms of autonomic dysfunction are numerous and vary widely from person to person. Since autonomic dysfunction is a full-body condition, a large number of symptoms may be present that can greatly alter a person's quality of life. Each patient with autonomic dysfunction is different. Some are affected only mildly while others are left completely bed-ridden and disabled.

The primary symptoms present in patients with autonomic dysfunction are excessive fatigue, excessive thirst, lightheadedness, dizziness or vertigo, feelings of anxiety or panic which are not mentally induced, irregular heartbeat and a sudden drop in blood pressure, sometimes resulting in fainting. My having autonomic dysfunction is a result from the brain damage I suffered at birth, which also caused me to have cerebral palsy. Usually, my condition was a precursor to my getting very sick, such as the contraction of the flu or pneumonia.

I remember Wayne always giving me a dollar when he saw me.

"If your dad ever gives you any trouble, you just let me know," he would always whisper to me. "I'll come get him and take him to jail."

One time, I took him up on his offer. Once when I was probably about five, I remember arguing with Dad about something, then proceeding to the phone to call the sheriff at home.

"Come get my daddy," I told him.

Wayne showed up in a police car and I got a dollar. I've had faith in our local law enforcement ever since.

\* \* \* \* \* \* \*

On October 19, 1987, Dad was amongst the hype that was caused when UFO sightings were reported all over Wythe County. The national television show *Unsolved Mysteries* got involved and before long, we were in the national spotlight.

As the Fredericksburg, Virginia newspaper reported that day, Wythe County sheriff's deputies were seeing lights in the sky that caused a local UFO craze, but they were not prepared to battle any space aliens.

"I'd rather have something else put us on the map," Dad told the Associated Press. "This brings all the weirdos out. Before this is over, somebody is going to have to see some little green men."

He told reporters that the department had received more than a dozen phone calls about UFOs in the previous few weeks, but he also pointed out that there were probably many more people who had seen the flying lights who simply chose to keep their mouths shut so that no one would question their sanity. Dad heard reports of flying objects swooping down and running cars off the road, but noted that the department had never received any such complaints.

"The UFO thing was crazy and there is a lot of stuff written and even on Fox TV about it," Wayne recalled. "We never degraded people over what they thought they saw. I tended to say that it was probably military aircraft or some explainable thing. We tried to quell fears and not fuel rumor. It was kind of funny."

Dad taught police science for a while at Wytheville
Community College in the early 1990s.

In 1994, Dad decided to move up the ranks and
accept a position as Chief of Police in Pulaski. I was never
happy about this decision because I never wanted to leave
Wytheville. Neither did my mom and sister. While my
mother kept her job as a social worker and we stayed in
Wytheville schools, we did eventually by a home in Pulaski
in 1996, which we sold a year and a half later. Even when
we had a home in Pulaski, Mom kept an apartment in
Wytheville at which we stayed a lot during the school year. I
never felt at home in Pulaski. Even though we had a home
there, I never felt like I lived there. I've always told people
I have lived in Wytheville all my life because that's what it
feels like in my heart.

"He went to Pulaski because that gave him an
opportunity to run an agency of his own and be the boss,"

Wayne said of Dad's move. "Anyone with management skills and desires wants to move up and they want to reach the ultimate in their career. I always encouraged people who worked with me to reach higher, even though you do not want to lose them. It is a compliment when an employee is selected for a high position. I have been blessed to have many who worked under me to become chiefs, state police officials, military officers, state training officials and business owners and much more. That makes me feel good and I congratulate them."

"I believe in always being polite and kind to everyone until they force you to be otherwise," Wayne said in closing. "I believe that people who, through no fault of their own are down and need help, should have help. I believe that people who put themselves in that situation through laziness and or crime and bad conduct, have to suffer the consequences. I do not believe in a hand out for those who do not want to work but are physically able to do so. However the world is full of those who are not. They make up stories and lies in order to have self gain. I have no use for these kinds of people. My dad was a hard-working man who raised eight children and he never made hardly any money. He paid his bills and kept us safe and I have always loved and respected him for that. He never had many opportunities but he did his best and came through. He never asked nor got any handout. He did it all on his own. He was uneducated and an unknown person but he is an icon in my eyes."

## Chapter 6
## A Brother Figure

Throughout my life, Danna "Teny" Underwood has been a constant presence and treasured friend. I have countless memories of her bringing me balloons after surgery or throwing me a birthday party at the Sheriff's Office. To all of us who were children of Wythe County deputies, she was an honorary aunt. To the rest of Wythe County, she has been a symbol of safety and protection. On October 1, 2015, Teny ended her 35-year career as a police officer.

A lifelong Ivanhoe resident, Teny was hired in 1980 by Sheriff Wayne Pike and my dad, to work as a dispatcher. After a year, she was offered a jailor position and worked the next several years at the Wythe County Jail. Later, she would graduate from the Law Enforcement Basic Academy obtaining a variety of additional certifications.

"It all happened so fast," Teny said. "I was just happy to do whatever was needed whether it was dispatching, jail, civil, courts or transports."

Although Teny was hired with only a high school education, her full-time job on alternate shifts enabled her to earn a degree in Criminal Justice and Corrections from Wytheville Community College. She has also obtained many other certifications throughout her career at various criminal justice academies.

She credits many of her colleagues along the way with helping to contribute to her success during her 35-year career, including former Sheriff Wayne Pike, my dad and uncle, Herb and Doug Cooley, both of whom were former chief deputies for the Wythe County Sheriff's Office, and current Wythe County Sheriff Keith Dunagan. She also mentioned the other two former sheriffs for whom she worked, Kermit Osborne and Doug King.

"There are too many more to mention whose faith, support and encouragement have gotten me through these 35 ½ years," Teny stated.

She also credits her parents, the late Everett and Bea Underwood, who instilled a work ethic within her that made Teny the dependable, hard worker she has always been.

"They always told me that you had to work hard and stick with whatever job you were given," she recalled.

As one of the earliest female officers hired in Wythe County, Teny admits that although many of her jobs were geared toward her own gender, she was always amongst the action of her male colleagues. She appreciated the mutual respect and teamwork that has always resonated throughout the department. Throughout her career, Teny has worked with the department to become what she believes to be one of the best law enforcement agencies around.

"The Wythe County Sheriff's Office has been highly respected and I have travelled all over the United States and Canada to accept awards that we received from organizations such as the Virginia Sheriff's Association and the International Association of Chiefs of Police for our programs in traffic safety, seatbelt awareness and crime prevention working to protect and serve our county," Teny explained. "These awards weren't my awards, but I was honored to represent this great organization."

Over the years, Teny has initiated the Drug Abuse Resistance Education program, which educated elementary and middle school students about the dangers of drug use. Interacting with so many students and teachers has been one of the most rewarding aspects of her career.

Also among Teny's career highlights is the time she spent working with interns from area colleges who came to the Sheriff's Office.

"The students need to know what it's like to be a police officer and we allow them to see the different areas of law enforcement first hand," she told me. "Many have been hired and continue to move up within the department."

Throughout her career, Teny has often found herself flying across the nation to bring prisoners back to Wythe County for trial. She has experienced every form of weather from the sunshine of California to the bitter winter of Montana. Affectionately dubbed as the quartermaster of the department, Teny has been issuing uniforms, badges and guns to children of her former colleagues. This has led her to consider retirement to travel and do things that her job has required her to cut short in the past.

Teny plans to return to the department for special activities and projects such as the Cliff Dicker Memorial Scholarship Committee and Golf Tournament, which annually honors her friend and colleague who was gunned down in the line of duty on December 6, 1994.

"I just can't leave this behind," she said in closing. "The folks here at the Sheriff's Office are my best friends and I will miss every one of them."

As sad as it was to see Teny go, no one deserves a retirement more than her. She has devoted more than half her life the service of Wythe County and has earned our eternal friendship and respect in return. We wish Teny all the best, which is nothing less than she has always given us.

Teny was probably the interview to which I was most looking forward because she was a dear friend, a straight shooter and one of my dad's biggest champions. She stayed close to all of us over the years and is still a great blessing to our family. Her and Dad have remained a mutual admiration society to one another amidst there decades long friendship.

"I always thought of your dad as an Andy Taylor sort of character," Teny told me during our interview. "The inmates all liked him, but they knew to follow his rules."

She illustrated her point by telling a well-known story about a prisoner who jumped over the fence of the Wythe

County Jail on Monroe Street, attempting to escape by Wither's Park. Dad was around the back of the jail in uniform, but had no weapon. He quickly shoved his thumb and index finger into his pocket to make the prisoner think he was reaching for his gun.

"Freeze," he shouted. "Get on the ground!"

The convict obeyed. As the officers handcuffed him, leading him back to jail, he whispered to Dad.

"You didn't have a gun, did you?" he asked.

"Nope," Dad smiled. "I sure didn't."

"The prisoners befriended him, but they knew that had to do what he said," Teny said. "All he had to say was 'freeze' and that guy knew he wasn't going anywhere."

"The guy's name was Graham Craig and he was a fugitive from Texas," she added. "Those guys were known for being in trouble and were some of our most fearsome prisoners. But, for Herb, they just stopped."

Much like the fictional TV sheriff of Mayberry, if you were compliant with the rules, Dad would be your friend. On the flipside, if you were belligerent and defiant, he could reciprocate in that manner just as easily.

"He had a lot of respect within the community as well as those who worked and lived within the jail," Teny remarked. "He treated everybody right and they appreciated him for that."

In the early days of the Pike-Cooley partnership in the Wythe County Sheriff's Office, everything had to be started from scratch. As a result, Wayne Pike left little room for error among his newly refurbished department.

"A lot of times, people didn't make the cut in those days," Teny explained. "Herb kept Wayne calm and saved a lot of people's jobs by convincing him to listen to what they had to say."

"Let's talk to them," Dad would say. "Let's hear their side of the story."

"In situations where Wayne would overreact, Herb would be willing to offer a second chance," Teny added. "He had faith in people. If he liked you and knew your capabilities, he stood by you."

She recalled a specific incident in which he did the same for her. Teny had just started the newly initiated Drug Abuse Resistance Education (D.A.R.E.) program in 1987. She had rolled a television across the street to the adjacent Wytheville Recreation Center from the Sheriff's Office to present a video on the department for Career Day within the school system. On the way back across 4th Street, the TV inadvertently slipped off the cart and landed in the street in shambles.

Another officer came out to warn Teny that the sheriff had witnessed the accident and planned to fire whoever was responsible. She quickly went in and told Dad what had happened. He and Wayne came rushing outside.

"I'm going to fire whoever broke that TV," fumed the sheriff.

"Wait a minute," said Dad. "It couldn't be helped."

"Herb took care of me on that one," Teny laughed.

She also gave special notice to Dad's extracurricular community efforts including his presidencies in both the Wytheville-Wythe-Bland Chamber of Commerce and the Wythe County Transportation Safety Commission.

"When he was over that group, they did all kinds of things to make sure our roads were safe," Teny commended. "Herb put more patrollers out and there were more monitors on speeders in the most crucial areas."

She also noted that Dad went the extra mile to make sure his officers maintain good morale and physical fitness. He organized and coached a softball team for adults.

"That's where I met you," Teny told me. "I used to babysit you when he would bring you to the softball games."

"I knew you from day one, but the softball games were where we first bonded," Teny noted.

That bond continues to this day, as Dad and I both count Teny among our dearest and most cherished friends.

"Herb always organized a team of us to play in tournaments whenever we could," she recalled. "It kept us in shape and we always had a good time."

While most of the team was comprised of members from the Wythe County Sheriff's Office, the team also included civilians such as my maternal grandfather, Bruce Arnold, and members of the Virginia State Police.

When my parents were first married, they were known for hosting the best known Halloween parties in town. They hosted the Sheriff's Office and their spouses every year. I've seen the pictures and some of those costumes are really something.

Before my sister and I were born, Mom and Dad were known for throwing the best Halloween parties in town.

Wayne Pike recalled a particularly fond memory of one party.

"On one occasion of one of the Halloween parties, Herb and I dressed up in giant white rabbit costumes that were just hilarious," he remembered. "We got into a car with a prisoner cage and were transported to the jail and you should have seen the passersby looking at what they thought were probably two inebriated Halloween celebrants being taken to jail. At the jail, we went to a holding cell and then a supervisor came in who was not aware of what was going on. He was told to come see these two in the cell. He could not believe it and was shocked when he realized who it was. It was just a little innocent fun to relieve stress from a demanding job."

"We never missed those parties," Teny remembered happily. "Herb was always the one initiating these gatherings because he wanted us to do things together as a family."

"We really were a family in those days," she added. "Herb and Doug Cooley have always felt like brothers to me."

Never knowing my parents to be very extroverted outside of work, I expressed my surprise at the seemingly happening occasion they were hosting.

"We were fun before we had kids," Dad responded.

The Sheriff's Office really was a family in those days. I know because I grew up feeling like a very big part of that, largely thanks to Teny.

"Wayne and Herb made our department what it was," Teny remarked. "They initiated all the safety programs, many of which are still in place today."

The previous sheriff, the late Buford Shockley, had only two or three deputies on the payroll. There were no programs in place, the initiation of which made the department not only more effectively run, but more accessible to the general public.

"It created more positions for officers and more opportunities to move up," she stated. "Their programs saved so many lives and we learned from the professionalism that Herb and Wayne brought to the Sheriff's Office."

She and her fellow officers became more professional in turn.

"Wayne was the boss, but Herb was a key player in the planning and execution of all those programs," Teny attested. "There are still a few of us around from that era that carry with them the dedication that learned from Herb and Wayne."

The public image of police could very well have been one of fear and distance. Dad's arrival on the scene in Wythe County helped to establish a rapport between its citizens and law enforcement. Dad, Pike and their team helped people to know that while members of the Wythe County Sheriff's Office were to be respected, they would earn their respect by protecting local citizens and being friendly towards them.

"He helped our agency receive recognition on a state and federal level and went out of his way to show that our work was appreciated within the department," Teny explained. "His awareness programs also helped us be more appreciated by the general public."

She noted that he did the instilled confidence in all of his officers.

"If he believed in you, he gave you the chance to move up and take steps you needed to take," Teny said. "That gave you more confidence in yourself and the way you performed your job."

Dad's confidence in his officers and the ideas he proposed usually resonated favorably throughout the department.

"Most of the time, anyone who worked for the good of the department agreed with whatever Herb said," she noted. "We all knew that pretty much anything he suggested was needed."

Among some of the first female officers ever to be hired onto the Wythe County Sheriff's Office, Teny says she never felt ostracized as such.

"I think Herb was the reason why," she emphasized. "He always made everyone feel of equal importance and value."

She added that Dad and Pike made her feel safe on the job, especially as a woman who never married or had children. She also credited Dad and Pike with hiring Paul Bailey, the first African American officer hired in Wythe County to her knowledge.

"If you could do the job, Herb and Wayne would give it to you to do," Teny told me. "It didn't matter if you were male, female, black, white or whatever."

Being in a position of authority never prohibited Dad from staying in step with his colleagues, according to Teny.

"He would never ask you to do anything he wouldn't do himself," she stated. "He was always by your side as you were doing the job as well."

Having worked together in High Point where trailblazing ideas such as interracial and female officers weren't as taboo, Dad and Wayne brought these ideals of equality with them to Wythe County.

"They knew what would work," Teny affirmed. "They gave everyone the same chance no matter who they were."

Despite feeling a big loss when Dad left Wythe County for the Chief of Police position in Pulaski, Teny said that his brother, my uncle Doug, did a great job as his replacement.

"He really helped me out a lot," she said. "He helped push my ideas forward."

"I know all of Herb's officers in Pulaski and Vinton thought as much of him as we did," Teny added. "He was firm but supportive leader and a true gentleman."

Teny will always have a special place in Dad's heart, as he always regarded her as his "pet."

"If he needed something done, he always gave it to me to do because he knew he could count on me," she laughed. "He gave me a little extra to do than everyone else, but that's alright, because it made me stronger."

Teny is also special because Dad refers to her as a "junior Hazel," referring to my great-great aunt Hazel Stoots. Hazel never married or had any children of her own, but had a motherly hand in raising every kid in the community. Teny was certainly similar.

Hazel raised my mom in Austinville while officiating the after school program for all the area kids in the recreation center located in the bottom of Austinville Elementary School. As a result, Teny knew my mom before she ever met Dad.

"I was older than her, but I was from Ivanhoe and I remember her cheerleading for all the ballgames at Fort Chiswell High School," she told me. "Your Dad liked her right away."

She also recalled Dad and Hazel hitting it off early on.

"Hazel was the best and Herb knew it," Teny recalled. "I can remember her face lighting up whenever he was around, too."

"People lit up like that when Herb was around," she added. "He was a very special person. I know my friend Maxine Waller thought there was nothing like him."

Dad was always a big collector of things. One of his more prevalent items was police uniform patches from agencies across the globe.

"He started collecting police patches whenever he would travel out of the county or state to extradite a prisoner or something like that," Teny noted. "He helped get my collection started and now I have all kinds of them from all over the place."

Teny credited dad for making the Wythe County Sheriff's Office a familial unit.

"Herb was the glue that held us all together," she said with a smile. "He knew how stressful our job could be and he always made sure we did things together that made our job more enjoyable."

She also mentioned her fondness for my dad's parents.

"I really liked your Granny Cooley," she told me. "She was a good woman and a very pretty woman."

My dad's parents, the late Herbert W. and Irene Cooley, with Mom and Dad on their wedding day on August 11, 1984.

I agree. My Granny, Irene Cooley, was something special. We didn't have her nearly long enough. We were extremely close, but she died when I was seven years old of pancreatic cancer on May 17, 1992.

"There have been many times that your Dad would go to Galax to see his parents and I would go along with them," she said. "They were great people and I miss them, too."

Teny also noted how he included me in his work.

"You had your own desk in his office," she said with a chuckle. "We all looked after you and you had your own place."

I can remember Teny giving me my own mailbox at the Sheriff's Office and filling it with candy and balloons. I know that when I had surgery in South Carolina at the Shriner's Hospital at the age of eight in order to release my hamstrings, the whole department sent me a packet of toys, coloring books and puzzles. When I came home, Teny showed up at my house with the biggest bouquet of balloons I have ever seen.

Living true to her nickname, Teny was always very small. As she walked up our long driveway, a big gust of wind came along. Teny and the balloons went airborne like Mary Poppins. That's an image that will never leave my mind. When I was very small, I can recall coming to the jail and getting a carton of milk. Given my obsession with the color red, I had to have the milk in the red carton. I remember thinking that those prisoners were lucky to get some of the coldest milk in the country.

Whenever I see Robert Burnette, who is now sadly confined to a wheelchair due to his declining health over the years, he still recalls my visits to the jail.

"You called it Robert and Teny's house," he said to me. "You always said you wanted your dad to take you to Robert and Teny's house."

"You were always the most fun kid to be around because you laughed at everything," Teny added. "Everything I did or said to entertain you, you would laugh."

I think that was due in large part to Teny's gregarious personality, universal sense of humor and her own infectious laugh.

There are many who have said, especially since Teny's recent retirement, that she could have easily been Wythe County's first-ever female sheriff. However, this was never an aspiration she would ever have desired to reach in her career.

"I would much rather be a helper than someone who takes charge," she told me. "I will take charge of certain projects if I'm asked, but I am not a political person and I would much rather be a worker behind the scenes than to have the responsibility of working on the front lines."

She felt that Dad or my Uncle Doug, on the other hand, would have been ideal candidates for the job.

Teny and Dad worked together in the D.A.R.E program for years.

"They were both excellent supervisors and it would have been great for me if either of them had decided to run for sheriff," Teny remarked. "It was a big loss for both the Wythe County Sheriff's Department and to me personally when those guys left."

She also had high praise for Wayne Pike, the man who hired her on to the department.

"When my mother passed away last year, Wayne was one of the first people to call me and offer his condolences," she told me not long ago. "Wayne was always really good about things like that and I'm really glad that I have had the chance to tell them both recently how much I have always appreciated the both of them."

I can attest to the kindness of the Wythe County Sheriff's Office in times of sorrow in my own family. When my grandfather passed away on August 15, 1997, Dad was Chief of Police in Pulaski and Doug was Chief Deputy in Wythe County. At my grandfather's funeral, most of the officers from both agencies were there.

I was equally touched when my Uncle Mike passed away suddenly of pancreatic cancer at the untimely age of 63, to see a Wythe County Sheriff's Office car in the parking lot of the funeral home when Emily and I pulled up. Inside, Chief Deputy Keith Dunagan, who would become sheriff in 2014, was there with Teny as well as other members from the department.

"I was really worried about your dad after that loss," Teny said to me. "I was afraid he would really get down after that."

I was equally concerned. Dad had experienced heart problems since about 2005 and we were really scared for quite a while. Just as his health seemed to be on the upswing, we got the horrible news of Mike's terminal diagnosis. I think Dad expected to pass on before his younger brother and outliving him was almost more than he could bear. Still, he handled the loss with his trademark rock solid courage and dignity. I was proud of him.

Keith Dunagan, who served as sheriff when Teny retired, made her a lieutenant just before she hung up her badge. This ranked her just under the chief deputy. Teny also praised Dunagan for the job he has done and is continuing to do as the leader of the Wythe County Sheriff's Office.

"Keith is one of the good guys that came from the era of officers when the Wythe County Sheriff's Department was a family," Teny stated. "That was the way Herb and Wayne taught us to be and that's how it should be."

Teny also said in closing that the stellar reputation that the Wythe County Sheriff's Office continues to maintain is due in great part to a legacy that Dad left there.

"I think the Wythe County Sheriff's Office does a great job of protecting people and helping all the citizens of Wythe County to feel safe," she stated. "I don't think any of these things would have ever happened had Wayne Pike and Herb Cooley not entered into the picture."

Dad has attested to Teny's integrity many times.

"You will never find Teny gossiping about anyone or not telling the truth," he has said many times about our dear friend. "She is one hundred percent down to business and that's it. There is absolutely no nonsense about Teny."

I think Dad would be proud to know that she credits him with the learning of her work ethic.

Dad judging a fire prevention event

"It was Herb who really taught what it truly means to be a good officer," she said. "I have told him how much I appreciate him and I believe he feels the same way about me."

Courtesy of the Kegley Library Archive, Dad became
the new Chief Deputy for Wythe County on January 1,
1980.

## Chapter 7
## From Puppet Shows to Dead Cattle

On January 23, 1981, Dad served as master of ceremonies when Wythe County Sheriff's Department Members performed a puppet show at Speedwell Elementary School as an ongoing crime prevention campaign sponsored by the department and funded via contributions from Wythe County citizens. The skits were performed on the stage of the school gym to the entire student body, which ranged from kindergarteners to seventh graders. All responded enthusiastically to the lighthearted approach to the serious issues of crime prevention and safety taken on by the puppets.

Dad introduced the show to the audience, competing for their attention with Marvin, a puppet with a dry sense of humor. Marvin, who had the responsibility of introducing his fellow cast members, had difficulty relinquishing his share of the limelight, which led to some amusing antics. Eventually, Dad retreated to the wings to let Marvin and the other puppets have the run of the show. Puppets with serious messages were animated by Deputies Tommy Horton and Ray Howell.

The dangers of talking to strangers were expounded by a puppet called Officer Holley. After several interruptions from Marvin in his relentless attempt to steal the show, Officer Holley went on to explain the seriousness and importance of fire safety at home and everywhere. Reggie, a puppet who walked to the park alone, cut between two parked cars to illustrate the theme of traffic safety.

"*Watch out for traffic. Never dash into the street,*" he sang. "*Cross at a corner. Wait for cars when crossing. Never chase a ball into the street.*"

A youthful puppet named Danny talked about bicycle and skateboard safety. He also had a song for the audience.

*"I know what I'm saying. I've had a ticket or three,"* Danny sang. *"The law's for obeying. Take it from me."*

Vandalism was addressed by the cowboy puppet Vandalism Vick who stressed the overall self harm in the long run that is in store for those who steal. Stan Star, an actor puppet and former drug user, released details about his new movie, *Death of a Doper*, which deals with details about the effects of drug use and explains that friendship and fun can be better implemented without them. Puppet comedian Milton Murrow warmed up the audience with a few wisecracks but found no funny jokes about hitchhiking. Murrow managed to get a few laughs before stressing the negative repercussions of riding with strangers.

The only nonprofit member of the show troop was Dexter, the police dog who belonged to my uncle Deputy Doug Cooley. Dexter had been trained in the detection of illegal substances. After demonstrating his adeptness at finding drugs, Dexter attacked a deputy wearing a training pad to protect him from the dog's proficient blitz. This drew a great reaction from the crowd.

With a final bow from the entire puppet ensemble as well as the human cast, Deputy Tommy Horton performed a serious song called "Little Flowers," a morally poignant ballad that served as well-received finale to a successful show. Principal Tommy Eller of Speedwell Elementary School commended the Wythe County Sheriff's Office for their program.

"Our school had sponsored an earlier program on shoplifting presented by the drama club as the result of a parent and teacher cooperation through the PTA," he stated. "Skits of this nature are commendable because they make children aware of different social views and install a respect for values."

The Crime Prevention Unit owned its own sound system, the puppet stage as well as its own store and transportation units. No county funds were used in this project and all of the officers contributed their own time on a volunteer basis. The following month, they were invited the Bristol Police Department to attend a Police Equipment and Exhibition Show. The unit also toured Wythe County, performing the puppet show for various other schools.

\* \* \* \* \* \*

Wythe County's police dog, Dexter, assisted the Smyth County Sheriff's Office in the capture of a cache of drugs on Tuesday night, January 27, 1981. This was the second drug case that Dexter helped close related to drug charges in Smyth County. Dad, Doug and Dexter, all being from the Wythe County Sheriff's Office, assisted the Smyth County deputies in securing the arrest and subsequent charge of intent to distribute.

Arlie Tex Roberts of Smyth County was charged with the possession of a large quantity of marijuana, Quaaludes, preludin, valium, and a smaller quantity of crystal P.C.P. Wythe County Sheriff Pike believed that this arrest and seizure would prevent another array of drugs from entering into Wythe County. He credited Smyth County Sheriff Jerry Archer and his deputies for doing a top-notch job and said Dexter sniffed out the evidence immediately.

On March 5, 1981, Sheriff Pike reported that the Wythe County Sheriff's Department had just received a grant in the amount of $7,300 from the Department of Transportation Safety. The grant money was to be used in the purchase of speed detection equipment in a safety program directed in the school zones throughout Wythe County. A portion of the grant was also used to compensate deputies for their work after hours in the operation of the equipment. This freed all deputies to be able to perform their normal duties while still provide overtime pay for time used to work the school zones during the deputies' off-duty hours.

"Captain Herb Cooley, vice chairman of the Transportation Safety Board, has worked with board chairman Grace Scott to bring about this grant and program," stated the sheriff. "Also, this would not have been possible without the work of Danny Dean, a local employee of the state, who helps to coordinate these grants. Danny Dean means a great deal to our county in acquiring these types of programs."

Late on the evening of July 1, 1981, Dad and Doug arrested 23-year old Janice King of the Gutton Park section of Wythe County near Max Meadows and charged her with possession of marijuana with the intent to distribute to an inmate as well as contributing to the delinquency of a minor. She was arrested and charged at the Wythe County Jail. Attempting to distribute drugs to an inmate is classified as a Class 5 Felony and is punishable by 1 to 10 years in prison in a state penitentiary and/or a $1,000 fine. King was released on bond pending her July 20, 1981 hearing in the Wythe County General District Court.

A week later on July 8, 1981, Dad along with Deputy Tommy Horton, arrested another young Max Meadows woman on drug charges. Twenty-two-year-old Sharon C. Gravely was arrest in Wytheville and charged with the possession of marijuana with the intent to distribute. Her apprehension came after an extensive investigation in which her vehicle was seized after a large quantity of drugs was found inside.

This was the third grant that was secured by the Wythe County Sheriff's Office at the helm of my father within his first year on the department, which was in an effort to decrease the burden of Wythe County taxpayers. The Wythe County Board of Supervisors as well as its administrator, out of concern for its citizens, was very hopeful in their support of these grants, which they were pleased were successfully awarded.

On July 21, 1981, a fourth suspect was named in a theft the previous month of more than $100,000 in heavy equipment from the Fort Chiswell Construction Company with his arrest forthcoming. Three Goldsboro, North Carolina were arrested the previous week as the result of an investigation conducted by the Wythe County Sheriff's Department, the Scotland County, North Carolina Sheriff's Department and the North Carolina State Bureau of Investigation. They were Rubin Earl Dail, 42, Charles Edward Chesnutt, 36, and John Steven Claurer, 27. An extradition hearing for the suspect was scheduled for August 13, 1981 in the Scotland County, North Carolina circuit court.

There was a possible connection in this case to other thefts in Wythe County, which Dad was busy investigating with his friend and colleague Deputy Ray Howell. According to a police spokesman, the serial numbers on the equipment had been changed in addition to the painting of the equipment. A Mack truck and low boy trailer, valued in excess of $40,000 have been identified by their owner and returned to Wythe County.

Between the hours of 1 p.m. on August 23 and 1:30 a.m. on August 24, 1981, Deputy Marty Stallard discovered a break-in at the Fort Chiswell Grocery while he was on routine patrol in that area. Minutes later, he and Sargeant Jackie Kitts discovered that the Fort Chiswell ARCO and Tastee-Freeze had both been broken into as well. With that, the two deputies initiated certain departmental procedures, which included notifying Dad and Investigators Lephew and Vaughn.

As the result of the follow-up procedure and investigation, Johnny Crockett Shipwash, Richard Tracy McKinney and Michael David Armbrister, all of Ivanhoe, were charged with breaking and entering. Ivanhoe residents Lucy McKinney, Francis Shipwash and Shirley Ayers were also charged with the concealing a weapon. Cases were cleared at Fort Chiswell Grocery, ARCO, and Tastee-Freeze as well as the Virginia State Police Highway Maintenance Shop in Fort Chiswell with approximately $1,000 in recovered merchandise. At the time of his arrest, Johnny Crockett Shipwash was out of jail on bond awaiting trial on another breaking and entering charge, which had originally ended in a hung jury. This result came after one juror held out his not guilty vote against eleven votes for conviction. After a long delay, the judge declared the jury hung. Shipwash was also awaiting sentencing on September 1, 1981 after being convicted of that charge in federal court.

Also at the time of his arrest, Richard Tracy McKinney was awaiting trial for breaking and entering charges in a case cleared by the Wythe County Sheriff's Department after several hundred dollars of property belonging to a local church was recovered. On August 1, 1981, the residence of Harry Walk, near Ivanhoe, was entered and as the result of investigative work performed by Doug, Lt. Lephew and Investigator Vaughn, subjects Gerald Weatherman and Robert F. King of Ivanhoe were arrested and charged with breaking and entering, which involved the theft of stereo and speaker equipment.

"These arrests have a great deal to do with the good patrol system which we now have and enable us to give better service, especially during late evening hours throughout the county as well as through certain intelligence information," commended the press. "Our patrol sergeants and deputies do a great job and, as time goes on, we should see an even better result from the new system we now have."

On August 30, 1981, a 25 year employee of a Wytheville business was arrested and charged with the grand larceny of $598 of heavy equipment parts. William R. Burress of the Sand Mountain section of Wythe County was apprehended following an investigation by Dad and Sgt. Ray Howell of the Wythe County Sheriff's Office conducted in Wythe and Carroll Counties. Burress was released from custody on bail pending a hearing as Dad and his deputies continued their investigation into the theft.

Dad and his brother Doug worked together to confiscate a series of marijuana plants from a Wythe County field on Thursday, September 10, 1981 were suspected to be of the sensimilla variety. However, until lab tests were conducted, this could not be confirmed. If indeed it was determined to be sensimilla, this type of marijuana is said to be 150 percent more potent that domestic marijuana. According to police reports at the time, this type of drug was selling in the streets for more than $3,000 per pound. The Wythe County man arrested for growing the 68 plants was said to have had a manual in his home specifically instructing him on the growth of sensimilla type of marijuana.

On Wednesday, October 28, 1981, 22-year-old Stanley Edward Richardson, son of Edward Richardson, pastor of the Wytheville Pentecostal Holiness Church, was killed after an apparent hunting incident. He was pronounced dead at the scene after suffering from a single gunshot wound. The shooter, Gary Chitwood Walker, was arrested at the scene by Wythe County Sheriff's Department personnel and subsequently charged with second degree murder. A resident of Wytheville, Walker was later released on bond pending a preliminary hearing in Wythe County General District Court.

My Uncle Doug told reporters that the shooting occurred around 5:30 p.m. in the Muskrat section of Wythe County. Richardson was reportedly looking for deer signs with a companion, Garland W. Hagee, a resident of the Muskrat community. Hagee told the deputies of the Wythe County Sheriff's Office that he and Richardson were standing in an open field preparing to smoke a cigarette when someone started shooting them. The two young men began to run when Richmond suddenly clutched his arm and fell to the ground. Hagee retreated to the cover of the woods until the shooting ceased before returning to check on his fallen friend.

When he discovered that Richardson had been shot and was unconscious, Hagee ran to his home to call the Wythe County Rescue Squad. Doug reported to the press that Richardson was struck with a single bullet that entered through one arm making its way into his chest. He reported that the bullet was apparently fired from a 7 millimeter rifle. Witnesses told authorities that five shots were heard while Walker claims to having been shooting at deer in the area.

As Halloween 1981 approached the Wythe County Sheriff's Department collaborated with the Wytheville Police Department in the preparation of effective measures to ensure that Halloween was safe and happy for all citizens of Wythe County. According to local law, a curfew of 9 p.m. is established for all trick-or-treaters, all of whom are not to exceed the age of twelve. No person over twelve is permitted to trick-or-treat within the streets, parks or any public place within the town limits of Wytheville. Furthermore, it is unlawful for any parent or guardian of a minor to allow such person to violate any part of the regulation.

"Town ordinances governing the celebration of Halloween in the Town of Wytheville will be rigidly enforced and no vandalism or any unlawful act will be tolerated," advised Wytheville Police Chief Warren Z. McAllister in a release to the press. "Violators of the law will be prosecuted to the fullest extent of the law."

Chief McAllister also ordered extra members of his force to be on duty for Halloween night for extra enforcement all lawful acts which might be violated.

Dad was responsible for completing the patrol schedule for the entire Wythe County Sheriff's Department during local Halloween festivities. He ordered all department personnel on duty for the entire evening to ensure that the law would be adequately enforced over all sections of Wythe County.

"It is the desire of Wythe County Sheriff G. Wayne Pike and the entire Wythe County Sheriff's Department that all citizens have a safe and happy Halloween," Dad stated. "We intend to keep vandalism down and insure that our children are kept safe and secure."

On April 15, 1982, Danny Gordon of the *Southwest Virginia Enterprise* reported that a six-month long investigation, in which Dad had directed, had finally drawn to a close. This was thanks to surveillance across three states on behalf of law enforcement, extensive undercover work, as well as the use of informants. It concluded with the arrest of a Wytheville businessman on drug and drug paraphernalia charges.

Clyde "Buddy" Carroll, owner of Carberry's, LTD of Wytheville, was arrested on Tuesday, April 13, 1982 after search warrants that had been issued for Carroll's property resulted in a cache of drugs and drug paraphernalia. The violator was also the owner of Upper South Distributors in Rocky Gap, VA. Under Dad's direction, the Wythe County Sheriff's Department initiated the investigation which led to Carroll's arrest in Bland County with the aid of the Virginia State Police Narcotics Division and a deputy from the Bland County Sheriff's Office. The Wythe County Sheriff's Department, assisted by the other two agencies, seized all the evidence after announcing their raid at 10 P.M. that Tuesday evening. The search warrants produced more than $100,000 of drug paraphernalia, an estimated one pound of marijuana, a large amount of cash and a sizeable amount of unidentified pills, Quaaludes and several grams of cocaine.

A 1977 Dodge motor home was confiscated following the raid along with an enclosed 1980 Ford Van. According to Wythe County Sheriff G. Wayne Pike, although members of Caroll's shop staff were involved in the investigation, he did not expect any charged would be filed against Carroll locally as he had just returned to the area from a three day stay in Knoxville, Tennessee.

By April 20th, the Virginia State Police had filed charges against Carroll on four counts of intent to distribute marijuana, cocaine, amphetamines and a Quaalude known as methaqualone. The law enforcement agency valued the drugs at an estimated $10,000. Additionally, Carroll was charged with possession with intent to distribute more than $100,000 of various drug paraphernalia including bongs, scales and cocaine kits.

Dad told the press that his arrest came after a tip from an informant had been received that Carroll had a large amount of drugs and drug paraphernalia in his possession. He passed the information along to the Virginia State Police Narcotics Division and then accompanied agent Bob Woodard to the location of Carroll's warehouse in Rocky Gap. After obtaining search warrants for his Bland County property, Carroll was arrested and his two vehicles, which were parked outside his warehouse, were confiscated. He was freed on a $50,000 property bond pending his June 8, 1982 hearing in Bland County General District Court.

* * * * * * *

On the afternoon of Saturday, February 19, 1983, a prisoner at the Wythe County Jail bled extensively before being apprehended by jail official before escaping. According to the officer in charge of corrections, Lt. Ray Howell, prisoners were in the recreation area at about 1:30 P.M. when a "minor diversion" provided 42-year old Graham Craig with an opportunity to climb over the top of the compound fence.

"The fence had recently been topped with razor wire in compliance with state regulations," stated Howell. "The escape appeared to be planned."

The wire severely cut Craig's arm, leaving a trail of blood as he ran 200 yards before being captured by Dad in the Withers Field ballpark area. Dressed in regulation red jail clothing, Craig was taken to Wythe County Community Hospital where he was treated and received several stitches. His freedom lasted a total of two minutes.

According to Howell, the Bristol, Tennessee was sentenced to 20 years in a state penitentiary by the Wythe County circuit court for breaking and entering the home of Fort Chiswell resident Agnes Davis as well as the home of Virginia State Trooper N.W. Dowdy near the Pulaski county line. Craig was also facing an additional five year sentence for breaking and entering in Bristol and was also wanted in South Carolina for violation of parole. At the time of his attempted escape, Craig was waiting to be transported to a state facility. Lack of space at the state prison has prevented his immediate transport.

On February 24, 1983, Dad made front page headlines as the *Southwest Virginia Enterprise* read, "Captain Cooley Puts Finger on Escapee."

Dad speaks to a crowd at Wytheville Community College.

\* \* \* \* \* \* \* \* \* \*

David "Dave" Loren Battistoni was arrested on Monday, March 13, 1984, was arrested in connection with the death of thirteen purebred Black Angus beef cattle. He is charged with cruelty to animals and thirteen counts of failure to properly dispose of carcasses. Wytheville veterinarian Dr. K.E. Hall was called by the Wythe County Sheriff's Department to assess the dead cattle.

"I've never seen anything like it," he stated.

The arrest was made after the Wythe County Sheriff's Department responded to an anonymous call complaining of cattle carcasses being spread all over the Stringtown area farm. Dad, having recently been promoted to major, and Captain J.B. Jackson, drove onto the farm conducting a preliminary investigation, after which they quickly returned to town obtaining search warrants for Battistoni's arrest. The apprehension was made without incident and Dr. Hall immediately began autopsies to determine if malnutrition was indeed the cause of death.

Hall told reporters that he had been called to the residence two months earlier. During this visit, he examined two dead cattle to determine that they had died from the ingestion of poisonous cherry laurel. The later autopsies revealed no such toxins.

The live cattle on the farm numbered approximately 125 head as of the time of the investigation with many showing signs of apparent malnutrition. Others appeared to be infested with lice and had large areas where the hair has been rubbed away leaving splotches of bare skin. Cattle bawled loudly as they followed Dad, Captain Jackson and Dr. Hall all around the farm during their investigation.

Battistoni was not the owner of the cattle or the farm, but was an apparent contractually hired caretaker for an investment firm in New York. While the owner of the livestock was not definitely established, the land was leased to Battistoni by Max Meadows owner James "Eddie" Hagee. Both cows on which Hall originally performed autopsies were pregnant. One was eight months and the other nine. Both were black. Upon inspection of the adult carcasses, Dr. Hall found tattoos in the right ear of one of the dead cattle, which is a generally an identification purpose used for more expensive animals.

"No one would bother to tattoo a worthless animal," said Dr. Hall, who estimated each pregnant carcass to weigh about 750 pounds each, a full 350 pounds under the normal weight of a cow that size and in that condition. Formerly employed by Tartan Angus Farms in Max Meadows, Battistoni was incarcerated at Wythe County Jail on $3,000 bond. He later made bail.

According to Sheriff Wayne Pike, unless arrangements were made by the following Monday evening, he believed the next course of action would be the implementation of a court order to aid the starving animals.

"The vet says they're on the verge of starvation and need silage or at least good hay immediately," stated the Wythe County sheriff. "If worse comes to worse, the court could order that any available feed might be given to these cattle. If that doesn't work, a court order could be issued to seize the cattle and arrange for their care."

When Monday night arrived, the mid-March weather remained cold. Sleet or snow was predicted. The only hay that could be seen on the farm was fenced away from the cattle and seemed to be of poor quality. The cattle would be turned over to the legal system the next day, after spending another night in the cold, wet and hungry outskirts of the desolate Stringtown farm.

## Chapter 8
### UFOs and Matricide

With a newly publicized salary for the fiscal year of 1984-1985 of $21,793, Dad was busier than ever cracking cases. Meanwhile the Battistoni cattle starving case reached an end on April 9, 1984 when David Loren Battistoni was convicted in Wythe County General District Court on a single charge of cruelty to animals on the basis that he did deprive his cattle of necessary food, drink and/or shelter. A baker's dozen other charges of unlawful failure to cremate or bury the carcass of each of his dead cattle were dismissed.

Battistoni's attorney, Danny Bird, said that the Commonwealth had amended the warrant from "did engage in cruelty to animals, namely cattle" to "deprive an animal of necessary sustenance."

"It really didn't change what he was charged with," stated Assistant Commonwealth Attorney Willard Lester. "It simply changed the wording of the warrant to the exact wording of State Statute 18.2-392."

The deprivation charge was a Class I misdemeanor, according to Lester, which is punishable by a maximum of a year in jail and $1,000 fine. Battistoni had pleaded not guilty on all charges with Judge James Joines imposing only a $50 fine for the single charge. The Commonwealth introduced evidence indicating that the defendant was not the owner of the cattle. Judge Joines dismissed the thirteen counts of faire to properly dispose of the carcasses noting that the county ordinance could only be applied to the owners of the cattle and that, based on the evidence presented by the Commonwealth, nothing could be done.

"Class IV misdemeanors are not extraditable offenses," Dad concurred when reporters questioned him on the matter. "There is nothing the Sheriff's Department can do."

Dr. K.E. Hall, the Wytheville veterinarian who conducted autopsies on the dead cattle on the day the Wythe County Sheriff's Department placed Battistoni under arrest, served as principal witness on behalf of the defendant.

Hall testified that he had performed two autopsies on adult Black Angus cows that had died as a result of either primary or secondary malnutrition.

"Mr. Battistoni was caring for the animals and was tending to one when the vet arrived," Bird noted before calling his witnesses. "Last summer's drought was severe and nearly every farmer in Wythe County lost animals. In every herd, there will be more dominant cattle that will get more than their fair share at the expense of other animals. "They're like a bunch of kids. Some push the others out."

"These cattle were killed," Lester objected.

"You cannot strike that charge against the defendant," refused Judge Joines.

Bird called more than half a dozen witnesses including Bill Brown of Wythe County.

"I was down there in November or December and nothing seemed unusual," Brown stated. "Anytime you've got 125 cows on a 500-acre farm, some of them are going to get pretty weak. He and I had bought some hay together from a Huddle fellow from up around Roanoke. I started feeding his cattle around March 15."

"What condition were his cattle in?" Bird asked.

"I didn't see that they looked any worse than some I own," Brown answered.

Lester objected.

"The court is not interested in your cattle or the good or bad job you are doing feeding them, Mr. Brown," interrupted the judge. "Have you been on that farm and seen what's left?"

"I had been down on the farm to load some cattle," he replied.

"Well, didn't it look pretty well picked over?" Joines prompted.

"Most everywhere does this time of year," Brown answered.

After hearing the remainder of the defense witnesses, court recessed for a lunch hour. After reconvening, the defense rested. On behalf of the prosecution, Lester submitted a photograph of one of the dead cattle as evidence.

"That animal is in bad shape and there is no question that the cattle weren't fed enough," Joines concluded after examining the photo. "On the other hand, you've got to feed them what you've got. Now what do I do?"

"I don't see what the court can do but find you guilty, but I don't think it was cruelty or a willful act," Joines concluded. "When it comes to not feeding them enough, Mr. Battistoni is an experienced cattleman and should know better. I find you guilty and impose a fifty dollar fine."

Bird immediately called for an appeal.

\* \* \* \* \* \* \*

On Saturday, August 11, 1984, my parents, Rhonda Lynne Arnold and Herbert Gray Cooley were united in marriage at 11 a.m. at the home of Mr. and Mrs. John W. Spurlin in Climax, North Carolina. John Wayne Spurlin was Dad's childhood best friend and served as his best man. The two of them always called each other by their last names, so he was "Spurlin" to all of us. As I remember Mom telling me, Spurlin wanted Mom and Dad to get married on his birthday, but it fell on Sunday, August 12. Eventually, they agreed to have it on Saturday.

"Have it at my house and I will pay for the reception as your wedding gift," Spurlin told my parents.

The double-ring, poolside ceremony was performed by Woodrow Albright of High Point, North Carolina. The music preceding was performed by my mother's oldest friend, the late Nancy A. Ward, whom she met on the first day of kindergarten. With the accompaniment of Les Hilton, Mom's brother-in-law at the time, Nancy sang "Tonight, I Celebrate My Love" and "The Rose." She also served as a bridesmaid along with Mom's best friend, Debbie King, and her then-sisters-in-law, Karen King Cooley and Rhonda Cooley. Mom's sister, my Aunt Pam, served as her matron of honor.

Nancy had an incredible voice that I still remember clearly. She left us much too soon when she died tragically of pneumonia at the age of 52. Karen King Cooley, daughter of Wytheville Vice Mayor and Town Council member Jackie King, also died suddenly at the age of 45. My Uncle Mike, who served as Dad's groomsman as did Doug and Wayne, is gone now, too. It's really sad to realize that.

Mom and Dad on their wedding day, August 11, 1984.

Dad still says Mom was the most beautiful bride
he's ever seen.

My maternal grandparents, Mr. and Mrs. Bruce C. Arnold of Piney, were stopped for speeding along the way, just behind Wayne Pike and his wife at the time, Regina, who attended the guestbook.

"I'm on my way to my daughter's wedding," my grandfather told the officer. "I'm following a county sheriff up ahead and he's flying."

The cop let him go. He made it in time to give his daughter away in marriage. The wedding was directed by my dad's coworker, Thelma Milgrim, who designed the floating pool and poolside floral arrangements with Carol Lee Rhudy.

Following the ceremony, a catered dinner of Famous North Carolina barbecue and chicken was enjoyed by all.

*********

On Halloween Eve in 1984, police advised trick-or-treaters to beware of any pranking. Wytheville Chief of Police Robert A. Doyle suggested that all trick-or-treaters be accompanied by a parent or responsible adult and that all treats should be inspected prior to consumption. Both area hospitals agreed to go the extra mile in this effort agree to X-ray all treats that could be contaminated with metallic objects free of charge.

Wythe County Community Hospital offered this service from 8-9:30 p.m. on Halloween night. The Wytheville Hospital Corporation made their X-ray equipment available on the following day, November 1, from 1-3 p.m. Doyle also advised that costumers were light colored clothing or use flashlights or reflectors for protection. Motorists were asked to be especially cautious in all residential and rural areas.

"All personnel in our department will be working Wednesday night to ensure a happy and safe Halloween for all," Dad said on behalf of the Wythe County Sheriff's Office. "We hope that people will remember that

Halloween is for the young folks because we will not tolerate vandalism or other related acts."

Apparently, Dad's warnings were ignored. Law enforcement officials had every reason to be prepared when vandals slashed more than one hundred tires in Wytheville on Halloween night 1984. According to Captain Roy Fowler of the Wytheville Police Department, the street-side of more than 60 vehicles ended up with flat tires. The police station in the town of Wytheville was still receiving complaints late in the afternoon hours of the next day.

Dad gave out many awards as President of the Wytheville-Wythe-Bland Chamber of Commerce from May 1992-May 1993. Courtesy: Wytheville-Wythe-Bland Chamber of Commerce

"Things were going pretty well until this happened," stated Fowler who noted that their appeared to be no pattern in the vandalism, which were part of a pending investigation. "Reports have been coming in from all over town. Whoever did this did not discriminate. They did it to big, small, old and new cars. The only pattern was that the flattened tires were on the street side."

Dad said that the Wythe County Sheriff's Department was also expected to be busy on the eve of All Saints Day in 1984.

"The trees in the Gunton Park section had already been notched," he said. "We expect to be pretty busy."

\* \* \* \* \* \*

On Wednesday, May 22, 1985, Captain Roy Fowler of the Wytheville Police Department reported that Emily King Grossi of Wytheville had died the previous day from brain injuries at St. Luke's Hospital in Bluefield, which were sustained in Main Street accident on May 11$^{th}$ in Wytheville that sent 10 people to the hospital, including my father. Initially, Grossi was not reported as being injured or even involved in the double car accident. According to Wythe County Sheriff G. Wayne Pike, Grossi was transported to the Bluefield hospital for a CAT scan as well as orthopedic surgery from Wytheville Hospital.

She was among eight passengers in a car being driven by Mable Dean Gravely, who reported was heading west on Main Street when she reportedly swerved, crossed four lanes of traffic and hit Dad in his patrol car head on, sending him through the windshield. He was flown to Roanoke Memorial Hospital, where I was still in the incubator unit as a premature six-week-old baby. He was treated for head injuries and released a week later. I came home the next week.

\* \* \* \* \* \*

On Jaury 27, 1986, Dad reported that the Wythe Alcohol Safety Program, known as WASP, had just completed its third year with excellent results. Funded each year through grants via the federal highway commission, the program helped to reduce the number of alcohol related accidents and deaths in the county. Ten thousand dollars had been awarded each of the previous three years, which provided extra man hours for road checks and other community transportation safety programs.

"We are one of the few localities to get funding for the second year, let alone the third," Dad said gratefully. "The grant also allows us to have the extra coverage that is really a benefit to the county. We put in 19,281 miles on patrols that were paid for by this grant and while the deputies are patrolling for WASP, they are also on duty for any other need that might come up."

The federal highway commission also issued Wythe County an additional $10,000 grant for seatbelt use in 1986, making us the only county in the surrounding thirteen to receive any grants at all that year. WASP was responsible for 2,302 traffic checks, 177 alcohol related arrests and an additional 78 arrests that were not connected to alcohol.

Ten members of the Wythe County Sheriff's Department had also successfully completed the Breath Alcohol Operator's Course through classes offered at the New River Criminal Justice Training Academy in Radford during the week of December 2-6, 1985. The course was under the supervision of the Bureau of Forensic Science, a division of Consolidated Laboratory Services. Prior to taking the actual course, candidates were required to pass an intricate mathematical pretest. The course itself involved chemical analysis, electronics, mathematics and other skills which qualified each member to be licensed to test suspected drunk drivers.

A substantial number of the certified breathalyzer operators were employed at the Wythe County Jail, which made more personnel available to complete testing at the jail. Thus, the operators were able to assist the town and state police agencies. Those completing the course successfully were Deputies Sandra M. Johnson, Douglas W. King, Danna M. "Teny" Underwood, my uncle Jeffery B. Arnold, Thomas E. Reese, Jr., Douglas W. Hudson, Jr., D.

Mike Anders, Gerald A. McPeak and Terry L. Montgomery.

On February 13, 1986, Dad told reporters that if the deputies of the Wythe County Sheriff's Office are overweight, they have six months to get in shape before being dismissed from the force. In January and June of each year, the department has a twice annual weigh in for all officers based on a height-weight scare approved by local physicians. According to the January 1986 weigh-in, four of the department's 38 deputies were overweight.

"If they are overweight, they have to weigh in once a month for six months," Dad explained. "If they don't lose the extra weight, they are off the force."

Dad noted the people do not expect law enforcement officials to be in poor physical condition, but that most of their time on duty is spent in the patrol car.

"Fifty-six percent of all law enforcement officials are overweight," Dad said. "In the last few years, a large number of law enforcement officers have suffered heart attacks and died after being involved in a chase or some type of struggle."

Dad said that he and Wayne actively encouraged their officers to become involved in some sort of organized physical activity program in addition to the weight management program. He suggested such activities as basketball, aerobics and weightlifting.

\* \* \* \* \* \* \* \*

The morning of Sunday, November 13, 1986 was quite and damp in Wythe County, Virginia. It was certainly not good weather for travelling up and down Sand Mountain. Three fugitives from Buchanan County found that out the hard way and were forced to surrender to the Wythe County Sheriff's Department. By time churchgoers had settled in their pews, they were in custody and on their way back to Grundy.

Dad told reporters that three men and three women had stopped at the Petro Truck Stop in Fort Chiswell at approximately 5:30 a.m. when an altercation developed between them.

"One of the women claimed she had been abducted by the men, but further investigation revealed that all six subjects had come to Wythe County together to escape Buchanan authorities," Dad said. "Additional investigation revealed that no offenses were committed by any of the fugitives while in Wythe County for approximately four hours before being captured on State Route 634 with the aid of State Trooper Dave Brook's bloodhound."

Wanted by authorities were Brian Stacy, 22, and Stephen Bandy, 18, who were both charged with breaking and entering and grand larceny, twenty-four-year-old Jack Bostic, for two counts of aiding a felon to escape, nineteen year old Linda Carol Stacy, for one count of aiding a felon to escape and twenty-year-old Brenda Gibson, for one count of receiving stolen property and two of aiding a felon to escape.

One juvenile was also charged with two counts of aiding a felon to escape.

Dad and the department were also busy with plenty of other crime at that time. Three men were charged with possession of marijuana and contributing to the delinquency of a minor when a reported was filed by three county law officers who witnessed the three men pick up a 16-year old and subsequently expose the youth to alcohol and marijuana. As a result, my Uncle Doug, Keith Dunagan and Sam Burcham arrested William Dunn and Ronnie Dunford of Rural Retreat and David Osborne of Wytheville. A preliminary hearing date for all three men concerning the possession charges was set for January 14, 1987.

\* \* \* \* \* \* \*

It was certainly Friday the 13th in February of 1987 when Mark Holmberg of the *Richmond Times Dispatch* was interviewing a Fort Chiswell whom who identified herself as Huggy Bear in the break room of the *Southwest Virginia Enterprise* office about a UFO sighting. That was proof enough that the media coverage of the UFO sightings in Wythe County produced as fantastic of a scenario as the sightings themselves. My father was forced to be in the middle of all the madness.

In the Wythe County Sheriff's Office, there was a map outlining the zones that deputies would patrol on Halloween nights. Around the margin of the map were pictures of ghosts and goblins. In the bottom center of the map was the drawing of an alien beaming down from a flying saucer to confront a deputy standing by his patrol car.

The sightings were first reported by deputies of the Wythe County Sheriff's Department as well as Rural Retreat Chief of Police Bob Lewis on October 5, 1987. For the next two months, the sheriff's department was bombarded by calls from news media outlets nationwide. Wythe County

Sheriff Wayne Pike said he had received dozens of calls from reporters wanting to know more about the sightings. So many newshounds were calling that Dad, being the second in command, was enlisted to field media calls along with the dispatchers on duty. On February 11, Wayne received a call from television reporters from Norfolk and Tennessee requesting interviews regarding the sightings.

With the news of the sightings first hit the national news wires, a disc jockey from Washington, D.C. called Wayne and asked him if his deputies were allowed to drink on the job. He was later asked if his deputies were required to pass a mental test before they were hired. Those calls aside, Wayne said that most of the news people with whom he had conversed had been respectful and that the members of his force had tried to cooperate with the inquiring reporters as best as possible.

"I'm surprised at the way some reporters have ignored the mundane explanations that could be given for the sightings and focused instead on possible visitations from extraterrestrial beings," Wayne said. "I thought there was a perfectly logical explanation for the sightings and I chalk it up to military exercises over Wythe County."

As an Air Force native, he knew that both the Air Force and Navy had classified aircrafts. WYVE Radio news director Danny Gordon described himself as a victim of a media blitz, literally receiving hundreds of calls from reporters and UFO researchers regarding the sightings.

"I believe I am providing a necessary service by acting as a responsible clearinghouse for information about the UFO sightings," stated Gordon. "As a newsman, I hope that the story can be brought to a conclusion and think my role in disseminating information to the media can help bring about this conclusion."

* * * * * *

"I shot them, but I don't know why," Celeste Ann Bane concluded in a statement given to Wythe County Sheriff Wayne Pike in the early morning hours of August 11, 1986.

Earlier that morning, her mother, Rebecca Pearl Bell, was murdered by a shotgun with her live-in boyfriend, Frank Alley, wounded as they were in bed asleep. On Monday, October 26, 1987 the trial for Bane began. She was charged with the murder of her mother as well as the attempted murder of Frank Alley in his Austinville home. Additionally, Bane was charged with two counts of using a firearm in the commission of a felony. If Bane was found guilty on all charges, she would face a life sentence as well as an additional fourteen years in jail.

Celeste's estranged husband, Robert Allen Bane, was convicted of Bell's murder in June 1987 as well as charges of breaking and entering with intent to commit murder and two counts of using a firearm in the commission of a felony. The jury recommended he be given the maximum sentence for all charges, which totaled two life terms plus fourteen years. Robert Bane confessed to the murder after discovering his wife had been arrested and charged with the crime. The sheriff's department subsequently corroborated these confessions through various pieces of physical evidence.

No such physical evidence has been introduced to suggest Celeste Bane to the crime. Assistant Commonwealth Attorney William Lester was depending heavily on Celeste Bane's statement made to Wayne as well as a statement in which she had written out in order to win the case. Lester also said in his opening statement that it was unlikely that Celeste could have slept through the firing of the shotgun, as she later claimed, having been allegedly awakened by Alley calling for help from the kitchen. He also argued that Celeste and Robert acted together to murder Bell and Alley.

In his opening statement to the jury, defense attorney Thomas Hodges attempted to disassociate Celeste Bane's personality from that of her husband by describing his client as shy and unassuming in contrast to Robert's domineering boastfulness.

"Any details of how Celeste Bane carried out the crime were conspicuously absent from the statement she made to Sheriff Pike and the statement she wrote out herself," stated Hodges. "Much of her statement was written in the form of a question."

"It was as if she was questioning whether or not she did it rather than making an admission of guilt," he argued.

The first witness called for the prosecution was Frank Alley, who recounted the events of the shooting.

"I was awakened by a loud boom that morning," Alley recalled. "Since I was sleeping face down, I didn't see who shot me. I looked over at Rebecca and discovered she had been shot in the face."

Alley climbed out of bed and went into the kitchen, where he claimed to have fallen and was unable to get up. Calling to Celeste for help, who had been staying with them since separating from her husband the previous June. Celeste went into the bedroom and discovered the dead body of her mother.

"Mom can't talk," she repeated over and over as she screamed in horror.

Exiting the kitchen, she called the rescue squad after being prompted to do so by Alley.

In his cross examination of Alley, Hodges elicited that Celeste had been hysterical upon the discovery of her mother's body and that Celeste had never been any trouble and seemed to love her mother.

Lester called Marty Stallard, an investigator for the Wythe County Sheriff's Department, to the stand. Having interviewed Bane at the scene of the murder, Stallard said it sounded suspicious that she could not hear the shotgun blast, especially since only one wall separated their rooms. He testified that, although Celeste told him to she was deaf in one ear, she heard him perfectly when he lowered his voice.

The real drama started when Lester called Lt. Thelma Milgrim and Sheriff Pike of the Wythe County Sheriff's Office to the stand as to the statements made by Celeste Bane on the morning of August 11, 1986.

Milgrim stated that the statement began between 3:30 and 4 a.m. in Dad's office.

"She told me she has been anxious and nervous about her divorce, that she was angry with her mother and that she and Mr. Alley were happy," she testified. "Her mother had sent her to the doctor several times and she was seeing a counselor."

"I did not remember anything after I went to bed that night," Bane stated. "I knew where the shotgun was kept in the house. I may have heard it being fired and might have even held it in my hand."

"I must be blocking something out," she shouted repeatedly. "I need a psychiatrist!"

"She may have seen the gun lying on the table," Hodges noted. "She may have been trying to kill herself or might have meant to kill Frank and her mother before killing herself."

Upon reviewing Milgrim's notes on the case, he discovered that Celeste Bane had denied shooting her mother and firing the shotgun.

"Why has this denial not been brought out before now?" Hodges questioned.

"I had never been asked if she had denied the charge," Milgrim replied.

Hodges then asserted that Bane was rocking back and forth during the interview while clutching a teddy bear, while the prosecution rested at around 2:45 p.m. on Tuesday, October 27, 1986.

The defense began calling its witnesses that same afternoon, trying to establish Bane's separation from her husband and the solidarity against him, which she shared with her mother whom she loved.

Hodges called Roberta Littlefield from the Family Resource Center in Radford, who had counseled the Banes before their divorce. She testified to Robert's domineering hold over Celeste and that he frequently physically abused her. Ann Turpin, who worked for a lawyer at the time of the murder, testified that the law office wrote Robert Bane two letters requesting he refrain from seeing his wife or any member of her immediate family.

"I have not spoken with my wife for about four weeks before the murder," Robert Allen Bane testified when called to the stand before invoking his rights to self incrimination when asked about statements he made to police and other people about the mother.

Much of the afternoon of Wednesday, October 28th was therefore spent in the process of deciphering his contradictory statements.

"I killed Rebecca and wounded Frank by myself," Bane allegedly confessed to Rev. Rae Mullins about a week after the murder. "Celeste had nothing to do with the shootings. "I even numbed her with ether before I shot them."

"Celeste had called me on Saturday, August 9th and said her mother was driving her crazy, pushing her to divorce me," Robert Bane told Wayne on September 4, 1986. "I told her that if I killed Rebecca, I would have to kill Frank, too, because he would probably come after me. Celeste told me to do whatever I had to do."

"Celeste shot Frank with his own shotgun while I killed Rebecca with a shotgun I stole from my father's house," Bane told Milgrim the following day. "I asked Celeste to leave it with him, but she said she couldn't because it couldn't look right."

The trial ended on Friday, October 30th with Celeste being acquitted.

## Chapter 9
## A Battle for Clerk of Court

In 1991, Dad decided to run for Clerk of Circuit Court in Wythe County in an effort to unseat incumbent Hayden H. Horney. Dad understood that the heritage of Wythe County was rich and that its past has provided our community with a strong foundation on which a bright future could be built. In the 1990s, Wythe County needed leaders who would serve with a deeply founded community spirit. They needed leaders who would understand the importance of striving daily to protect the heritage of our community while moving forward to build a sound quality of life for everyone.

Dad believed that any elected leader, regardless of the position held, should serve as a community leader, which meant being willing to wear many hats in order to uphold a variety of responsibilities. He was certainly no stranger to wearing many hats in Wythe County. He was a lot more than a police officer to this community.

Dad oversees a bicycle obstacle course for kids sponsored by the Wythe County Sheriff's Office

In addition to serving as Chief Deputy for the Wythe County Sheriff's Office, he was also an adjunct faculty instructor in Criminal Justice Services at Wytheville Community College. At that time, he was vice president of the Wytheville-Wythe-Bland Chamber of Commerce, eventually becoming president. He was also chairman of the Wythe County Transportation Committee and vice chairman of the Wythe County Local Emergency Planning Committee. Dad also served on the incident management team for the Virginia Department of Transportation as well as the juvenile education committee for the Wythe-Bland American Cancer Society. That makes me smile as I would serve as a team captain for the Mt. Pleasant United Methodist Church Relay for Life, which serves the American Cancer Society, for four years.

A family publicity shot for Dad's campaign in the autumn of 1991.

Dad also served on the Wythe County Rural Retreat Lake Authority and as a member of the Virginia Farm Bureau, Ivanhoe Civic League, Wytheville Masonic Lodge #82 and American Legion Post #229. That's not even counting his service to the High Point Police Department and the 18th Judicial District of North Carolina as well as his experience as an insurance adjuster and real estate broker. Just that year, Dad had received his Master's of Science Degree in Criminal Justice and Administration from the Virginia Commonwealth University in Richmond. He also received certificates from the University of Virginia in Charlottesville in both the Leadership Development Program and the Criminal Justice Graduate Program. This is all in addition to his being a graduate of the FBI National Academy in Quantico, Virginia and his Associate and Bachelors of Arts and Sciences Degrees from Guilford College in Greensboro, North Carolina.

Dad's campaign brochure cover

Bearing that in mind, let's remember that this is only just a little more than halfway through his career. He still had twenty years to go. During those two decades, he would garner countless more achievements and accolades.

Dad's campaign slogan was "Preserving our heritage while working for the future—leadership for Wythe County." He really worked to change the face of that position. He wanted to work together with the citizens of Wythe County to come to grips with many issues facing the community at the time, there were several crucial topics specifically wanted all the citizens of Wythe County to address including the environment of children in the community, economic development, natural environment and the overall enhancement to the quality of life in Wythe County. I'm sure that the issues concerning a healthy community environment for children had a lot to do with my sister and me. I was just six years old at the time and my sister, Tara, had just been born earlier that year on January 11, 1991.

A campaign headshot

As an elected official, the Wythe County Clerk of Court has a responsibility to be a leader in all aspects of the entire county. The position of the Clerk of Court is a vital one that requires a great deal of dedication and integrity. Dad respected the extraordinary seriousness with which the clerk must take the court's recordkeeping. Recording sentences issued by the judges, deeds, marriages and other related documents must be done with the utmost care and accuracy.

The budget for the Clerk's office is comprised entirely of revenue generated by the taxpayers of Wythe County. Therefore, the position demanded efficient management to the highest degree. The clerk must also realize that the office is solely responsible for the preservation of the history of Wythe County. Few other records are as precisely indicative of our local societal operations as well as how the current citizens of our community will be viewed by those of future generations.

Dad understood these things and had the management skills and leadership ability to serve the people of Wythe County above and beyond the call of duty as their Clerk of Court. Serving the community had been his only profession. Had the voters of Wythe County elected him to serve, it would have continued to be his only occupation.

By 1991, Dad had already accumulated a quarter of a century in experience with the criminal justice and judicial system. He had already served for nearly a dozen years as the Chief Deputy of the Wythe County Sheriff's Office, a job which concentrated on administration. As a law enforcement officer, Dad understood the care which must be given to the preservation of court documents. Thousands of dollars in revenue have been brought to Wythe County through grants that Dad personally pursued. His grant writing ability would have brought enhancement to the office of the Wythe County Clerk of Court in an unprecedented manner.

The quality of life enjoyed in Wythe County is intricately related to many community features including youth, environment and economy, just to name a few. Dad knew that the leaders of Wythe County must join with the citizenry to build an environment that can produce positive outcomes for the present and future. He believed this could also be done by developing a future plan based on the strengths from the community's past. These included a thriving economy and a safe environment in which nature can flourish and children and grow and prosper.

Dad demonstrated his commitment to this philosophy through his extensive community involvement. In 1990, he was instrumental in bringing Averett College's Bachelors and Masters Degree programs to Wythe County. In October 1991, Dr. Harold Henry, dean of Adult and Continuing Education at Averett College in Danville, Virginia, presented Dad with a mug in appreciation of his efforts to locate a branch of the college in Wytheville. A business administration program was already underway with an M.B.A. program slated to start that December. Dr. Henry credited Dad with being instrumental in attracting Averett to Wythe County. The cup of appreciation was presented at the Joint Industrial Development Authority's quarterly dinner.

Through lectures to youth groups, churches, businesses and civic organizations, Dad strived to educate the community about drug problems and safety issues. One of the initiators of the Drug Resistance Abuse Education (D.A.R.E.) program, Dad worked hard to educate the young people of Wythe County learn about the dangers of drugs while attempting to build their own self-confidence. He understood that the youth of Wythe County needed guidance during their teenage years and, as a result, founded an Explore Scouts program which assisted young people from the ages of 14 to 20 in developing their own professional skills. Dad was also an active supporter of the volunteer fire departments and rescue squads throughout the county. As the then vice president of the Wytheville-Wythe-Bland Chamber of Commerce, Dad always concerned himself with business and industrial growth in Wythe County. He believed that caution must be exercised when working to create economic prosperity in order to preserve a quality environment for the county.

As the Election Day drew closer, there seemed to be a lot of support surrounding Dad for Clerk of Court, not the least of which came from his friend and boss, Sheriff G. Wayne Pike of Wythe County. In an October 24, 1991 letter to the *Southwest Virginia Enterprise* editor, he publicly endorsed my father. He begins by stating that, since he had served as an elected official longer than anyone else in Wythe County with the exception of the Commonwealth attorney at the time, he felt as qualified as anyone to endorse Dad based on his knowledge of the inner workings of our local government and its mechanics.

"I have seen local government workers and officials come and go and I have seen some good and some not so well," Wayne Pike wrote. "I have known Cooley longer than anyone in Wythe County and for once, I can really look at candidate for what he is for which he stands."

Wayne wrote that he was endorsing Dad not for political reasons but for the good of Wythe County. He said he had seen him advance in his education and career one step at a time over the many years of their professional partnership, noting this campaign as a continuation of his initiative and ambition to be the best man he can.

"He is a gentleman, who has conducted himself as such throughout his campaign, refusing to make derogatory remarks about persons or personalities and has tried to distance himself from those who do," he commended. "Cooley may be the most qualified person to run for local office here in Wythe County."

Sheriff Pike also noted that he and Dad had both worked hard for Wythe County and have both shared the same concern about not only public safety, but about many other issues as well, such as wildlife and natural resources, our youth and the safety of the youth and elderly within the community, not to mention the community in general and its governmental leaders.

"He holds a masters degree and aside from his great contribution to our community, he is a military veteran and has spent a lifetime of service in our court and justice systems," lauded Pike. "Cooley is one of the few people in Southwest Virginia today who is a graduate of the FBI National Academy. Not only is this significant to his education and training, but it means that we have a candidate here who that able to withstand an FBI background investigation. How often does this happen?"

Wayne also noted the large amount of revenue Dad had sought successfully in terms of grant funding toward the enhancement of Wythe County from many state and national corporations. He added that Dad's work would continue in this vigorous manner as clerk of court.

"Cooley's work has helped to see that less than ten percent of our department budget is paid for by local funds," he explained further. "Today, our department is paying its own way thanks to people like Cooley."

The county sheriff referred to the Webster Dictionary definition of the word "audit," which is listed as "an official investigation and verification of financial accounts and records. He stated that the Wythe County Sheriff's Office had undergone successful audits with positive outcomes every year since they took office. Pike credited Dad for this in terms of his good leadership within the department, adding that men like him were needed in order to effectively lead Wythe County through the increasing challenging years that lay ahead.

"I believe that Cooley could bring special leadership to the office of the clerk of court," Wayne stated. "As we approach the year 2000, Wythe County will have special needs and problems that only a highly qualified and staffed government can face."

He also noted that while other constitutional officer salaries have remained in the $40,000 range including sheriff, treasurer, the commissioner of revenue and Commonwealth attorney, the clerk of court salary had risen to $64,100.

"This is not a job to be taken seriously and I do not believe Cooley thinks so either," Pike said in closing. "It is a job for the best person we can find. I hope that each of you will set aside political parties and vote instead for good government as I will when I vote Herb Cooley for Wythe County Clerk of Court."

Marie G. Flanagan, the former Clerk of Court in Wythe County who was the predecessor to Hayden Horney, also endorsed Dad. In her October 23, 1991 letter to the editor of the *Southwest Virginia Enterprise*, Flanagan stated that she was pleased to serve as the clerk of court in Wythe County from 1976 to 1984. For seven years prior to that, she served as chief deputy clerk to the elected clerk of court James E. Crockett. Being well aware of the of the office of Clerk of Court and the procedures necessary in our order for the office to function properly, which included dedication above and the call of duty, Flanagan knew that Dad was the candidate who would closely involve himself with the job. He refused to be just a figurehead.

"The record of Herb Cooley as an official of this county demonstrates that he can serve responsibly and well," she wrote. "He is known throughout the town and county as a fine citizen."

Based upon his vast education, experience as both the chief deputy sheriff of Wythe County and civic community involvement, she publicly placed her support behind Dad in his pursuit of her former position.

Dad's friend and fellow police officer in the Wythe County Sheriff's Office, Don Crockett, also endorsed him, saying he will accept the responsibility of making Wythe County better in the position of the clerk of court.

"I have had the privilege working with Herb Cooley for their past 12 years," Crockett wrote in the same edition of the *Southwest Virginia Enterprise* in a letter to the editor. "I have found him to be a very honest, hard working person and an excellent supervisor."

Crockett said he felt that Dad was the person who could capably and responsibly serve as the Wythe County clerk of court. He was pleased to offer his endorsement for Dad and implored the voters of Wythe County to cast their ballots for him on Tuesday, November 5, 1991 as their newest clerk of circuit court.

"His win will be our gain," wrote Crockett.

In Wythe County, the clerk of circuit court has two sets of duties. First, there are the responsibilities associated with the judicial proceedings in the circuit court. Secondly, the clerk of court is responsible for the recording of all the documents relating to land transfers, deeds, deeds of trust, mortgages, births, deaths, marriages, wills and divorces that occur within the county as well as the recording of all the county election results. The clerk of court also issues each and every hunting, fishing and marriage license distributed within the confines of Wythe County. The clerk of circuit court serves a term of eight years per election. In Wythe County, the annual salary for the position in 1991 was $64,146. The compensation is established in the annual appropriations act and is derived from fees and commissions collected by the office of the clerk of court, which includes a staff of four full time employees as well as one part time worker.

As Chief Deputy for the Wythe County Sheriff's Office, the decision to run for the Wythe County Court of Circuit Court position was not made lightly.

"I thought about running for a long time," he told reporter Debbie Maxwell for the October 26, 1991 issue of the *Southwest Virginia Enterprise*. "Before running for any office, you have to determine if there is a need. Secondly, you have to ask yourself, 'Am I the person who can best meet those needs?' I felt there was a need for leadership and management skills with the clerk's position."

Dad felt he had the skills to meet those needs.

"I have an effective combination of administrative and managerial skills as well as an education and experience in the judicial system. I have 29 years of public service and 25 years of experience in the judicial system and over half of that time included management and administrative duties.

Dad was also a former licensed real estate broker and explained to Maxwell that he understood the duties of the clerk's office. He stated that the clerk's role in county government was a vital one.

"It is the focal point for all legal matters in the county, especially the circuit court," he said. "He is the register of deeds, the probate judge, and he deals with all aspects of the circuit court. The clerk's office contains all the vital records of our county and our history. The clerk is the record keeper of our office."

Had he been elected, Dad said that contrary to recent rumors, he would not hire a new staff.

"The rumors that I would fire the whole staff are simply untrue and unfounded," he said. "The only reason they would not remain is if they resigned or if, after a period of time, I find them to be negligent in their duties."

Dad told the reporter that he would like to see better accountability for the civil and criminal files in the clerk's office.

"While I understand the public needs to have access to these files, there needs to be a procedure implemented where the files remain in the clerk's office at all times," Dad explained. "This could be done by having copies made for the person who needs them and simply having a check out system."

Dad also said that he would like to see the historical records within the office better maintained, possibly by using microfilm.

"This could possibly be done through the use of historical grants as well as the use of college interns, work study students and historical scholars who would like to volunteer."

When discussing the qualities necessary for the clerk's office, Dad noted the importance of efficiency on behalf of the clerk as a skilled administrator.

"The position of the clerk's office is so important and so vital that there is virtually no room for error," he stated. "Twelve years ago, I set up the existing record system for the Wythe County Sheriff's Office and the Wythe County Jail. I was later responsible for having these records computerized. I presently administer a budget of approximately $1.5 million and I have helped reduce the funding to the local sheriff's department to ten percent. I am also responsible for the supervision of thirty seven full time employees."

As Election Day drew nearer, Dad took out an ad, which displayed his eight stops across the county on the day prior to the opening of the polls. Beginning at 8:30 a.m. on Monday, November 4, 1991, he held public meet and greets in Rural Retreat, Cripple Creek, Speedwell, Ivanhoe, Austinville, Barren Springs, Max Meadows and finally Wytheville were he would be appearing at the Bingo Room of the Wytheville Community Center with other candidates. The appearances would not be over until 7:00 that night, which made for a very grueling day to say the least.

"During my campaign, I've worked diligently going door to door to meet all over you personally," he said to Wythe County in the advertisement. "However, with time restraints, scheduling conflicts and the election only a few days away, I realize I will not be able to personally see each of you. Therefore, to meet as many people as possible, I've scheduled visits throughout the county. All Wythe County voters are invited to come and talk with me on Monday, November 4th.

Dad worked hard on his campaign. In fact, my entire family and all our friends did as well. Even at six years old, I can remember all our lives being consumed with Dad's getting elected whether we were putting up signs, painting them or giving away hats and pens. He really tried to knock on every door in the county.

His loss was big and I remember being devastated by it. I handed out his campaign gear to my first grade class and can remember going with him to all his campaign rallies. I helped put up signs and felt certain he would win because he was my dad. I remember pulling the lever to vote for him in the booth and crying when I listened to the election results being reported over the radio with my great grandmother, Rose. When he finally came home about 10:30 that night, I remember the dejected look on his face. My heart broke for him. My whole family was heartbroken. Robyn Melton, his campaign manager, bawled and bawled that night. It was a very sad time. I learned a lesson very early in life that I have never forgotten. Politics are ugly. The further time goes on, the more this is true.

"The clerk of court is a big job and pays big," Wayne Pike told me. "He felt a need for a better operation and he would have been great but it is hard to unseat a person in an office. The county lost when Herb lost but he never dwelled on it. He moved on."

The clerk of court salary was a guaranteed $64,000 a year for eight years, which makes sense to me now as to why

Dad chose to seek the office. I can't help but think that if he had won, he may never have left Wythe County. Twenty five years later, that annual salary had topped six figures of over $100,000.

Dad credits Robyn Melton with getting him involved in the campaign. Now back to her maiden name of Underwood, she was head of the Wythe County Republican Committee at the time with former Wytheville mayor, the late Dr. Carl Stark, leading our local GOP party. Robyn says the in addition to her, there were several who wanted Dad to seek the Clerk of Court office.

"He was already a leader in the community and we felt he would be a great asset to the county as an elected official," Robyn told me. "I guess I was part of the steering committee."

Originally volunteering to oversee his campaign, she felt she wasn't doing an adequate enough job. Robyn credited Dad's brother, Doug, along with current Wythe County Sheriff Keith Dunagan for intervening midway through the campaign and taking the lead while she still enjoyed coordinating social and fundraising events.

"I felt your Dad was the best guy for the job because of his character, work ethic, and his education," Robyn stated. "He also loved the people of Wythe County and all of us knew he would serve them well."

She also can recall working behind the scenes painting signs, fundraising, door-knocking, coordinating meet and greets and working the polls on Election Day. While Robyn doesn't recall any specific memory about the campaign, she has a general recollection of how well Dad interacted with the public.

"He was just a great people person," she recalled. "He never came across as the typical politician."

Dad never really liked political parties, although his parents were staunch Democrats. That's why I am a little surprised in retrospect that Dad ran on the Republican ticket.

"I think during that time we were in the Reagan-Bush era and most of us were Republicans," Robyn explained. "I think your Dad's principles aligned with the GOP at that time so I think it was just natural that he would run as a Republican."

Robyn also recalled her devastation, as well as that of all of us who believed in him, when Dad lost.

"I felt strongly that your Dad would win because of his popularity in the county, his credentials and the hard work of everyone who was behind him," Robyn said to me. "I really felt that Wythe County would go his way."

I realize that Herb Cooley is my dad and that leaves it difficult for me to look at this race objectively. However, I believe that when you review the changes he was planning to make to the clerk's office, many of which would still be useful a quarter of a century later, it's pretty easy to see that voters made a mistake in 1991. While Robyn says Hayden Horney has served the county well as clerk of court, she agrees with me that Dad's loss was an equal one for Wythe County.

"I just believe that your Dad would have been a new voice for the county with new ideas," she stated in closing. "He served the county unselfishly all the years he was with the Sheriff's Department and we all knew he would do the same as our Clerk of Court."

## Chapter 10
## The Man with the Plan

For the current local sheriff of Wythe County, W.
Keith Dunagan, law enforcement was in his blood just as it
seemed to have been for dad. The Marion native and high
school graduated hadn't been out of the army long when a
friend got him a job as the manager of the Pizza Hut in
Wytheville. It didn't take long for Dunagan to realize that
this wasn't the line of work for him. His uncle, Larry Ratliff,
was the first-ever helicopter pilot for the Virginia State Police
and Keith was ready to apply for membership on that force.

As fate would have it, Ratliff stopped in to pay his
nephew a visit on the very day he was set to apply for a job
with the state police. Ratliff had been flying around
Wytheville on a marijuana eradication case. When
Dunagan told his uncle the news, his reaction was less than
encouraging.

"Don't do it," he warned his nephew. "If you want
to spend the rest of your life writing tickets on the interstate,
it's a good job. If you want to do real police work, you need
to talk to the young new county sheriff here. His name is
Wayne Pike and he's a real pro-law enforcement kind of
guy."

Fate intervened once more for Dunagan, when a
couple of days later, Pike walked into Pizza Hut for lunch.
He asked Wayne for a job and he handed Keith an
application. He went to work in March of 1983 and met
Dad on his very first day on the job.

"I found him to be an easy going guy," Dunagan
recalled. "It seemed to me like he was going to be a pretty
easy guy to work for and, as it turned out, he was."

The current sheriff also attested to what the rest of
Dad's Wythe County colleagues had said. While Pike had a
reputation of being a hot tempered perfectionist, Dad was

the one who offered his officers a second chance by hearing them out and giving them the benefit of the doubt.

"Your Dad was the only chief deputy that could get through to Wayne in that way," Dunagan told me. "There was several in that position that weren't as accessible to Wayne in that way."

"They had a long working relationship and a strong faith in one another," he added. "So I guess Herb could say things to Wayne or cause him to consider certain things in a way that nobody else could."

Before becoming sheriff, Dunagan served as chief deputy under the administration of previous Sheriff Doug King.

"I inherited the Herb Cooley scissors," Keith stated proudly.

When Dad was chief deputy for the Wythe County Sheriff's Office, someone had "Captain Cooley" scratched into the scissors in his office with a pair of metal scissors. Ever since Dad left that position, every one of his successor are given ownership of these scissors for the tenure of their service as chief deputy.

"Charlie Foster has them now," Keith said, noting his second in command.

He added that since becoming a leader of the department, there are many of Dad's leadership tactics that Dunagan says he has attempted to implement as the current sheriff of Wythe County.

"Herb never belittled people when they messed up," Dunagan recalled. "He was never the kind of cop that would scream at you or curse at you. He would just bring you in, sit you down and talk to you. Depending on the seriousness of the offense, he would tell you what was going to happen. Luckily, I never saw anything too bad happen during the arrests he made."

As even tempered as Dad could be, if you angered him, just as memorable of an experience could be impressed upon you.

Once, after a drunk was jailed for a weekend, he came into Dad's office claiming that the supervising matron of the Wythe County Jail, the late Betty Vaught, had stolen his jacket from him. In reality, Betty had tried to return his jacket, which he had left at the jail. After he complained to Dad two or three times, he had finally had enough.

"The entrance to the Sheriff's Department at that time was on one end of the hall and your Dad's office was on the other," Keith explained. "All at once, we heard all this racket and Herb came out dragging this guy up the hall and out the door with one hand on his collar and the other on his belt buckle."

"Don't ever come back," Dad shouted as he slammed the door behind the disgruntled prisoner.

"Well, somebody's pissed Herb off," Dunagan and his colleagues muttered amongst themselves with a chuckle as they nonchalantly went back to work.

"Herb kept the Sheriff's Office seeming more like a second family than going to a job," Dunagan told me. "I have tried to keep it like that today even though it's much bigger now than it was back then."

"When I first started there were only a dozen road deputies, two investigators, your Dad and Wayne," he elaborated. "Now, we have sixty five employees including about twenty patrollers, school resource officers, six investigators, a major, a chief deputy and me."

During Dad's tenure as Chief Deputy, he was the only major on the force. Dunagan explained also that his current payroll includes a lot of part-time employees. Many of these men and women have already retired from their full-time positions as either deputy sheriffs or correctional officers.

There are many programs started during the administration of Dad and Wayne Pike the help keep the department in tip-top shape today.

"We didn't have a narcotics officer when I first started there," Dunagan noted. "We have two now."

The Wythe County Sheriff's Office is also on a Drug Task Force. This was first introduced to the department in 1988 by Dad and Wayne. The two of them also started a TACT team to handle especially high risk cases, which still exists today, as well as a scuba diving team.

"I was the first diver the Wythe County Sheriff's Office ever had," Dunagan stated when the scuba team was initiated in 1988.

Wythe County Sheriff's Office first Tact and Dive Teams.

The photo from left to right, back row to bottom is:

Mike Edmonds, Doug Cooley, Doug Hudson, Gerald McPeak, Doug King, Terry Montgomery, Herb Cooley, Mike Anders, Marty Stallard, Dub Ford, Kent Vaughn, Keith Dunagan. Courtesy: Wythe County Sheriff's Office

That was also the same year that the Wythe County Sheriff's Office became a founding member of the Tri-County Anti-Drug Task Force. It was forced to withdraw its partnership with Smyth and Bland Counties three years later due to budget cuts made by the Wythe County Board of Supervisors. Thankfully, the Wythe County Sheriff's Office is now a member of the Claytor Lake Anti-Drug Task Force.

Dad was also responsible for the first-ever grant awarded to the Wythe County Sheriff's Office from the Virginia Department of Motor Vehicles concerning seatbelt safety.

"Your dad got some of the biggest grants that DVM gave out at the time," Keith informed me. "He was also able to get a grant that enabled Thelma Milgrim to work with women who were victims of violent or sexual abuse crimes."

Today, Keith's department has both a paid officer and another grant subsidized female who performs the same duties today.

"The officers help female victims get the protective orders they need and will sit with them in court to help them if they need to testify," he explained. "Basically, the help prepare them for everything they will go through within the judicial system before it happens."

Dad gave out many awards as President of the Wytheville-Wythe-Bland Chamber of Commerce from May 1992-May 1993. Courtesy: Wytheville-Wythe-Bland Chamber of Commerce

Keith regards Dad as the greatest teacher and boss he ever had.

"I spent many years as a narcotics investigator and then as a criminal investigator and when I would have trouble with a case, Herb was always the first person I would ask," he stated. "He would always have an 'Old Joe' story for me that related to every case."

Keith labeled all the stories Dad would tell Keith from his days as an investigator in North Carolina as 'Old Joe' stories.

"Herb," Keith would implore my dad. "I'm stuck on this break-in case and I am just not getting anywhere."

"Well, I had this old guy in High Point," Dad would begin in a long story. "He had a case like this and this is what he would do."

Keith would lay out all his collected information and Dad would review it carefully when ask to catch anything he might have missed. He not only ever belittled his prisoners, but he always wanted the best for his officers, even if it meant leaving his department.

"He tried to get Doug and me to join the federal law because he knew that's where the money was," Keith told me. "I always considered Herb a good friend and I hated it when he left the Sheriff's Office."

He noted that his brother, Kip Vickers, had worked as Dad's right hand man when he was chief in Vinton.

"He was very influential on Kip's career," he said.

"Herb was very good about seeking grant money for things that most officers wouldn't even consider," the current Wythe County Sheriff stated. "He kept our eyes open to things that the department needed that we would have never thought about having."

The second place winner in the Chautauqua Window Decorating Contest was Blue Ridge Books. Chamber President Herb Cooley presented the ribbon to Caroline Wing. Other chamber representatives are: (far left) Admi...

Keith says he has tried to implement those same skills as leader of the Wythe County Sheriff's Office, which he says he learned from Dad. Examples of this include the victim witness and female violence officers that he has hired. He also noted that, even after he left Wythe County, he would call the department and encourage them to pursue certain grants he thought would benefit Wythe County.

"Over the years, he has kept my eyes open to certain grants that I didn't know about," Keith told me. "If there was a place where we could obtain funding that he knew we didn't have, he would call and tell me about it."

He also noted that when Dad went to work as chief of police in Pulaski, he hired officers to specifically deal with drugs, which are a huge problem in that area to this day. Oftentimes, Pulaski drug cases would cross county lines, which meant that Keith would be able to work with Dad again.

"I don't know whether any officers had ever worked specifically with drugs in Pulaski before Herb took over the department, but they definitely did after he got there," Keith recalled. "That was always an issue that was very important to him."

"Ever since Herb left Wythe County, he has always managed to look after us," he added. "I never met anyone who worked for your dad that didn't like him. If you cared about your job, you couldn't help but appreciate and learn from him."

Dad was certainly a friend to all of his deputies. We got together at each other's homes a lot outside of work. My mom and his wife Tammy were pregnant at the same time on two different occasions. Keith's daughter Tabitha and I are the same age and went all the way through school together. My sister Tara and his youngest daughter Kelly did the same and were very close friends for a long time.

I remember being in the same kindergarten class with Tabitha when both of our dads came to read to our class in representation of the Wythe County Sheriff's Office. We were the proudest two students in Kirstie Smith's class that day. Just this past year, Keith repeated the honor for his youngest granddaughter Kylie who just completed kindergarten.

**Window decorators**
The first place winner in the Wytheville-Wythe-Bland Chamber Commerce's Chautauqua window decorating contest was United Cities ( Accepting the ribbon are (left to right) Kathy Repass and Rita Richard

On the day I interviewed Keith Dunagan, he was on his way to the Cliff Dicker Memorial Golf Tournament, an annual event held in Wytheville in honor of the only deputy to be gunned down in the line of duty in the history of the county. On December 6, 1994, he was murdered by 15-year-old Shawn Wheeler, who shot him in the back of the head as he attempted to make a drug arrest in a home.

Dad and Cliff were good friends and he was an avid supporter of all things the county did in his memory. When he would have awards banquets for his own officers, he would always include a moment of silence for Cliff.

"Herb would go get him a cup of coffee at the jail where Cliff would be working first thing every morning before he did anything," remembered Keith. "It wasn't unusual to come by the jail early in the morning and find Cliff and Herb talking over a cup of coffee together."

Keith added that this was the saddest time in the history of the Wythe County Sheriff's Office. It was only a couple of months after Dad left to take the chief's position in Pulaski.

"You could have heard a pin drop for months after Cliff died," the sheriff recalled. "We were the saddest group of guys I have ever seen."

Keith also clearly recalls campaigning for Dad heavily when he ran for the Clerk of Court in 1991.

"Doug and I put up hundreds and hundreds of signs up for Herb all over the county," he stated. "I still have my Herb Cooley button and pen from that election."

Keith also couldn't resist commenting on Dad's famous arrest of the Wythe County Jail escapee with his finger.

"Herb was notorious for leaving his gun in his patrol car," he laughed. "That's why he ended up having to arrest guys with his finger."

Dad did tell me once that he never had to shoot at anyone during his forty five years as a police officer. Keith concurred, along with his other fellow officers, that Dad was respected by most violators because he treated them like human beings. He never belittled anyone.

He also agreed with me that Dad would have helped the county in an unprecedented way had he been elected and that he probably would have never left Wythe County had he won.

"If you needed an answer to a question, you asked Herb," Keith continued. "He knew more about the budget and all the other operations within the sheriff's office than anyone in the department."

Keith worked with my uncle Doug Cooley in the narcotics division for many years. They remain close friends to this day and the duo had a lot of fun working with Dad, who oversaw all their investigative work.

"He would join in on a lot of investigations with us, especially if there was a big drug bust to be handled," recalled the sheriff. "Herb was probably the first person on the scene at every major crime committed in Wythe County while he was chief deputy."

It was clear to me that Dad was not just a figurehead that sat behind a desk and sent his deputies to do the dirty work. He was out there in the midst of everything, never afraid do to the same work he asked of the other officers. Keith attested to this, noting Dad's customary appointment of a half a dozen or so deputies to work a nightshift detail every year at Christmastime. This was a particular time, he said, the crime seemed to spike in Wythe County.

"He had us out all over the county checking stores and patrolling streets and we would be talking and laughing the whole time," he recalled. "We would work until two or three o'clock in the morning and then we would all go eat breakfast together at the end of the shift. Those were good times and Herb was the ringleader of all of it."

As chairman of the Wythe County Transportation Safety Commission, Dad spearheaded a January 1991 campaign to send a proposed seatbelt law to the General Assembly in Richmond, which made it legal for motorists to be stopped and fined if not wearing a seatbelt. Previously, the single violation was not enough for officers to stop drivers, but motorists could be fined for not wearing a seatbelt if they had been stopped for some other violation. Sgt. Bob Ratcliff of the Virginia State Police told my friend Marcella Cockerham Taylor on January 30, 1991, who was then a staff writer for the *Southwest Virginia Enterprise*, that the seatbelt law of that time was virtually ineffective.

"I have seen a lot of cases where a seatbelt would have made the difference between life and death," Dad stated.

"If approved, this new law will bring up a new generation that will buckle up and more lives will be saved," added Maxine Manuel who served as vice chairwoman and treasurer for the commission.

A motion was also approved by the commission to send letters supporting the proposal of the seatbelt law to State Senator Danny Bird and Delegate Tom Jackson. It had already received a stamp of approval from both the Virginia State Police and the Virginia Department of Motor Vehicles. The commission discussed several safety requests received from the citizens of Wythe County and approved a speed study on Route 94 in the Piney community of Fort Chiswell, which would change the speed limit to 55 MPH as the area is primarily residential. Also discussed was the possibility of widening a bridge of U.S. Route 21 South near Galilee Church in Wytheville.

"I have contacted the highway department six months ago about the narrow bridge," stated commission member Bobby Williams. "Signs were put up indicating that the bridge was narrow."

"Crosswalks are still needed at the intersections of U.S. 52 and State Route 94 at Fort Chiswell High School," state the late commission member Bob Dean. "This will ensure the safety of students when crossing the roads."

The commission also cosponsored a bike rodeo safety program on May 4, 1991 with the United Telephone Company, which was held along with a cookout for children and their parents.

"I would like to see the commission incorporate the Child Identification Program at the bike rodeo," Bob Dean added. "It would be a good time for the program."

Commission members agreed and asked Dean to bring some brochures for the program to their next meeting. They also agreed to recognize the Wytheville Lady Ruritans, of which my mother Rhonda was an active member at the time, with a resolution commending their being named second in the nation for their transportation safety activities.

"The local Department of Motor Vehicle offices will soon be getting information from the Virginia Department of Children," notified commission member Danny Dean. "A public information campaign is being launched where people who spot children in vehicles without safety seats can inform the DMV, which will send letters to the parents with information on the child safety seats and where to purchase them. There is no law violation involved in the department's campaign."

Below Marcella's article on the meeting there was a notice stating that the Wythe County Sheriff's Department had received at least one report that a mother who had sons involved in Operation Desert Storm, saying that they were missing in action. Police wanted to notify the public that the armed forces always sends a representative to notify their next of kin in person when a serving member of their family has been killed or is missing in action. It is horrible to think that something like that would happen at such a scary time in our community and nation.

\* \* \* \* \* \* \* \*

On January 31, 1991 at 10:55 a.m., Emzy Monroe Walls of Bland turned himself in to the Bland County Sheriff's Office as the fourth person to distribute drugs stemming from a lengthy undercover operation. He was taken to the Smyth County Jail where he was being held on a $500,000 bond after a warrant was issued for conspiracy to distribute methamphetamine, a Schedule II controlled substance.

The Tri-County Drug Task Force, which was headed by the Wythe County Sheriff's Office, began around Christmastime 1990. On January 25, 1991, two Bland County residents named Ronald W. Dillow and Anita K. Matney were arrested in Marion after they allegedly sold a pound of methamphetamine valued at $45,400 to an undercover Wythe County officer. The next day, A.C. Matney, also of Bland, was arrested in his residing town. All three were charged with conspiracy to distribute a Schedule II controlled substance.

Searches were conducted at homes both in Wythe and Bland Counties, at both of which property including real estate, vehicles and weapons were seized as well as more than $90,000 worth of drugs. The value of all confiscated property totaled approximately $600,000. Wythe County Sheriff Wayne Pike reported that an additional $45,000 was confiscated from a bank account, which was turned over to federal agents.

"If the money is forfeited in the court system, the funds will be returned to the law enforcement agencies involved in the operation," he stated. "Wythe County is hoping for a substantial amount."

"A drug bust of this magnitude couldn't happen without an organization such as the Tri-County Drug Task Force, which combines the manpower of Smyth, Bland and Wythe County Sheriff's Offices," Dad pointed out, stressing the interagency cooperation. "Small law enforcement agencies couldn't conduct such operations alone."

With money for public safety scheduled to deplete in March with an overall state budget cut of 50 percent in 1991, Sheriff Wayne Pike announced big changes to the operation of the Wythe Sheriff's Office for 1992. He explained his dilemma to the Wythe County Board of Supervisors back in November 1991, asking the county to allocate additional funds to his department for mileage. By mid-December, Board Chairman Tom DuPuis and committee member George Johnstone were still undecided in the matter.

The committee had to major concerns which the requested the sheriff investigate. One was the complaint that deputies used the patrol cars for personal reasons. The second was a concern about the amount of time officers spent answering calls from the Factory Merchants Mall in Fort Chiswell.

"I realize the mall had no security force, but I asked Sheriff Pike to request that such a force be hired," Dupuis said.

Dad represented the Wythe County Sheriff's Office at the Wythe County Board of Supervisors meeting on December 13, 1991.

"We cannot ignore calls for assistance from the mall," he told them.

"The charges of my deputies using vehicles for personal use are unfounded," Sheriff Pike said in a statement to the press the next day. "I have repeatedly asked for information on these alleged instances, such as who was involved and where it happened. None of this information could be given to me. All I was told was that it was an anonymous call made prior to the election. I can't wait on the board to take action. I have to plan now to stretch the money as far as possible.

"The structure of law enforcement that this sheriff's office has had for the last twelve years is dead," he added. "Until I get some financial support from the county and state, unfortunately, that's the way it will stay. I realize that the state made the cuts and the county is in a tough financial situation. I'm not blaming anyone. I'm caught in the middle. I'm trying to provide public safety, be a good manager and serve the people."

In an effort to make cutbacks, the Wythe County Sheriff's Office was forced to withdraw from the Tri-County Drug Task Force of which it had been a founding member since 1988. The drug dog was also retired, which eliminated training trips to Richmond and back as well as special calls that would require the drug dog. The business checking program and long distance calls with the exception of those pertaining to the placement of prisoners were stopped.

As the department received no funding for police supplies in the 1991-1992 fiscal year, photography and fingerprinting were reduced, which made investigative efforts much more challenging. Deputies were sent only to schools that were mandated and were required to drive their own personal vehicles for covering all events for other agencies such as school ballgames, as many of the cars in the departmental rolling stock were parked.

"We're looking at every program that requires money," Pike stated further. "If it doesn't bring in revenue and isn't self-sustaining, we'll have to cut it."

"The reason Wythe County has such a low crime rate is that my personnel is dedicated and honest. That's the reasons citizens have supported us. They know we'll be there no matter what time of day or night. We've stopped big time drug dealers before they got a foothold on this county and developed education programs in the schools. Even before D.A.R.E., we did puppet shows. To continue operating in this manner, the office needs financial support from the county and state," he went on. "We have provided millions of dollars for this county and jobs for families. We've spent money here, which boosts the economy. People here look at the sheriff's office with pride, but I see all of that disappearing because of a lack of financial support."

"This isn't a feud or a disagreement between personalities, but a huge money problem," Pike said after a morning meeting with Dupuis on December 14, 1991. "I'm doing everything I can without compromising the safety of our citizens. We need the support of everyone and I hope everyone will bear with us."

Chapter 11
An Admired and Witty Colleague

Doug King was hired by then Sheriff Wayne Pike in June of 1983 and reported on July 1, 1983. The hiring process was rather unique when he was approached by Sheriff Pike with a job offer.

"I had never thought of working as a deputy although I had, several years before, flirted with the idea of becoming a Game Warden only to be told I was too short," he told me. "Anyway, after mulling over the offer, I went to see Sheriff Pike at his office and asked him if he thought I could do the job; after all, I was only 5'7" tall and 155 pounds at *that* time."

Sheriff Pike assured Doug that his size would not be a drawback so he accepted. Doug had previously met my father on a social basis after the election of 1979, as he was the Chief Deputy. Though there were numerous occasions in which they gathered as friends over the years, the ones that stand out to Doug the most were his famous Halloween parties that were held at his house in the Muskrat section of Wythe County.

"The best way I could describe them was hilarious," Doug recalled happily. "These parties continued for several years and they were always very much anticipated as there was a lot of people there, good food, good drink, and the chance to mix with all types of Law Enforcement Officers that, I believe, were and are some of the best people in the world. I still feel that way about these Officers after 33 years and will never change my opinion of them."

King did not immediately work under Dad.

"When we first met, my impression of him was that he was friendly, *extremely* witty and a welcoming person," King explained. "This still remains my impression of him."

King told me that Dad continued to be a calming influence on him with his experience and management style.

"Herb always had a wry comment to make about any situation that developed even though, at the time, it may have been extremely tense," the future sheriff stated. "As the lowest man in the structure of the Sheriff's Office, my contacts with Herb were limited at first. There was a rigid chain of command and I reported to others that were between us in the line of direct communication."

It was only later, after he had been promoted, that Doug had a working relationship with Dad and that was very brief, as he left the Sheriff's Office shortly after. Most of their interactions occurred when he was Chief at Pulaski and Vinton, where he completed his 45-year career. However, there was one very vivid incident in his career during which Doug referred to Dad as his savior, as he prevented Doug from enduring an intense internal investigation.

"I had stopped a motorist that I suspected was driving under the influence and was subsequently arrested," Doug remembered. "Herb had heard my stop and radio traffic and pulled in behind me on the highway. I briefed him on the facts; he observed the subject and agreed with my decision to make any arrest."

Later, the family of the suspect made a complaint to Sheriff Pike that Doug had been extremely belligerent, having allegedly kicked in the taillights of the suspect's vehicle to break the lenses in an effort to provide an excuse to stop the subject initially.

After the family presented the vehicle to Sheriff Pike for inspection, he mentioned this complaint to Dad who immediately informed him that he was present at the stop and arrest, stayed with the vehicle until the wrecker arrived and had not seen any damage to the vehicle. The damage had occurred sometime after the vehicle was towed away.

"As a result of Herb's eyewitness account of the event, I was immediately cleared, though I did not learn of this whole episode until a good deal of time had passed,"

Doug recollected with gratitude. "Such was the mettle of Herb."

Another humorous event Doug relayed to me came from Dad directly. Doug wasn't present, but recalls Dad telling him about the service of a search warrant on a suspected drug dealer's home. The suspect offered unarmed resistance and was bodily thrown down a line of deputies who were part of the serving team. Sheriff Pike threw him to Dad who then threw him to the next deputy in line and it continued until the last two subdued him. After the subject was placed in handcuffs and transported away, the serving team was in the process of searching the resident. The mother of the suspect was present and, in typical fashion, loudly protesting her being removed from the house during the search.

More Chamber of Commerce photos from 1992.

"In the midst of her ravings, another deputy who was known for his down home style of personal interactions began inquiring of the woman about a stove that was standing in the yard and whether or not she planned on throwing it away as he would like to have it," Doug told me. "She was completely disarmed by this line of questioning and Herb would practically howl with laughter about the manner in which this entire event unfolded. Herb has a way of putting a humorous spin on any event, as I have previously related."

Doug noted that Dad's belief that there was no reason to panic at any time and his calm presence was infectious. "It promoted a clearer picture of events and resulted in a more thoughtful approach of how an incident should be handled. I strove during my stint as Chief Deputy, and afterward as Sheriff, to emulate his calm."

"Panic is contagious and I always tried to defuse situations with humor that would give everyone pause in their demeanor. Notice I said 'tried'," he added. "Not every situation can be calmed; such as a suspect who takes it upon himself to start firing shots in direction of others or yourself. Sometimes you have to move fast and the situation is chaotic. The time for calm can come later."

On a side note, one of the funniest incidents in Doug's involvement with Dad occurred after he had retired. Sgt. Teny Underwood came into his office at my request and asked if he could go down to my house and install a child safety seat in my van.

"As I had a lot of experience in that, I went to your house and was met by Herb and a man that may have been your father-in-law," Doug recalled. "Herb and the other man were frazzled by the effort that they had expended into attempting to install the seat without success. I looked at the seat and had it installed in under a minute. As usual, Herb thought that this was hilarious that someone had easily accomplished a task that was completely foreign to him. He is self-effacing if nothing else in this world!"

I remember that incident well. It was Friday, May 30, 2014 and we had just brought my daughter home from the hospital, who had been born that previous Tuesday at 9:04 p.m. Isabella Marie Cooley was my father's seventh grandchild and my mother's only. My father-in-law had driven Emily and Bella home in his car while Dad drove me behind them in my handicapped accessible van. They had gotten the seat out of Dave's car, knowing that it needed to be permanently placed in my van. This seemingly easy task quickly turned disastrous. Reading the instructions seemed to befuddle them all the more. After a half-hour that seemed more like a day, I finally intervened.

"Why don't you call Teny and have her send Doug King down here to put it in?" I asked Dad.

We had been told that the Sheriff's Office was always available and being a nervous wreck and overly cautious, I wanted the absolute safest plan for my baby. I live just down the street from the Sheriff's Office and he came right away. Doug was our saving grace that day and I will never forget it.

"Like every man, Herb's direct influence can last only as long as the careers of the people that he worked with at the Sheriff's Office," Doug reasoned. At the time of this writing, there are only a few deputies that worked with Herb that are still employed. Many have retired, as have I. That being said, the influence is, hopefully, still present and being reflected in the operations of the Sheriff's Office. The supervising style being utilized by current deputies that were trained by those who did work with Herb certainly should the beneficiaries of his personality."

Personality is defined by the perception of a second person," the retired sheriff added in closing. "In the opinion of this 'second personality,' Herb Cooley is someone I have always admired and respected. His career was long-lived with several Law Enforcement agencies, he performed well with all, and I miss the interaction that I had with Herb throughout our careers."

Another kindness I can recall from Doug King was when my wife was working for CareNet as a telephone triage nurse with callers from across the nation. She was required to have nursing licenses, many of which required that she be fingerprinted. Having pushed her deadline to the limit,

Emily and I went into the Sheriff's Office praying someone would still be in the fingerprinting room. Doug was the only one in the building. Without a hitch, he took her fingerprints and even mailed her information off to the licensing office free of charge. He was our saving grace again that day and I shall always be grateful to him. Emily eventually became licensed in all fifty states, thanks to the kindness and help of Sheriff King and our friend Teny Underwood.

* * * * * * * *

During the first week of February in 1993, legislators in Richmond decided whether or not Virginians would be limited on handgun purchases as part of Governor Wilder's three step plan to keep weapons out of the hands of criminals and sever the image of the Commonwealth as a haven for gun runners. The other two steps in the plan would allow State Police officers to keep gun record purchases valid for a year as opposed to a month as well as to prevent teenagers from having access to gun except in such limited supervised activities as target shooting.

The biggest controversy for local citizens surrounded the one gun per month proposal, which had many loudly vocalizing opinions at a public hearing at George Wythe High School concerning the issues of violent crimes that involved firearms, which drew more than 400 locals who opposed gun control. This included representatives from such organizations as the Virginia Chamber of Commerce, the Virginia Sheriff's Association, the Virginia Association of Chiefs of Police and the Blue Ridge Association of Chief of Police. These organizations were among several others who supported the governor's legislative package that contains seven other violent crime opposition measures. Several people echoed the opinion that the solution to crime control should not be through the limitations of guns.

"Virginia's escalating reputation as a handgun supermarket is unraveling the reputation of our Commonwealth as a good place to do business, work and live," Virginia Chamber of Commerce Chairman Robert T. Skunda.

"We don't see what guns do in the big cities such as children being shot down in the streets," Dad added. "The only part of Governor Wilder's plan I would question would be the limit of the number of guns a person could buy. If someone is going to commit a crime, they only need one gun to do it, but I understand the gun running measure. We need to cut down on the number of guns people may be selling for profit."

"While I have some reservations, we have to have some measure of gun control," Dad continued in representation of the Wythe County Sheriff's Office as chief deputy. "At the same time, we don't want to be known as a gun running state; we really need to look at this issue. All in all, I think what the governor is trying to do is a good measure."

Dad didn't seem to think that the gun purchasing limit would have that big of an impact on the people of the area.

"I can't afford to buy a gun myself every month," he said. I also don't see how this would impact the sales of any other type of gun, such as a hunting rifle. We have a number of legitimate people in our area, such as sportsmen and collectors, who own guns but I don't think people such be able to walk into the streets and buy a gun. A waiting period is a good thing."

"We have to do everything legitimate we can to stop criminals," Dad added. "There are always going to be criminals that will be able to obtain guns, but we shouldn't let that be an excuse to say 'They'll get them anyway.' It doesn't mean we can throw the door wide open. We must do what we can to control the criminals and prevent them ready access to hand guns."

"I don't really see the problem with the gun measures that have been taken," commented Wytheville Police Chief Bobby Doyle. "As far as police officers being concerned, we won't notice a big change locally in terms of what the legislators do. Big cities like this will see more effects from this sooner. In looking at the limit of one gun per month, it wouldn't bother me if legislators decided to set aside some provisions on hand guns.

"I don't believe the purpose of the proposed legislation is to impact the sales of sport or collector guns," he added. "It may affect people who hunt with hand guns."

Hillsville's annual Labor Day Gun Show in neighboring Carroll County was expected to see some repercussions from this proposal by the General Assembly.

"These types of shows may be part of what is contributing to the problem," continued Doyle. "A dealer has to obtain the history of anyone purchasing a gun, but individuals who are not licensed as dealers can sell to anyone. I don't think they should be blamed for the crime problems in New York City and Washington, D.C. They've have problems long before there were Virginia gun laws. A new law is not going to make any difference to drug dealers. Also, I don't think it's right to punish honest sportsmen who are already abiding by the laws on the books because of what these criminals have done. It's going to be difficult to separate this."

Manager of Outdoors and More in Wytheville Diane Woolheater also weighed in on the subject.

"I don't think this is going to solve anything," she said of the proposed legislation. "The crooks have always been able to get their hands on a gun and they'll still get them."

Although the store where she worked was not licensed to sell guns at that time, Woolheater felt that the new law would only create more paperwork for her if it was passed.

"Licensed gun dealers have always had to fill out multiple forms with gun sale reports. A new law will only create more paperwork and I'm opposed to Governor Wilder's plan. There should be more crime control, not gun control," she said. "We're a hunting community, not a killing community. I'm not saying that anyone who buys a gun is a criminal, but this one gun per month law won't stop the criminals. I don't think there are that many people in our area who would buy more than one hand gun a month. Around here, most people only buy rifles or shotguns."

Woolheater added that she didn't think that this legislation would affect the sale of hand guns, but felt that there would eventually be legislations to affect other types of guns. She also noted that this proposed law would stop drug trafficking and gun runners.

"The criminal doesn't care about what the laws says," she remarked. "He is just going to do whatever he wants to get what he wants. I don't think this is going to affect local businesses that sell guns or the people in our area. The hunters aren't going to mind this thing. If a hunter wants a pistol, he's not going to buy more than one a month anyway."

Billy Moore, owner of Moore's Gun Shop in Max Meadows, disagreed entirely with the proposed legislation.

"It's just a way for the state to get more money," he said. "When you limit the number of guns that can be sold to a person, it is just another form of communism. Limiting the number of guns that can be sold to a person over the time period of a month will not help. A crook will get a gun no matter what the law says. This won't take any more guns off the street like they say it will. It won't help a thing. It's just another form of harassment."

He also felt the gun control measure would be a stepping stone to the eventual limitation of guns such as rifles and shot guns that could be sold to a person.

"Although I understand that most people cannot afford to buy more than a single hand gun per month, I think that people should have the right to purchase as many guns as they want at any time," Moore added.

At H and H Guns N Stuff in Max Meadows, shop owner Johnny Huddle said he did not see how the numbers of guns that could legally be sold to a single individual over the time period of a month would help to stop drug dealers or any other sort of criminal for that matter.

"They have tried to regulate drug and alcohol crime in the state and it has not worked," Huddle stated. "The makers of the law need to concern themselves with the criminals. This proposal just limits the rights of our honest citizens and does not touch the people who commit the crimes. The law is only as good as the people who uphold it. The judicial system needs to enforce the laws that are already on the books instead of releasing criminals back into the streets in a matter of days or even hours of committing their crime, only to repeat the same offense."

Both Huddle and Moore agreed that the proposed gun control legislation would not deter the criminal element in the least.

"A crook is going to steal or kill for a gun no matter what kind of law there is," Moore stated. "However, I am sure it will affect me. On top of everything else, there will be more paperwork to do."

"I don't think gun control will have any affect at all," added Huddle. "Lawmakers need to keep criminals in jail and stop returning them to the streets. If the law of one gun per month is passed, it might hurt my business some, but not much. A lot of the people I sell guns to aren't criminals. They just like guns. Besides, if I sell more than two handguns in a five day period, I have to report it to the tobacco and firearms people."

\* \* \* \* \* \* \* \*

As Dad reached the end of his tenure with the Wythe County Sheriff's Office, he joined the local police forces in support of a new and more stringent law against drunk driving that would lower the legal blood alcohol level to .08. As Jeffrey Simmons, my future boss, reported on March 30, 1994, Sen. Jack Reasor stated that new DUI legislation, including the Omnibus Alcohol Safety Act of 1994, was awaiting the signature of Gov. George Allen. This legislation was one of several alcohol safety related bills that had been recently passed by the General Assembly.

"Virginia has one of the lowest crimes rates in the nation; only 17 states led us in that important category," Reasor stated in a statewide press release. "Hopefully, when the new laws are enacted, we will see a decrease in the crime rate."

Local police agencies believed that if the laws were signed into action by the governor, more drunk drivers who were classified as borderline, which was .10 at the time, apprehended and off the road.

"More and more people involved in recent traffic stops were on the borderline level," Lt. Rick W. Arnold of the Wytheville Police Department told reporters, noting that approximately 11 to 12 percent of the drivers who were stopped and submitted to breathalyzer or blood tests fell between the .05 and .09 range. "It would give us teeth by being able to take a more aggressive stand and get drunk drivers off the street at any level. It would take away a lot of these borderline cases and put them in jail."

As Chief Deputy of the Wythe County Sheriff's Office, Dad told Simmons hat lowering the legal limit of blood alcohol content would relay a much needed greater threat to the general public not to drink and drive, keeping those who would off of the road.

"There are a lot of borderline cases involving people who should be charged because they are drunk," Dad stated. "Unfortunately, these drivers were not charged with drinking and driving because of the courts' strict adherence to the .10 blood alcohol content law."

New laws also addressed the issue of drivers refusing to submit to blood and breathalyzer tests, providing for an immediate seven-day suspension for any driver's license who is arrested for a DUI violation if the person unreasonably refuses to submit to a breathalyzer test. This is effective for any offender who has had any prior violations from six months to one year prior to being apprehended.

Arnold also added that 15 percent of those who were arrested for drunk driving refused to submit to any testing in 1993.

"We had a few more refusals in 1993 than in the past," he told Simmons.

Along with the suspension of licenses, new legislation would feature a zero-tolerance policy for underage drunk drivers. The safety act imposed a six month forfeiture of the license of any underage individual in addition to a $500 fine if the driver has a blood alcohol content level of .02 to .08. Another provision of the new alcohol safety legislation includes a 30-day administrative vehicle impounding with the offense of driving without a license if it was revoked or suspended on any previous violation relating to alcohol. Neither town nor county police maintained an impoundment facility. However, both departments had other means of storing confiscated vehicles.

Additional pieces to the anti-crime legislation from this session of the General Assembly awaiting signature on the governor's desk include a bill that would make it a Class I misdemeanor offense to make a verbal threat to kill or harm any employee of an elementary, intermediate or secondary school while on a school property, bus or attending any activity sponsored by a school. A law was also featured that would enhance the penalties for simple assault and trespass in which the person or property targeted by the crime was intentionally selected based on race, religion, color or national origin. This particular bill would add a minimum mandatory sentence of six months of incarceration, thirty days of which cannot be suspended. Another bill would add carjacking to the list of felonies for which a separate penalty would be prescribed if a firearm was used. A final legislation, punishing the crime of adult abuse and neglect as a Class VI felony if the offense results in serious bodily injury or disease, was also on the agenda for proposed implementation.

## Chapter 12
### The Ultimate Cool Big Brother

My dad and Uncle Doug were brothers who didn't really grow up together. Dad was sixteen years older and left home when Doug was just two-years-old. Their other brother, my late Uncle Mike, came along right smack in the middle of Dad and Doug. It was as if my grandparents had planned to have a boy every eight years.

"I don't think it was planned at all," Doug said with a laugh. "In fact, I'm quite sure I was an accident."

Douglas Heath Cooley, born June 18, 1958.

When it comes having a typical brotherly relationship complete with fights and competition, the Cooley boys were too far apart in age to have that. In fact, Doug grew up in the small home on Delhart Road that I knew as my grandparents' home, as opposed to the large pre-Civil War family home in which Dad and Mike grew up. My grandparents moved to the house at 1348 Delhart Road in 1963 when Doug was just five. Dad was already a young husband and father at that point.

"I do remember a little bit about the old house," Doug recalled. "I can remember Herb taking a bath in a washtub behind an old woodstove."

A clearer memory happened with Dad when Doug saw his oldest brother come in dressed in full motorcycle cop attire, complete when the shiny boots, leather jacket and helmet. After Dad took him for a ride down the highway on the back of his Harley, Doug knew his fate was sealed.

"I knew from that moment on that I wanted to be a policeman," he told me. "He was *the* cool big brother and I wanted to be just like him."

The Cooley brothers, circa 1963.

Dead set on joining law enforcement, just like his big brother, Doug joined the military police unit of the army training drug dogs straight out of high school.

"Then I went to work for Herb," he chuckled.

"I would just hear him and his buddies talk and then I was just taken by it," he said. "I went into the Army as Military Police and handled dogs in there."

Doug came to work for his brother by mere coincidence.

"When Wayne Pike was running for sheriff, he wasn't actually elected for sheriff, I was home on leave, and I saw him somewhere over here in town when he was campaigning," he explained in reference to acquiring his job with the Wythe County Sheriff's Office.

"If you get elected I'd like to have a job," Doug said to Wayne.

"I get elected and there's an opening, come over and you'll have one," Wayne promised him.

"It just so happened that about the time when I was getting ready to come out, a deputy and a dispatcher ran away together and created an opening and that's how I got my job here," he told me.

For Doug, having his brother as his boss was no big deal.

"Herb was a laid back boss," my uncle recalled. "Herb kept the place at an even keel. He had to go behind Wayne and put out the fires that Wayne started, that's pretty much what he did. As a boss, Herb was good."

After Doug's first promotion, he remembered questioning himself to his brother.

"You know what to do," Dad assured him. "Just make the decision and I'll back you."

"He just supported you," Doug said of Dad. "Herb was never the kind of boss who was mean to anybody. "You'd just go in and do your job, it was all good. You couldn't have a better boss. He just happened to be my brother."

That sort of treatment was not exclusive to Doug.

"That's the way he did with everybody," he stated. "You did your job, Herb would support you. He left you alone."

When Doug was promoted to position of authority, Dad was in role model in terms of his administration tactics.

"If somebody does something under you, take care of it," Dad warned his brother. "Do something because if you don't, Wayne will go off and fire them. Do what you have to do, but do something and make sure it's done when it comes to the sheriff's attention."

When Dad left Wythe County to accept the position of chief in Pulaski, Doug would replace his brother as Chief Deputy, achieving the rank of lieutenant colonel before leaving the Sheriff's Office.

"He probably helped me get that job in the sense that in the years leading up to the time, he said. "He and Wayne helped me get the opportunities for the pro-training and education that were needed."

Doug credits his brother with helping make him a better person and police officer, which Dad did for all of his police officers. Dad was always focused on the big picture, something Doug saw a bit of when he became captain of the patrol division.

"You didn't just have to worry about patrol anymore," Doug said of being promoted to Chief Deputy. "You had to worry about investigations, the jail, and civil matters. You had to worry about everything."

According to Doug, the Chief Deputy was responsible for running the department by dealing with the day to day operations of the sheriff's office.

"He essentially left Wythe County for other opportunities," Doug said of Dad. "He prepared himself and he basically did the same thing he taught us to do."

Probably the crowning achievement of Dad's career was graduating from the FBI National Academy, for which Doug said it was an honor just to be selected.

"I think it was just an opportunity that came along at just the right time. "I just never had that opportunity, but I kind of moved on and worked for the State and then, interestingly enough, he did the same thing I did."

"I wasn't looking for a job and I'm not sure he was," Doug reasoned. "He saw an opportunity and he took it."

While Dad went on to be chief of police in Pulaski, Doug accepted a position as field representative of Southwest Virginia for the Department of Criminal Justice Services.

"Our main office was in Richmond but my job was to ensure that all the training academies and all the police agencies in the region of Southwest Virginia were in compliance with employment and training standards," he explained. "So, I went to all the different agencies around this end of the state and the academies to make sure they were in compliance with employment standards."

From there you went to the Police Academy in Bristol as director, a position from which Doug says he is likely to retire.

"I really enjoy it," he said. "It's one of the most rewarding jobs that I've had from the training aspect of it."

I have found interesting that, because Wytheville is where my home is, that when Dad had a job in Pulaski and Vinton and you went to Richmond and to Bristol, you all maintained homes in Wythe County for most of that time.

"When I got the job at DCJS, they had advertised that you had to live within a 25 mile radius of Roanoke," Doug told me. "After I got the job, my boss said even though logistically Wytheville was as good as anywhere because I had to go from Lee County to Lynchburg. The compromising point was Pulaski. I never did go to Richmond where the main office is. I had been there about a year and they changed the administration at the very top."

"I don't care where you live," Doug's new boss told him.

"I'm going home, which was to Wytheville," he responded. You know even though we were from Grayson County, Wytheville had basically become home for both of us."

Although Doug had never thought about it before, he agreed that losing the Clerk of Court election may have been an ultimate factor in why Dad ultimately decided to leave Wythe County for good.

"There's no doubt in my mind that Herb would have done a superb job in that position," he noted. "It was the typical "knock on the door" campaign. I'm not really into that kind of thing but I did it for him. I can remember Herb saying after the election that he was not a politician. He's just who he is."

Wayne Pike was a consummate politician. According to Doug, he could work a room like no one else. That's why he was in the top job. He never stopped campaigning. My uncle illustrated this by recalling the story of a suicide they investigated.

"The guy had shot himself, but he had shot himself with a .22 and just barely had a trickle of blood and he's sitting in a chair slumped over," he told me. "Wayne comes in and is working the room and proceeds to shake hands with the dead man."

"Wayne," Doug told his boss. "You ain't gonna get that vote, buddy."

Doug told another funny story involve Dad and their late brother Mike.

"He and Mike came up when we lived in Pulaski, past the house and over the hill," Doug recalled. "We went camping over there. Well, he and Mike decided they were going to sneak up and scare us, but what they forgot about was a German shepherd named Nelson. So Nelson started barking then he took off. I saw some people running, well I had a bow and arrow and I think I had a machete and we took off and started chasing them and they got so tickled that the joke backfired on them."

"Mike always wanted to scare somebody," he added with a laugh. "I remember growing up and we slept in the same bed and our closet was a piece of wire going from the chimney to the wall and that's where we hung our clothes. He took a piece of fishing line and tied it to the plug and when we got into the bed and it would knock against the bed. He did stuff like that all the time."

The Cooley brothers in the summer of 2013, shortly before we lost Mike in November.

My grandmother was the most compulsive worrier, which was a trait I unfortunately inherited from her. Having two sons who were policemen could not have been as easy reality for Granny. So, Doug's way of breaking the news of joining the army must have been awful for her.

"Nobody even knew I was thinking about going," he told me. "I just went downtown and talked to a recruiter and came home."

"Guess what I just did today?" he asked his unsuspecting parents.

"Mike, of course, didn't go into the military," Doug noted. "He's the only one that had any sense."

Doug, however, knew his fate was to be a cop.

"I was so eat up with wanting to be a cop like my brother that I went to college for a year and my goal was to become a trooper and then when I realized when I graduated from college, I still wouldn't be old enough to become a trooper and I couldn't wait so I decided to join the military and be an MP," he explained. "The first time I ever saw him get real excited was in a car chase down in Speedwell. This car came by us with no headlights on and I turned around and started chasing him right up the mountain and he finally stopped and Herb jumped out and run up to the car, grabbed that boy by the collar.

"Boy," Dad shouted. "What are you doing running from the police?"

"I'd never seen him get excited before," Doug chuckled. "Herb was one of those people who'd get mad but it'd go right away. He just didn't let things bother him."

In working with Dad, Doug learned a number administrative tactics from his brother, which he implemented during his administration as a supervisor.

"One thing, I remember Herb saying that always stuck with me," he noted.

"The hardest thing you will ever have to deal with is dealing with different people and just because somebody is different, doesn't mean they're wrong," he remembers Dad advising him.

"I think one thing I've tried to do but I don't think I've accomplished it as good as he did is to keep a calm demeanor and to maintain a calm, level-headed approach," Doug stated. That was something I tried to emulate in the way I approach things because it worked."

He learned that, of course, from Dad.

"People did respect him," Doug said of his oldest brother. "That was probably one of the biggest ways I tried to emulate him in the way he treated people. I wasn't as nearly successful as he was. I try not to make rash decisions. I try to think things out."

It always surprised me, and saddened me in fact, that Dad or Doug were never appointed or elected to be Wythe County Sheriff. In the summer of 1998, Doug was considered for sheriff and said that, had he been appointed, he would have taken the job.

"I had a petition signed by almost every deputy on the force in support of my being sheriff, but it didn't happen," Doug told me. "I think Herb took a different path, but he was headed in that direction. After he left, I was headed in that direction until another opportunity came my way."

Nevertheless, I always appreciated the sheriff's office because from the time I was born, I felt like I was one of their little mascots. That was a fun place to go. I went to work with my daddy and Teny gave me milk and candy and everybody treated me like family."

Doug credits Dad for making the sheriff's department feel like a family.

"That's something that Herb was trying to make that place feel like and he did," he recalled. "Back then, we all played softball together and we all had Super Bowl parties. He did those things like softball games to keep the guys in shape and to also have fun at their jobs. The camaraderie meant so much."

I saw that camaraderie when my grandfather died in 1997 and nearly the entire force from both Pulaski and Wythe County showed up at the funeral in Galax. Five years earlier, when my grandmother passed away, both Dad and Doug worked for Wythe County. Granny and I were very close and since, at seven years old, that was my first experience with loss, my mother thought it was too much for me to attend the funeral. Doug told me that, during her procession, there was a Wythe County deputy at every intersection. I know that would have touched her. It did me, having heard it for the first time, nearly 25 years later.

"I guess I never witnessed her worrying about me because I wasn't there to see. She was a worrier; she imagined the worst about everything," Doug said of his mother. "So you know it drove her crazy but she never expressed it,"

I know Teny got her a scanner and she had that thing tuned to Wythe County.

"Let's see if we can hear your daddy or Doug," Granny would tell me, getting very excited if they happened to come on.

"You know I never thought about that," Doug said before taking a pause. "All those nights I was working that she was in a chair listening. I guarantee she was."

The most difficult thing for Doug to recall about his parents was seeing his father weep as he dropped him off for boot camp.

"He took me to Beckley, WV to drop me off the day I joined the military where you did your intake processing," he remembered. "From there, you took a plane to Atlanta and from there to Alabama, but I remember getting out of that car and seeing that big lip quiver and that about tore me all to pieces. It didn't dawn on me because, you see, it was peace time. Dad was in WWII and I can only think about what was in his mind sending his son off into the army."

"Sending your boy off into the military, the visions of the military he had, you can only imagine. I had never heard him talk about it until my father in law at the time, a veteran in the Korean War, and my Dad were standing out there in his garage and they got to talking. It was first time in my life I ever heard him talk about it."

He credited his fellow officers with also being his good friends.

"Those guys were there from the beginning. Keith, Mike Edmonds and all those guys were just like brothers. We used to go canoeing together," he said. "Herb and I used to take the guys on days off and just go fishing and canoeing on New River. Talk about some good times. Mike Edmonds wasn't in the water 3 seconds until he had flipped that canoe."

Dad, however, had more skill.

"Herb was good with the canoe," Doug said. "He and Bill Collins used to canoe a lot."

"It was a unique experience to be able to work with your brother and your mentor at the same time," Doug said in closing. "He was always the boss and he still is!"

At Dad's retirement party, June 28, 2011, seated are my mom Rhonda and me. From left to right, my sister Tara, Doug, his wife Melba, Mike's wife Joy, Mike, Dad and my wife Emily.

\* \* \* \* \* \* \* \* \*

Retired Sheriff Kermit Osborne was already with the Wythe County Sheriff's Office when Dad took second in command of the force on January 1, 1980. Kermit came on the force five years earlier, joining the Wythe County Sheriff's Department in January of 1975 under the administration of the late Sheriff Buford Shockley.

"We were getting used to new administration coming in and, of course, we became friends and I think we're still friends," Kermit said of Dad.

Before becoming a police officer, Kermit was already well-known for his name, which he happened to share with a famous Muppet.

"Whenever I went to a school or anywhere and I was walking down the hall, I would always hear someone say, 'ribbit, ribbit,'" the Grayson County native recalled. "It didn't bother me at all. My name is Kermit so they just related it to Kermit the Frog. I just carried on with it."

That's how I remember Kermit. He would be walking down the hall of the Wythe County Sheriff's Office, poke his head into Dad's office and smile at me.

"Ribbit," he always said before going on his way.

"He was fair and he was like that to everyone," Kermit said of Dad as a supervisor. "He was a person you could talk to."

Kermit made mention that along with the new administration there were a lot of new programs, which involved many different things that hadn't been started there before.

"It really changed things for the better," he said.

"His mentoring and friendship helped me a lot," Kermit said of Dad's influence on him as an officer. Kermit served as sheriff of Wythe County for seven years until his retirement in 2005. To me, he was a wonderful sheriff because he was always very humble and didn't seem like the type that would want to be sheriff.

"It was never a dream of mine to be sheriff," Kermit told me. "I just wanted to be around and help people."

After being appointed sheriff in 1998, he was elected by a three to one margin, the biggest victory for the office in the history of Wythe County. Ironically, it was a win against Wayne Pike, who had recommended Kermit to the circuit court judge as his replacement. Pike vacated the position to accept a job on the state parole board. After his loss, Pike accepted an appointment by President George W. Bush as a U.S. Marshal, the position from which he retired.

"During my administration I had to shut the jail down and we moved into a new office building," Kermit recalled. "Before I was sheriff, I spent a lot of time transporting prisoners back and forth and things like that."

Kermit said he had nothing to do with the decision to close down the Wythe County Jail in 1999.

"The county did that," he clarified. "It was just a matter of doing the actual closing down of the jail and transferring the prisoners to the facility in Dublin and all the paperwork that's involved in that.

As a low key guy, handling the strenuous work of being sheriff might have been extremely taxing to someone like Kermit. As far as how he survived, Kermit gives all the credit to his personnel.

"I had a lot of help," he told me. "I had some good help!"

As far as his memories of Dad, Kermit most vividly recalls his inability to keep up with things, especially his keys.

"He had a thing with keys," he recalled One day, there in the office, he left and was going to a meeting and he went out and after a few minutes, he came back."

"Would you let me in my office?" he asked Kermit.

"Sure," he agreed.

"I opened the door to let him get in his office and he got his keys and stuff off his desk," Kermit told me. "He'd forgotten his keys. So, I just picked on him over things like that."

He still could because he still has those issues.

"Another incident I remember was when we were sitting in the office and had a call that one of the officers was stopping a vehicle that had an armed fugitive in it," Kermit added. "So, we jumped in the car to take off to back him up. So Herb got in the car with me. I was driving and he was in the car with me. So, we got out there to the scene where the stop was at and there were shots going off. Well, he was so scared at that time, but funny later. So, as I pulled up, stopped the vehicle and was trying to unbuckle my seatbelt so I could reach for my gun. Well, Herb, was trying to take my gun away from me. As usual, he'd left his gun in the office. He forgot to bring it."

Although no shooting took place, Kermit was adamant that, if there was going to be any gunfire, he was going to shoot with his own gun.

"I remember another time when he was gone on a trip somewhere," Kermit went on. "I don't remember where it was. We got a call that came through the office saying I needed to talk to someone in Roanoke. They called me at home. So, I was trying to find out what was going on and who I was talking to. Come to find out, it was somebody from Good Will. His badge and ID had shown up the Good Will in Roanoke."

"I think Rhonda had given some clothes and stuff to the Good Will," he explained. "On a serious note, you would say he's been a good friend and an influence on you as a good administrator and I look forward to seeing him when he gets back here. I don't know if I can go that far south to see him. I can't travel that much anymore."

## Chapter 13
## Hail to the Chief

On July 1, 1994, it was reported by the *Southwest Times* newspaper in Pulaski, Virginia that Dad was one of two candidates being considered for chief of police by the Pulaski Town Council. As chief deputy in Wythe County, Dad was indicated as having an edge over fellow front runner, Pulaski County Chief Deputy Jim Davis. Reporters were already predicting his appointment in an announcement to be made by the town council the following Tuesday, July 5th.

Despite having filled many other constitutional offices with hometown people at that time, Dad had Pulaski setting their sights elsewhere. At 51, some said his age was a factor. Council quickly revised their statement, saying it was his experience rather than age that gave him the lead in the running for the job. Pulaski was impressed with his education, which included a master's degree from Virginia Commonwealth University and a bachelor's degree from Guilford College in Greensboro, North Carolina.

It also didn't hurt that Dad had worked every facet of police work known to man during his nearly thirty year tenure as an officer, working his way through the ranks at High Point Police Department and the Wythe County Sheriff's Office. After nearly fifteen years as chief deputy in Wythe County, he had achieved the rank of Colonel after experience in every facet of police work from patrol to narcotics investigator. Dad told reporters that morning that, if offered the job, he would accept and most likely be moving to the area, much to my personal chagrin.

"I feel I would need to be a part of the community if I am offered the job and accept," he said.

The article mentioned that Dad was married and had two children and also noted his unsuccessful bid for Wythe County Clerk of Circuit Court as the Republican nomination, saying he was soundly defeated. I'm sure this fueled his reasoning for leaving Wythe County. Mom kept her job in Wytheville as a social worker, however, and we stayed in school there despite her having to reenroll me after the principal removed me from the roster assuming I had already moved.

Over the first half of 1994, the Pulaski Police Department had been rocked by a series of resignations of veteran policemen, many of whom were unhappy with pay and benefits. In some cases, benefits offered by other departments were more enticing than pay increases. As many as five patrol positions have been vacant at one time. This was capped by the resignation of Police Chief E.J. Williams effective May 1. Williams took early retirement through disability because of a leg injury. Williams became chief upon Dan McKeever's appointment to fill the town manager's position in December 1983, and previously served three times as acting chief.

Dad was named as Pulaski's Chief of Police effective July 18th with a base salary of $40,000. On the morning of Tuesday, July 5th, the town council officially held a meeting in which council officially appointed him to fill the position vacated when Chief E.J. Williams. Dad told reporters in an interview after the meeting that he didn't intend to be an "outsider" for long. At the time, he lived Wythe County but planned to move into the area as soon as possible. My sister and I were three and nine years old. Concerning, the Pulaski Police Department, Dad told reporters that he planned to go in and evaluate the organization of the department and see if there are any problems and what may need to be done.

"It might be a little wide, he noted, having already looked at the organization chart for the department. "Then again, it might be perfect for the department. I'll need to take a closer look before making any changes."

It was only the previous April that the council approved a reorganization of the police department. "I have no political ambitions," Dad stated further. "I'm here to be police chief. Democrat, Republican, makes no difference. I'm politically neutral."

Dad mentioned that he also hoped to work well with the Pulaski County Sheriff's Department.

"I think we can do a lot of things together," he noted optimistically. "Crime doesn't stop at the county line."

Dad's main competition for the position of chief was Pulaski County Sheriff's Department Chief Deputy Jim Davis. Davis, with 20 years, in law enforcement, held a bachelors degree from Bluefield College. He also worked his way up through the ranks, from patrol through narcotics investigations, and worked five years for the Commonwealth of Virginia. Davis was named chief deputy to Sheriff Ralph Dobbins upon the retirement of Max Campbell. Prior to that, Davis was in charge of the criminal investigation division for Pulaski County.

After nearly 30 years of answering to someone else, Dad would finally get to be the top cop.

As the new Pulaski Police Chief, Dad was not rash and wanted to look at his department a little longer before making any decisions on its organization. "At this point, there are no sweeping changes planned," Dad told *The Southwest Times.*

However, Dad still felt the department may be a little "top heavy." He intended to take a close look at the situation. "You've got to consider the man on the street, and I'm not sure we have enough patrolling put there at times," said Dad on the morning of July 19, 1994, as he begins his second day on the job.

**Pulaski Police Chief Takes Office**

Pulaski Police Chief Herb Cooley (center) was sworn in by Mayor Andrew Graham (far right) this morning in the council chambers of the Town Municipal Building with members of council, and Commonwealth Attorney Everett Shockley and Sheriff Ralph Dobbins in attendance. Also at the ceremony were Cooley's wife, Rhonda, and two children, Zach and Tara. Cooley replaces E.J. Williams, who retired earlier this year. Today is Cooley's first full day on the job. He was to meet with his entire department later today.

He described Monday the 18th as "a get-acquainted day," spending the afternoon meeting with department members, and telling them what he expects.

"Over the long-haul, I have three goals. First, I want to make Pulaski the safest and most crime free environment we can.   Second, I want the best trained and motivated force. Third, I want the department to provide the incentives and conditions and benefits that will attract and keep the kind of personnel we want working here," said Dad.

In the short term, he wanted to see what the department has and what is needed. He discussed the care of equipment with the officers.

"I told them if I fight for them to get good cars, and other equipment, I expect them to take care of them," Dad ordered.

At Monday's meeting, Dad was pleased with the look of the department with all officers in uniform and "looking sharp." He also expected the officers to maintain a sharp and neat appearance on duty.  On the job, Dad wanted to spend the first few days getting to know the town.

"Then, I'll get on with the task of deciding what, if any, changes should be made."

On July 19, Greg Rooker, publisher of the *Southwest Virginia Enterprise*, wrote a wonderful editorial to the Pulaski newspaper, *The Southwest Times*, explaining Dad's remarkable contributions.  In describing why Wythe County would miss Dad, he expressed why the Town of Pulaski would be lucky to have him leading their police force.

"The Town of Pulaski recently made an excellent decision in selecting Herb Cooley to head up Pulaski's Police Department," Rooker wrote.  "Cooley is a seasoned law officer with experience across the board and a reputation as an excellent administrator. Working with Wythe County Sheriff Wayne Pike, Cooley was directly responsible for much of the improvement which the Pike administration has brought. To say that the Wythe County Sheriff's Department has made quantum leaps forward in the last 15 years is an understatement. The department has undergone extensive modernization, most especially in computerization, communications and professional training for personnel. But Cooley's highest achievements may not have been in the professional arena. His involvement in the civic affairs of Wytheville and the county is what we will most miss. For the past six years, Cooley has been a mainstay of the Wytheville-Wythe-Bland Chamber of Commerce where he has served as president, vice-president, treasurer and as a member of the board. Community events would always find Cooley present if not shoulder deep in the work at hand. His involvement in community affairs have certainly taken a great deal of the little free time his position allowed. Cooley also served in the Rural Retreat Lake Authority, the Local Emergency Planning Committee, American Cancer Society Board of Directors and the Transportation Safety Commission of which he has been chairman since 1983. Cooley furthered his education, getting his master's degree in criminal justice and risk management from VCU and graduated from the FBT National Academy. But he wasn't satisfied with just getting more education; he wanted more educational opportunity for others. Through his work with the chamber, Cooley was instrumental in bringing Averett College's B .A. and M.B. A. programs to Wythe County. And finally, Cooley worked well with us at the *Southwest Virginia Enterprise*, Wythe County's community newspaper. He has always been open, fair and sympathetic to our needs and special problems. We will miss him greatly. As one of the deputies at the sheriff's office said, 'our loss is Pulaski's gain.' Nothing could be truer. His friends and neighbors in Wythe County will be wishing Cooley well and watching for substantial accomplishments within his new job and community. In all that he has done during his years, in Wythe County, he has been the epitome of a public servant. If the past is any indication of the future, Herb Cooley will serve Pulaski well."

That same day, the Pulaski Police Department was honored for its outstanding efforts in enforcing the state safety belt and child safety seat laws and promoting correct safety belt and child safety seat use. The International Association of Chiefs' of Police (IACP) announced Tuesday, July 19, 1994, the winners of the "1993 Chiefs' Challenge," a nationwide competition among law enforcement agencies to promote safety belt use and enforcement of state belt and child safety seat laws. Among these winners, the Town of Pulaski Police Department came in third place and was scheduled to be recognized at the LACP's Annual Conference in October 1994 in Albuquerque, N.M. The "Chiefs Challenge" program was developed by the Department of Transportation's (DOT) and the National Highway Traffic Safety Administration (NHTSA) as part of a major campaign by all levels of government, law enforcement agencies, and safety groups to achieve a higher safety belt use nationally. The national safety belt use that year rose to 62 percent, up from 11 percent in the early 1980's. Safety belt use laws have reduced traffic fatalities by seven percent per year. From 1984 to 1994, more than 30,000 deaths and 770,000 moderate-to-critical injuries have been prevented by safety belt use. These remarkable statistics demonstrate the importance of safety belt awareness and enforcement promoted by the "Chiefs' Challenge" program.

As the newly appointed chief, Dad commended his entire department for their efforts in promoting safety restraint usage and attributed much of the success of the "Chiefs' Challenge" program to retired Chief E.J. Williams, under whose administration this award was won. Also, Dad noted that the department has placed first, statewide, for the past three consecutive years. He further stressed that, under his leadership, the department will strive to ensure the safety of all citizens by continuing their efforts in promoting the use of safety restraints.

\* \* \* \* \* \* \* \*

Federal agents working with the Virginia State Polite and Pulaski Police Department have broken up an illegal firearms distribution ring which involved at least one Pulaski man, and a gun dealer from Blacksburg. Federal, state and local agents moved in early that same morning on James Roy Mullins of 1948 Memorial Drive and charged him with the possession and sale of unregistered silencers and a short barreled rifle. He was also charged for facilitating the unlawful purchase of a firearm. Patrick D. Hynes, Special Agent in Charge of Bureau of Alcohol, Tobacco and Firearms along with Virginia State Police Superintendent Colonel M. Wayne Huggins and my father announced in a press release the arrest of Mullins and the arrest of Paul David Peterson for violation of the National Firearms Act and of the Federal Firearms Laws. Peterson, a federally licensed firearms dealer, doing business as Peterson Sporting Goods from his residence at 1975 Mount Tabor Road in Blacksburg was charged with the sale of a firearm to a convicted felon and falsifying state and federal firearms transaction records.

The investigation was conducted by a firearms task force which consists of special agents from ATF, the state police and the Pulaski Police Department. The ATF, the firearms investigation unit of the Virginia State Police and the Pulaski Police Department began investigating the activities of Mullins and Peterson earlier this year. Agents allegedly learned that Mullins and Peterson were actively soliciting membership in an organization which has the goal of circumventing the state and federal firearms laws by disguising and falsifying the identity of the firearms purchasers. Agents in dark outfits scattered throughout the Memorial Drive area were spotted by some local citizens on their way to work. The U.S. Attorney's office in Roanoke planned a news conference for later that day in Roanoke.

"He did a lot of good work and was a big part of the operation," Dad commended Investigator Sheldon Ainsworth for his part in the undercover operation.

The investigation was initiated through a tip from a state trooper working another county. That tip was passed along to local and federal authorities, and a task force was formed of federal, state and local law enforcement officers. Mullins had been under investigation since March. Peterson had been investigated since May. If convicted, the penalties faced by the defendants were 10 years and a $250,000 fine for each count of possession and transfer or sale of unregistered silencers and short barreled rifles; 10 years and a $250,000 fine for selling or facilitating the sale of a firearm to a convicted felon and five years and a $250,000 fine for each count of falsifying records. Assistant U.S. Attorney Donald R. Wolthuis prosecuted the case.

There was a lot of talk that this case was politically motivated. Dad quickly dismissed this to the press.

"It caused me concern knowing some talked about killing a police officer. That's a subversive type of action. Guerrilla warfare is more than someone worrying about gun rights," Dad told reporters. "When someone talks about luring a Pulaski police officer out just to shoot him, I'm not concerned about politics."

Federal agents maintain that Mullins and Peterson hoped to avoid firearms laws by disguising the identity of gun buyers and to stockpile weapons. Court documents report as many as 15 people attended the three meetings held by the Blue Ridge Hunt Club. Mullins made his initial appearance in court Thursday, July 28 in Roanoke and Magistrate Glen Conrad ordered him held without bond. A pretrial hearing was set for August 9. Peterson also remained in jail as of reports conducted July 29.

* * * * * * * *

By August 15, 1994, Dad was busy reorganizing his department effective immediately with the anticipated approval of town council. That morning, he outlined his plan to the personnel committee. He proposed three division commanders to replace the positions at the time of a captain and two lieutenants. The captain's rank was held by Barry Buckner. The two lieutenants were Eddie Hogston and Ernie Taylor. All three were now to be division commanders. According to Dad, Buckner would be over administrative and support services. Hogston would direct investigations with Taylor leading the patrol division. No salary changes are involved. Cooley said it isn't a demotion for Buckner, who was named captain only a couple of months ago. "I see it as an administrative move that allows for more efficient operations and better communications."

Dad also preferred to call his plan "fine tuning" rather than an out-right re-organization.

"Some areas are over-supervised and some are under supervised. There is also a lack of flexibility to allow for lateral movement within the department. I'm not criticizing what was put in place, but communication is a key here, and the current structure hampers communication," Dad said. "The present patrol lieutenant will tell you is he is not an investigator, yet he's technically over investigations. This leaves much of the investigation leadership up to the sergeant of investigations."

"The sergeant is busy with narcotics investigations and working with the drug task force, with no time to properly supervise, leaving this as one of the under supervised areas of the department," he explained. "The captain is overseeing all areas, with no time to specialize in investigations. This leaves the detective with no immediate supervision or expert help. Patrol is classified by my father as an over-supervised area for the Pulaski Police Department at the time. The chain of command for patrol is chief, captain, lieutenant, sergeant, corporal, officer, which Dad described to members of the town council as "very cumbersome and demoralizing for the patrol officer as well as a total waste of manpower."

Instead, for patrol, the recommended rank order was chief, division commander, sergeant, and officer.

"This will cut unnecessary links from the chain of command and provide much better communication from top to bottom and vice versa," Dad explained.

Plans called for doing away with the positions of detective and corporal. However those currently classified as corporal would remain so until the position is vacated for any reason. The corporal position, once all are vacated, would revert to a rank of police officer first class. The detective rank would be eliminated. Investigator positions will be filled, as necessary, by either a police officer or a police officer first class. This offered the lateral movement Dad sought for his department.

"If investigators don't clear cases, then it gives more ability to send them back out on the road. This plan also allows for closer supervision," Dad told committee members on the morning of August 15th. Council was scheduled to offer its final approval of the re-organization plan at the council meeting the following day. Approval was unanimous.

One of Dad's first actions as Chief of Police was to ban smoking entirely in the municipal building area occupied by the police department, both in public and in police cruisers.

"You can ban smoking entirely for police and firemen. We haven't gotten to that point yet. Still, stress related illnesses are grounds for a disability claim for a fireman or police officer, so I've opted to ban smoking while our officers are on duty," Dad explained to members of the town council. "A police officer might smoke four packs of cigarettes a day. He develops heart trouble and it is automatically assumed to be work related."

Council considered an ordinance that would have banned smoking in all public areas as outlined by state law, not just town owned buildings. It would have also included a civil fine of $25. However, council didn't want to go that far. Instead, by resolution, council is expected to ban smoking in its own buildings at its meeting that night on August 16th at 7 p.m.

By October, the Pulaski Police Department filled 10 positions, with 40 percent of the available jobs filled with females. First, after his appointment as chief earlier summer, my Dad set about restructuring the department. Then he began the task of filling vacancies created by resignations over the past year and now has the department up to full force. Some of the vacancies were filled from within. Others were filled with veteran officers while others are new recruits. Dad noted previously that he felt a need to hire some officers with previous experience, who are certified, and who would be of benefit to the town immediately.

One of those vacancies was by the late Sandra Wilhoit as my Dad's administrative assistant. Originally from Austinville and a long time family friend, Sandy was playfully called "Mrs. Wiggins" by my dad after the *Carol Burnett Show* character. I remember her always bringing me different kinds of cheese from her vacations in the Amish country. Her mother, Annie Reynolds, is also a dear friend. Sadly, Sandy battled multiple sclerosis for years and died much too soon in 2011 at the age of 56. We miss her to this day.

Pulaski police officers displayed their new look Wednesday morning, October 20, 1994, as they passed their first public inspection conducted by Police Chief Herb Cooley. My dad assumed the duties of police chief in July of that year. With their new Stratton ranger-style hats atop their heads and Beretta 40 cal. semiautomatics at their sides, complementing their traditional policeman blue uniform, the officers stepped lively for inspection.

Police Chief Herb Cooley inspects Sgt. Wes Davis'
handgun during a department inspection.

An honor guard was provided by the Veterans of
Foreign Wars. The colors were presented as "The Star
Spangled Banner" was played on the trumpet by Chris
Stevens, a Pulaski County High School student. The hats
were a new addition since Dad's appointment. The semiautomatics were approved last year. Dad also changed the
paint design of the Pulaski Police Department cruisers,
opting for a two-tone style, with the front and rear fender
areas painted in blue, with white dominating the rest of the
car. He walked down each row of officers inspecting their
uniforms and weapons before dismissing them for a safety
speech presented by former Washington Redskins center
Jeff Bostic. Bostic reminded the officers they are role
models.

"I was always the type of guy who put his kids in safety belts and child restraint seats, but then I didn't buckle up," Bostic said. "On Oct. 21, 1984, I hurt my knee and had to have major reconstructive surgery. It taught me a lesson, and 1 never went back out on the football field without knee braces. I learned a similar lesson after attending a seminar sponsored by the Virginia Division of Motor Vehicles .on seat belts. We were shown the results of accidents where people didn't wear their safety belt. I was also impressed by the state trooper who told me that in 21 years he had only had to cut out one person from a car who was wearing a seat belt," said Bostic.

He also told of his neighbor whose son died from a car accident in which the car he was riding crashed while going 70 in a 25 mile zone. He was not wearing a seat belt. "It's tough to see a 17-year-old lying in a casket and think what might have been," Bostic stated soberly. "It's important to teach the children at a young age the importance of seat belt safety. We're a society that likes to copy success. That's why it is important for you as role models to set the example," Bostic encouraged the crowd of about 50, mostly police officers and town and county officials. Bostic's trip was sponsored by the Virginia DMV. He travels throughout Virginia speaking to various groups about seat belt safety.

Dad had met Bostic when he was still Chief Deputy in Wythe County. I never followed sports much, but remember being a big Redskins fan in 1992 when they won the Super Bowl, because my Dad was. Bostic signed a poster for me that said "Best wishes to a champion," which hung in my bedroom for years.

* * * * * * * *

In November 1994, Dad requested and was granted an upgrade of the parking enforcement officer to a grade equal to dispatcher. Dad planned to cross-train these positions to provide better coverage and enforcement. Since the parking enforcement officer would be required to be a certified dispatcher and regularly handle dispatch duties, he believed a position upgrade is necessary. The town's classification plan included one parking enforcement officer, three dispatchers and one part-time dispatcher. The pay range for the parking enforcement officer was $11,775 to $17,100. The pay range for a dispatcher was $13,005 to $18,903. The reclassification was also approved.

December 6, 1994 was likely the saddest day in my Dad's career when authorities say a Wythe County deputy sheriff was shot in the back of the head with his own weapon, execution style, as he lay wounded after trying to arrest a 15-year-old on a juvenile warrant. The Barren Springs resident was a 13-year veteran of the Wythe County Sheriff's Department.

The boy whom Deputy Cliff Dicker, 57, was trying to arrest Tuesday has been charged with capital murder and two firearms charges. The teenager was arrested a short time after the shooting by Wytheville police, who were called to the scene by a neighbor. Authorities declined to identify the youth because of his age, but he has been identified by others as Christopher Shawn Wheeler.

Sheriff Wayne Pike said Dicker was shot in the face with a .22-caliber rifle and, while he lay wounded, he was shot "execution style" with his own 9 mm weapon. Thomas B. Baird, Wythe County Commonwealth's Attorney, said he will seek to have the youth tried as an adult. If convicted of capital murder as an adult, he would face either life in prison or the death penalty. If convicted as a juvenile, he could not be held past his 21st birthday. The youth was transferred from the Wythe County Jail to a juvenile detention center in Christiansburg by Pulaski County deputies at the request of the Wythe County Sheriff's Department. The state police, who are investigating the shooting at the request of local authorities, said Dicker arrived between 9:15 and 9:30 a.m. at the house where the youth lived with his grandmother. He was attempting to serve the boy with a detention order, the equivalent of an arrest warrant for a juvenile. State police special agent Carroll Delp said Wytheville police had accused the youth of auto larceny and petty larceny.

"He lost his momma when he was 3. His daddy has been dead three, four months. His uncle was killed a year ago," Teresa Davidson, an aunt, told a Richmond newspaper. The boy was cleaning squirrels at the grandmother's house and apparently had been squirrel hunting earlier in the morning. He normally attended classes in an off-campus program for students with special problems, taught at the Wytheville Recreation Center, authorities said. Dicker, wearing a protective vest, was found a few steps inside the grandmother's house according to my uncle, Lt. Col. Doug Cooley, who replaced his brother as chief deputy of the Wythe County Sheriff's Office. He was pronounced dead at the scene.

Dad, who recently left as chief deputy in Wythe County to take the Pulaski chief job, described Dicker as kind, a good officer and a friend who was liked by everyone. He immediately went to Wythe County Tuesday after learning of the shooting to be with and console his fellow officers. Chief Cooley noted that Dicker had a lot of ties to Pulaski County and that he enjoyed activities on Claytor Lake such as boating and camping. Funeral arrangements for Dicker are pending at Bower Funeral Home in Pulaski. Dicker, who had a heart attack 18 months ago, recently was moved to the civil division, where he provided court security and delivered court papers, such as the detention order. Doug told the press that the youth charged in the shooting had had 'a string of run-ins with police, and had been served with 12 other detention orders prior to the shooting. Dicker retired from the Air Force after 20 years and had worked for the Sheriff's Department for 13 years.

## Chapter 14
## Tackling Another "Little Chicago"

After Cliff Dicker's murder, members of Pulaski Town Council wanted to be sure everything is being done that can be done to keep its police officers safe.

"We've had a death to the north of us and we've had a death to the south of us, and we've had an attack on one of our police officers," Councilman Roy D'Ardenne noted on December 21, 1994. "I'd like for the town manager and police chief to examine our policies and equipment to be sure we have what our officers need."

Dad said in an interview that same morning that a key to safety is "good policy and training to the policy." My father, on the job since July, had already emphasized the need for training within the department and now had eight certified instructors on his staff to do in-house training. After the first of the year, Dad planned to review all town police policies, revise and change those that need changing, and then train to them.

"Still, you can do everything right and someone still gets hurt once in a while. Before the knifing incident involving Officer John Goad, we hadn't had a serious injury in many years. It's rare," Dad told reporters. "Still, when you've had two officers killed in jurisdictions surrounding you, and then we have one severely hurt, you have to stop and think."

Concern was voiced about the fact that the pepper spray Goad used in this specific incident had no effect on Goad's attacker. Dad noted there are cases in which the spray does not work. A few people, he said, are not affected by the spray and sometimes, if a person is under the influence of drugs, it will not affect them. Dad was relatively satisfied with the personal protection his officers had for such cases.

The officers have protective vests and last year went to the semiautomatic style hand gun. Still, Dad noted, injuries can occur. Goad was cut on the arm and Wythe County Deputy Cliff Dicker, who was recently killed in the line of duty, was wearing his protective vest. But he was shot in the head. Some of the police vehicles aren't as well equipped as they need to be.

"Nowadays you have to have them stocked like a hospital with gowns and masks for infectious disease situations. Also, being close to the interstate, we have to think about potential hazardous materials. These are the more probable dangers we face, but hazardous material and hepatitis don't make the headlines like a shooting or knifing attack on an officer," Dad commented.

The Fraternal Order of Police in Pulaski, known as FOP, was probably thinking along the lines of F-L-O-P in their year-end fundraising drive for 1994. Several people were upset by the tactics used to raise money. You could list my father among the irate.

"These people, when they called asking for money, represented themselves as the Pulaski Police Department when they called in town, the sheriff's department when they called in the county and Dublin P.D. when they called there and that's not true," stated Dad. "We had a few complaints when the drive started and I thought we had taken care of that problem. Then, I guess earlier this week, they decided to make one more push for money and that's when the complaints started."

However, Dad wanted it understood the group did not represent the Pulaski Police Department. It did represent the FOP, which is an organization made up of area police officers, but no local officers were involved. Dad thought it to be even worse that only 25 percent of the money raised will stay here.

"If you're going to have a drive, use local people, get volunteers and let the community get to know the members of the FOP. Don't call in outsiders," he advised.

Pulaski policeman Terry Smith is president of the FOP and explained that there hadn't been a fund-drive by the local FOP for a couple of years. JAK Productions Inc. out of Atlanta, GA, handled a previous drive and there were no problems. For the last few previous years, the company had contacted the group asking about a drive and the idea was rejected. In 1994, the FOP decided to give JAK another try. Smith explained that he had talked with the project manager earlier when there were complaints and thought the matter was resolved. Then, on Wednesday, December 28, 1994, the complaints started rolling in, and Smith pulled the plug on the operation Thursday morning. Dad suggested the FOP issue an apology. Even though it wasn't local members of the FOP, it was a group brought in by the FOP.

"I just hope they haven't damaged the FOP or the area police departments permanently. Many people out there are going to think that it was us calling, and it wasn't," he told the press.

Dad also thought it was awful that the FOP would only be allowed to keep 25 percent of the money. Another 25 percent went to JAK and 50 percent is used to pay for expenses and salaries of those calling.

"It's not good business to let 75 percent of the money leave the area," Dad added. "I hope future fundraising ventures are handled in a different manner."

Pulaski Town Council received an encouraging report on the state of the Police Department my dad, Chief Herb Cooley on the evening of January 17, 1995, but he warned that there is a danger of losing well trained officers if salaries and benefits weren't increased.

"The Pulaski Police Department is a group of fine people who are highly trained and we need to keep them. But in four years, the town has lost 14 officers to surrounding jurisdictions because of pay and benefits," he began. "We need to be competitive and money's not always the answer, but it's hard to see a fellow officer in a nearby department doing the same job you are doing for a lot more money. It's more expensive to keep training new recruits."

"Others know Pulaski has quality people. Wytheville Police Department is just waiting for another opening to hire one of my men," Dad added.

At that time, the administrative staff for the Town of Pulaski was working on a new pay classification plan and possible benefits for employees. There were 30 pay classification plans and a study by Radford University students recommended cutting that to 15. Dad said he wasn't reflecting negatively on his predecessor with regard to the turnover and pointed to Pulaski's low crime rate as a credit to former Police Chief E.J. Williams.

"Pulaski has a low crime rate. Most of our crime is domestic in nature meaning driving under the influence cases and domestic violence," Dad noted.

In 1994, there were no murders and none have been committed in the town since 1992. There have been no armed robberies. "Last year, there were 18 burglaries and all but four or five were inner-family situations. This means the guys on the street are doing a good job," he commended as celebrated his six-month anniversary as chief the following day.

Dad pointed out that when he came to Pulaski, officer morale was low and that has gone up, but "the officers are waiting for better things to happen." At the last meeting of council, questions were raised about the training and preparedness of the police force due to a knifing incident in which two officers were injured and since the knifing followed the fatal shooting of a Wythe County Sheriff's Deputy.

My father told council that in the six month's he had been chief of the department, seven officers had been certified as criminal justice instructors and that training sessions were being conducted twice a month. Another 14 officers had been sent to special schools that teach officers how to handle high-risk situations. He also reported that Pulaski, Dublin and Pulaski County had also formed a special response team for special cases such as hostage situations and drug raids. However, Dad told council that the threats out on the street weren't the greatest danger to police officers.

"The number one killer of police officers is suicide," he pointed out. "Police officers are also number one in divorce rates and number one for hypertension cases. A police officer often suffers a death of the spirit. They're often understaffed, underpaid, undertrained, and underappreciated. "It's also hard to go to work every day when you know almost everyone you meet will be in an adversarial manner. No one wants that police car parked in front of their house. No one wants those blue lights to come on behind their car. They're often verbally abused. Then they have to go home and act like everything is normal."

"Pulaski PD is a group of fine officers who are highly trained and who we need to keep," Dad further advised. "There's no substitute for youth. Officer John Goad is back on the job, but Officer E.T. Montgomery still has a cast on his arm due to torn ligaments."

Pulaski was known locally as "Little Chicago" just like High Point due to its excessive crime rate. However, thanks to Dad's brief tenure as the chief of police, that had already turned around. An editorial in the Pulaski newspaper, The Southwest Times, reflected that.

"That was the good news reported recently by officials of the Pulaski Police Department 'during a meeting with Neighborhood Crime Watch coordinators," it read. "Their revelation is good news for us all. Starting way back in the 1950s and continuing into the '80s, Pulaski was known by some .as "Little Chicago," due to the high crime rates, including those for juvenile crime, property damage and violent crimes. All these factors contributed to the perception shared by some living within and outside the town that Pulaski suffered from many of the problems one would see in a city like Chicago, once known for being a hotbed of crime. That has all changed now. Sure, we still have crime in Pulaski. As a matter of fact, overall crime reports are up. However, police officials point to some silver linings within the clouds. While crime reports are up, serious crimes such as murder, robbery and assaults are down. Today, most crimes are cleared and often many of the break-ins reported have a cause associated with a domestic situation. Pulaski Police Chief Herb Cooley noted that property damage in the town is low and violent crimes are down. He reminded the Neighborhood Watch coordinators that there hasn't been an armed robbery here in several-years, and there hasn't been a murder in Pulaski for about two years. Cooley cited several reasons for the change. One is the higher professionalism of the police department in recent years and better response times. Another is tied to the economy. The market isn't here, he said, for a major crime problem as big crimes follow big money. Also, no doubt the growth of Neighborhood Crime Watch groups and the development of a better attitude toward teamwork between these groups and the police have helped as well. Certainly, Pulaski is not crime free. We're like most other towns in that we have our problems. But unlike some communities, we're improving and changing for the better. We can continue to see even more improvement if we'll continue to Work together in the fight against crime."

Staff photo by J.R. Schrader

### Tie One On For Safety

"Tying one on for safety" are, left to right, Dublin Police Chief Russ Gwaltney, Pulaski County Sheriff Ralph Dobbins and Pulaski Police Chief Herb Cooley stressing Buckle Up America Week. Red, white and blue striped ribbons are to remind motorists to buckle up and not drive while drinking.

By April 1995, junk cars within the town of Pulaski are becoming an endangered species. It was expected that by the end of June, the Pulaski Police Department would have had hauled away at least 100 of the inoperable vehicles. Pulaski Mayor Andrew Graham said Tuesday, April 21ª, during a meeting of town council, that he was impressed by Dad's efforts in the area of removing junk cars.

"A lot of people for a long time have complained about this problem of junk cars and now it seems something is being done," said Graham.

Dad said that same morning that his department first writes a letter to the property owner where the car is located. If there is no response, then the department issues a summons and has the vehicle towed away.

Beginning on Monday, May 22ⁿᵈ, those who had already been notified to move their vehicles and hadn't yet done so would be getting a visit from a police officer who will summons them to court. Fines ranged up to $500.

"It's cheaper to go ahead and move the car than to go to court," Dad advised, saying that about 30 letters had been issued and 75 more were ready to go out.

"Those of you with junk cars who haven't gotten a letter will be getting one," he promised.

Pulaski Town Council, in months prior, had asked the police department to enforce a junk car ordinance. The town is also still seeking people to mow lawns which are in violation of the town code. The town will pay mowers.

In addressing the town council in May, Dad proposed raising parking fines from $3 to $7 for over-time parking. It was noted that a parking study done by the Planning District Commission has determined there is enough parking downtown, but parking regulations need to be strictly enforced. To do this, Dad felt he needed two people working the streets instead of one. The extra person would give the staffing to write parking tickets-six-days a week. It was estimated that this would generate $42,000 in revenue, up from $4,000 in 1994-95. Dad explained that before 1995, the most parking tickets written in a year totaled 253. In February of 1995, 225 were written by one part-time person. Although he would not give any officer a quota for any type of ticket, Dad said the numbers break down to each of the two parking enforcement officers writing about 15 tickets a day, which he thought was reasonable.

The U.S. Marines were also helping to improve the quality of police training in the Town of Pulaski. Earlier in May, work was started on completely rebuilding the Pulaski Police Department's firing range located behind the National Guard Armory on Draper's Mountain. It was be an ongoing project through August, the target date for finishing the work. Dad noted the facelift for the firing range has actually been a town-wide project involving people from many departments, but has cost the town very little due to volunteers. John Hawley's Engineering Department developed the plans. Then Tom Compton and Barney Kemp used their own heavy equipment to haul in several truck loads of top soil.

The Marines arrived on a weekend, and in two days, they took up the old paving and built a strip of grass alongside the road. Then they put in the top soil that had been brought to the site by Compton and Kemp. Marine officers E.Z. Whitehead and Mark Elliot were in charge of that portion of the project and Sgt. Charles Epperly of the National Guard has also provided excellent cooperation, according to Dad. Members from the Recreation Department helped in re-seeding the site.

"It is a win-win-win situation. The community gets advantages from it, we get advantages from it, and I think that those who provide the service do as well," said Dr. Byrne from the Office of Emergency Medical Services. "We have field laboratories and in those situations you're using solvents and can run into hazardous situations. So, it is convenient to have a cadre of trained EMS people on campus should there be an emergency."

The only cost to the town had been in fuel to operate the vehicles.

Dad said the new firing range will allow for more realistic training of police officers.

"In the past, officers have basically gone up to the range once or twice a year, stood and shot at the target, totaled their score and that was it," he told the press. "Now, there will be more movement. Officers will have to drop and roll in the grass as they might need to do in a real life situation. They'll have to change their ammunition while on the move. They'll practice jumping out of an ear and taking cover. A gun is a deadly weapon and officers have to develop good habits in using that weapon, because when they pull that gun on someone for real, it will be a stressful situation. If we put more stress on the officers during training, it will make them better able to handle the situation in real life."

Later plans called for building a house out of tires to practice entering buildings. There's also the possibility of a 500 meter rifle range being built by the National Guard that will assist police tactical teams. "If it all comes about as planned," Dad offered. "It will be an excellent training facility."

The Department of Criminal Justice Services awarded three grants totaling $114,686 to the Pulaski Police Department in late June 1995. The state grant money would pay for two undercover narcotics officers and two secretaries. Dad explained that approximately 30 departments were denied these grants, while Pulaski was approved for three.

"We believe that this speaks well for our department's ability to obtain grant funding," Town Manager Tom Combiths noted.

While the town's match is estimated at $38,228, it's estimated that the general fund of the town will only have to absorb $9,750. Dad added that the undercover cops would not be permanent positions and that the two secretaries would be hired on a one-year contract basis. The drug enforcement grant was for $84,000. While the first grant was for drug enforcement, the second is for crime analysis and would require one person for data entry. A part-time salary would be reduced with a net impact of $1,234 to the budget. This grant was valued at $33,073. The third grant was for crime control planning.

This money would be used to enhance and develop procedures to prevent, reduce or control community crime and delinquency problems. A secretary would also be hired for the Drug Task Force and totaled $35,841. Cooley has also proposed that a new parking enforcement position be deleted to help in paying the match. Also, Cooley proposes to cross-train the two secretaries in parking enforcement to maintain the same level of enforcement as was proposed under the new position. The information was presented to council on June 15, 1995 and they seemed receptive to the grant proposal.

* * * * * * * *

"The Pulaski Governmental Employees outslugged. New River Media, featuring WPSK, 21-11 Sunday at Calfee Park in the Steve Quesenberry Memorial Scholarship Fund Classic. Pulaski County Sheriff Ralph Dobbins led the government team with a home run and two triples. Investigator Mike Hudson added a home run and triple while Commonwealth Attorney Everett Shockley batted 3-4 and scored three runs and Todd Litton slugged a long home run. State Delegate Tommy Baker, Town Engineer John Hawley, Liz Moore and Mickey Smith had two hits apiece for the winners which jumped on top with a nine run second. WPSK's Steve Holstein and Gary Muench batted 3-3 and scored two runs apiece for the Media Bunch. Jerry White, Chairman of the Board of Supervisors, was the winning pitcher with relief help from Micky Hickman. Marty Gordon batted 2-2 with a walk but took the loss for the Media and Southwest Times Sports Editor Kim Nelson batted 2-2 helping along a five-run sixth. As for the media squad, Tom Williams gets the Pete Rose "Charlie Hustle" Award, while Mary Kelly gets the Lenny Dykstra award for plowing over Chief Herb Cooley at the plate. The team spirit award goes to both teams and it is hoped that another game can he staged later this summer," read the sports page on June 27, 1995.

Dad took a pretty hard hit, both in a literal and figurative sense, from that June 25th charity game.  I remember his office blowing up the picture of his blunder, which was featured in the local newspaper and writing a mock story underneath it regarding a "hickey on the thigh." They presented it to him as a gag.

Staff photo by Aloma O'Dell

**WPSK's Mary Kelly scores as she plows into Pulaski Police Chief Herb Cooley causing him to drop the softball**

On Tuesday, August 8, 1995, the Pulaski Town Council's Ordinance Committee met concerning matters of animal control. The town adheres to the county's Dog Control Ordinance which requires that dogs be under the general control of the owner. There were, however, a significant number of complaints to the Pulaski Police

Department concerning barking dogs and dogs running at large.

"The police department is not equipped to handle animal control matters. This is a highly specialized area requiring special equipment including, but not limited to: catching devices, traps, tranquilizer guns, a pickup truck with animal cages, proper clothing, protective gear and training," Dad said some time before council addressed the matter. "The only way to efficiently handle animal control matters is with a specially trained and equipped animal control warden who would answer directly to the town manager."

Ordinance Committee Chairwoman Bettye Steger said council is discussing the dog issue because of concern for the safety of the public. It was noted that one parent some time ago brought a large dog on a leash to a recreation event. There was no problem with this dog, but some officials expressed concern that, with the large number of children usually present and those participating in activities, the potential for problems is there. Town Attorney Frank Terwilliger informed the committee that council could prohibit dogs from town parks at specific times, events, places or through certain other restrictions. Owners also take dogs to parks and the courthouse lawn to "do their business," causing other problems for children or others walking and playing there. All dog/animal complaints received by the police department are referred to the county animal warden.

"Due to the limitations of two staff members serving a large area on a 24-hour basis, it is unrealistic to expect a rapid response to complaints about dogs running at large," County Administrator Joe Morgan informed Town Manager Tom Combiths. "The county dog control ordinance states that a dog shall be deemed 'to run at large' while roaming, running or self-hunting off the property of its owner or custodian and not under its owner's or custodian's immediate control."

Dad informed town staff that outside of the regular hours, the dog warden would only respond to dog bite cases.

"This can create quite a problem for the police department since we are not equipped to handle animal complaints," Dad stated.

"Dangerous or vicious dogs have, on occasion, had to be destroyed if we could not contact county animal control or could not wait for them to respond," the police chief told the town manager. "The county warden has said that he would not be able to expand his workload within the town because of his present workload in the county."

Dad also pointed out that Wytheville, Blacksburg, Galax and Radford have fully equipped animal wardens working out of the town manager's office. County officials report that from January to August 1994, the animal control officers answered 1,204 complaints of 1,379 received. A total of 854 dogs and 234 cats were picked up during those eight months. Between 250 and 360 pounds of dog food were purchased each month and an additional 25 to 50 pounds of cat food were bought monthly during the same time period. County officials reported in October that dog tag sales brought in $10,066 in 1994-95 $13,066 in 1993-94, $16,353 in 1992-93, $14,160, 1991-92, and $15,677 in1990-91. At that time, it was reported that summonses issued for no tags ran slightly more than one per month, average. The 1994-95 budget detail for animal control shows total expenditures of $96,303 approved by the board of supervisors. This includes $55,566 for salaries and wages including $1,400 for selling of dog tags by veterinarians.

## National Night Out

Pulaski Mayor Andrew L. Graham (second from right) presents a proclamation Tuesday afternoon on National Night Out to members of the Pulaski Police Department and representatives
of the local Neighborhood Crime Watch Program encouraging participation in the nationwide
event which was held Tuesday night. On hand to receive the proclamation were (from left) Police
Chief Herb Cooley, Crime Analyst Specialist Sandra Wilhoit, Crime Prevention Specialist
Vanessa Hill, Triad Coordinator David East, and Neighborhood Watch Captain Colleen East.

Staff photo by Dee Ann Lindsey

The Pulaski Police Department learned on August 7, 1995 that an anonymous caller is contacting citizens informing them their dues for their Neighborhood Crime Watch membership must be paid.

"Please do not give anyone money for this purpose," said Vanessa Hill, crime prevention specialist for the police department. "The Pulaski Police Department offers the Neighborhood Crime Watch and all other crime prevention services at no cost to our citizens."

"There is no membership fee or cost for any service the department offers," Hill stressed. "Again, do not cooperate with these callers, or anyone else asking money for this or similar programs."

Dad reiterated the importance of the public contacting the police department or other law enforcement agencies when calls from unknown or anonymous sources were received. This was one way to stop those people who were using the phone and the mail in scams of all types. Also, town and county citizens were receiving calls soliciting funds for the FOP.  The caller did not identify where this Fraternal Order of Police was located, stating that for a specific sum, a decal and some other items would be sent to the contributor. Dad, Sheriff Ralph Dobbins and Dublin Police Chief Russell Gwaltney all said none of their departments were involved in this telephone drive for the FOP.

After just a year in office, Dad had reversed Pulaski's crime rate exponentially as Chief of Police.

Chapter 15
Modernizing a Department

Crime and the fear of crime have a powerful impact
on older Americans. Recognizing this fact and the growing
number of older citizens in Pulaski County, the three local
law enforcement agencies and the American Association of
Retired Persons formally joined forces to make a difference
in the lives of these county citizens. A cooperative agreement
of the Pulaski County AARP, Pulaski County Sheriff's
Department, Pulaski Police Department and Dublin Police
Department was officially signed Friday, August 18, 1995.

The formal name of the crime fighting organization
is Triad, which had its beginning when AARP, the
International Association of Chiefs of Police and the
National Sheriffs Association signed a cooperative
agreement to encourage the growth of local Triads and to
sponsor annual meetings to provide information and
support to local leadership. The National Institute of Justice,
which is the research and development arm of the U.S.
Department of Justice, recognized the value of the Triad
concept and supported the production of selected training
and technical assistance resources. Included were the Triad
handbook, a quarterly newsletter and a video. Triad means a
three-way commitment among the chiefs of police, sheriff
and older or retired leaders in the community. Involved in
Pulaski County were Sheriff Ralph Dobbins, my dad and
Dublin Chief Russell Gwaltney as well as David East, who
served as the Pulaski AARP representative. Attending the
official signing ceremony in Jackson Park was Randy
Marshall, associate state representative of AARP for
Virginia, Maryland and the D.C. office. East, chairman of
the Pulaski County Triad, acknowledged the assistance given
by Christiansburg Police Chief Ron Lemons and Officer
Connie Bishop to the Pulaski group. Also playing a role in

the county organization was the New River Valley Agency on Aging, where many of the meetings have been held.

Serving as vice chair of the local Triad was Carolyn Duncan, director of the Pulaski Retired Senior Volunteer Program. Marshall told the group gathered in the hot summer sun that the work really began with the signing of the agreement. The concept came after those living alone felt threatened and intimidated by scams and schemes plied by the unscrupulous among society. Marshall said he had talked with Gwaltney who sees Triad as a block program for the elderly across Pulaski County.

"These people are willing to be the eyes and ears in the community, giving them a positive outlook as they elderly become more aware and active," Marshall said.

"What we are doing this morning is symbolic," Dad addressed the crowd. "What's next is not symbolic when we will tend to the needs of those who've given so much to us and the community." Gwaltney pledged the assistance and cooperation of the Dublin Police Department and said the program would work out fine.

"The elderly in Dublin are looking forward to the program," he added.

"The joint effort is another piece of evidence the towns and county are working together," Dobbins chimed in.

Leaders were an implementation handbook detailing why the organization is necessary including guidelines on starting a Triad, making it work, what Triad can do, elements of Triad, fostering understanding through Triad, senior volunteers as well as evaluation and avoiding missteps. As a group, the elderly were proven to be a powerful and active force. However, as individuals, they can be vulnerable and may need help. Triad offered some assurances against that vulnerability and offer help in many ways. Officials said there was no such thing as a typical older person. An older person can be housebound and ill, or very active. AARP studies show that a few types of crime claim older victims more often than younger ones. In this category were frauds and scams, purse snatching, theft of checks from the mail and crimes in long-term care settings. The Pulaski Triad became involved in gathering information from older county residents through a survey. Forms were distributed and a number had been returned. An advisory council is a key element in any Triad's success. The council was made up of older citizens in the community, people who work with the elderly and law enforcement personnel. The suggested makeup of the council included the clergy, business community, health care professionals, and service or membership groups consisting of agencies working directly with seniors and aging professionals. The council, officially dubbed "Seniors and Lawmen Together," was better known as S.A.L.T.

Chief Herb Cooley, Sheriff Ralph Dobbins, Chief Russell Gwaltney and David East (back to camera) watch Randy Marshall, AARP, sign agreement

Meanwhile, Dad was still busy with the matter of getting junk cars moved out of town. In recent months, council has been receiving reports from Police Chief Herb Cooley about this situation with officers contacting individuals about the town ordinances. Ordinance Committee Chairwoman Bettye Steger reported September 6 that the chief said 28 vehicles were to be moved soon. A question was raised about screening the vehicles from view and what constituted proper screening or covering. Council has the authority to limit the number of vehicles which can be kept and screened. This authority is allowed by the state code, Town Attorney Frank Terwilliger informed council.

Dad continued his innovative work with the Pulaski Police department as the autumn of 1995 approached. The last week of September, he announced a trio of his officers who would serve on a very unique division of the police department. These three officers would make up a very special force known as Pulaski Police Department's bicycle patrol unit, something completely new to the area. Officers Rob Davis, Terry Smith and Vanessa Hill all volunteered for the duty, which was anything but easy.

Hill knew firsthand the hazards that can befall a cyclist, after a particularly nasty spill while in training. All three officers recently attended a special school on the campus of Western Kentucky University sponsored by the Police Mountain Bike Association. Hill, while learning how to take her cycle up steps, was tossed head-first over the handle bars. She had the scars to show the unsuccessful outcome of that accident. Still bruised and battered, she continued with her training along with fellow officers Smith and Davis. There were no other major mishaps among the local group, except for a few sore muscles. Smith actually took second place in skills-testing for the school. By October 1, they were back from school and ready to pedal. Dad told the press that he expected to have them on the streets and attending various functions throughout the town.

"The program is part police work, part community relations, and part public relations for the department," Dad offered. "People are more likely to talk to a police officer on a bicycle than they are one sitting or riding in a car. It makes sense to get these people out among the citizens."

"It's less threatening," Smith agreed, noting that while on the college campus people would talk to them often.

They all agree that the major requirement for the job was "knobby knees."

Dad described his three volunteers as "the cream of the crop."

"It's a demanding task to ride a bicycle eight hours a day. You have to be in top physical condition. It also can be a dangerous task," Dad noted.

Although they've all taken a certain amount of kidding from their fellow officers about their bike duty,

Davis said that there is a higher degree of danger on the cycle.

"The car is like armor," he suggested.

Davis, who works hard at keeping physically fit, liked the fact his new duties would allow him to use his physical fitness.

"It puts us into the face of what we're supposed to be doing and that is fighting crime," Hill agrees.

Although her work was primarily dealing with the Neighborhood Crime Watch groups, Hill was now a trained police officer and she sees not only the public relations angle of the bike patrol, but also the practical uses.

"Police cars can't go driving through people's yards. You can't really sneak up on someone if you're driving a car, whereas the bike is quiet. The bike can go so many places the car can't. If you are stuck in traffic, you can take to the sidewalk. There are advantages to the bicycle as a police tool," said Hill.

Davis remarked that the bicycle can also be used as a weapon.

"There is a take-down sweep you can use on a suspect if needed," he said.

Smith commented that the cycle can maneuver faster in parking lots than a car when tracking someone. All three had an interest in cycling prior to the formation of the unit.

Dad reported that the cost of the new unit has been practically zero for the town. Wal-Mart donated gloves and helmets. Shoes were purchased at a discount at Shoe Show in Pulaski, and the Diamond Back cycles were bought through a discount at CMT. The Division of Motor Vehicles had just awarded a $750 grant to the department for the unit.

"The DMV is a big supporter of the program," said my father whose cycle cops were also expected to be a big hit with kids in local schools.

He planned for his officers to occasionally present programs on bike safety. The officers knew they would be setting an example for youth and their bicycles as well as helping to keep the streets safe while they're pedaling on patrol.

## Crime Prevention Month Proclaimed

Pulaski Mayor Andrew L. Graham has proclaimed October Crime Prevention Month for the town noting that those of all ages must be made aware of what they can do to prevent themselves, their families, neighborhoods and workplaces from being harmed by violence, drugs and other crime. On hand for the signing by Mayor Graham (seated) were Pulaski Police Officers A.K. Anderson (left) and Vanessa Hill along with Police Chief Herb Cooley (right).

*Staff photo by Dee Ann Lindsey*

\* \* \* \* \* \* \*

In early October, a Hiawassee shooting incident took place in which a man allegedly shot his neighbor and began firing at police officers who arrived on the scene. The easy answer would have been to take the 60-year-old man out with a sniper's bullet. Regardless of age, anyone with a loaded gun can be a deadly force to citizens and police officers, and must be dealt with. Sheriff Ralph Dobbins called in the Pulaski County Special Response Team and they took down the man safely without firing a shot. To the men who comprise this team and their department leaders, this was a successful mission.

"Anytime we can save lives and prevent an injury, that's a success," said Dobbins. "No officers were hurt and the suspect was taken into custody."

These sentiments were echoed by Pulaski Police Chief Herb Cooley and Dublin Police Chief Russ Gwaltney.

It is volunteers from the three departments that make up this team.

"When an incident occurs in Pulaski, I'm in charge of the scene," Dad explained. If it's in Pulaski County, Dobbins is in charge, and when it's in Dublin, Gwaltney is in charge." "There's none of this where anyone is. pushing to be in charge. We all work well together, and the men think of themselves as a single unit,' not as members of different departments," said Gwaltney. Although the team has been in existence for almost two years, it maintains a low profile and is only used for special instances, such as the recent shooting, and in drug cases. Members of the team prefer not to be identified.

"It's a psychological element," added Gwaltney.

Dressed in black from head to toe, the team members are imposing in appearance.

"Imagine you are a criminal in your house and these guys come busting through the door. It's going to be a shock or they come up out of the woods as they did in the recent incident and the man never really knew what hit him until after they'd knocked him to the ground," said Dobbins.

"On a couple of drug raids, a few people are still trying to figure out who the turtles are," Dad noted.

Turtles refer to the look that was achieved via their head gear, which included a helmet, mask and safety goggles. The members of this special tactical team trained locally at least once a month and had also attended special schools that provide training for various situations they may face as a unit.

Rescue was their primary duty. They were trained to stop a fleeing vehicle with a dangerous suspect as well as take a person down with sniper fire or force someone out with tear gas who is barricaded in a building. All were volunteers.

"There is no extra pay for this extra duty, but we hope that will change in the near future," Dobbins said. Also, the members determined if a new addition to the team is selected because the group must work so closely together.

"It's important they get along well together and these officers do," said Gwaltney.

"In addition to being physically fit, the officers must also relate well to people and among themselves," my dad added. "While much of their equipment is standard police issue, they are still adding pieces of equipment to serve the special unit all the time and are continuously training."

"They they might not be needed often; when the team is needed they're ready," said Dobbins.

"A suspect won't even know they are there until it's too late," Dad pointed out.

It was also explained that the members of the unit did this work in addition to their regular duties as police officers in Pulaski, Dublin and Pulaski County.

\* \* \* \* \* \* \* \*

On November 4, 1995, a New Jersey man was arrested and charged with possession with intent to distribute "crack" cocaine after a search warrant was executed Friday in the Town of Pulaski. The warrant was served by the Pulaski County Tactical Response Team, which often works with the Pulaski County Drug Task Force, reported my dad as Pulaski Police Chief and Sheriff Ralph Dobbins. Upon searching the residence, officers found approximately 5 ½ ounces of crack cocaine already packed into $25 and $50 "rocks" for distribution. The crack was located inside of a food container with a false bottom. Street value of the confiscated cocaine is estimated at $19,000. Wilburt K.

Cooper, 26, whose home address was not available, was arrested at the scene for possession of the cocaine with intention of selling it. Also seized from Cooper was $2,286.03 in cash. Authorities said a 17-year-old female from New Jersey, who was also at the house at the time the search warrant was executed, was released. The Pulaski County Drug Task Force is comprised of officers from the Town of Pulaski Police Department, Pulaski County Sheriff's Department, Dublin Police Department, Virginia State Police and Virginia ABC Enforcement Division.

* * * * * * * * *

Two weeks later, the Pulaski Police Department announced that it would be receiving two grants from the Department of Criminal Justice Services totaling $46,826. The grants were to be matched with $15,608 from the town. Dad the first grant of $15,000 was for purchasing an incident based reporting system. He explained that this would enable the department to comply with state mandated reporting requirements well before the deadline of 1999. Along with a $5,000 match, the town police department purchased a fileserver to accommodate the software for the incident reporting system and link the entire police department to the system. The grant will also paid for training all users of the system. The second grant was for a Criminal Records System Improvement, which Dad noted would enable the department to replace outdated computer systems with new hardware, software and office equipment. The grant will enable the entire police department to be networked through Novell software.

With this grant, the department bought three workstations and printers, six to seven additional connections to Criminal Justice Information System software, computer aided dispatch software and hardware, 911 interface software to allow new reporting system of the offense number, four lateral file cabinets to centralize criminal records, one shredder to allow information that must be destroyed by the department such as criminal histories and driving records to be destroyed.

One of the most stressful occupations in society is that of police officer. Not only are there high levels of physical assertion, but there are also high levels of mental stress. With a goal of maintaining good health for all his officers, Dad had all his sworn personnel submit to a health screening, saying that each officer needed to know their present health status. Once the screening was complete, the results were given to each officer. Those results could be used as a measuring device in developing a personal physical training program.

"It will also determine each officer's fitness level and readiness for the police department's upcoming physical assessment in January," Dad explained. "At that time, each officer will be scored on pull-ups, sit-ups, 1.5 mile run, dexterity, bench press and other exercises." During the screening, which was conducted by Occupational Health & Safety Services of Pulaski Community Hospital, cholesterol, glucose, body fat, height, weight, vision, pulse, and respiratory peak were all evaluated. Plans also call for having another screening to evaluate any improvement made by the officer.

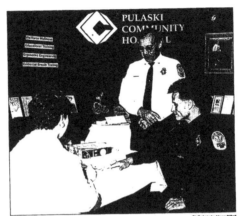

Officer Rob Davis has his pulse checked which Chief Herb Cooley looks on

\* \* \* \* \* \* \* \*

Lindsay Sarkis of Blacksburg believed her 18-year-old son, Jeremiah Scott, was being harassed by Pulaski Police and she took her complaint to town council Tuesday evening, December 19, 1995. Sarkis said she wanted to turn her complaint in before council because she is distrustful of the police. Dad said the next day that it wasn't uncommon to get complaints about officers and his philosophy was to be fair to the public and fair to the officers.

"We get complaints daily and I don't take them lightly," he told the press. "By the same token, I'm not going to let criminals run over the public by using threats of harassment against an officer, especially one with an exemplary record."

"I won't stand for any officer harassing any citizen, but I do have faith in my officers. They have a job to do," he added.

Sarkis claimed that the harassment goes back a couple of years, but only cited what she called recent examples. She told council that it started with a broken tail light for which Scott was cited in August. Sarkis claims he then was stopped several times without being ticketed with the officers asking to search his vehicle, which Scott allowed. In October 1995, Scott was stopped again with his pregnant wife and her friend, who was also pregnant. Sarkis said they were forced to walk home from Guida's Market in Pulaski because there was no licensed driver in the vehicle. Scott had lost his license when he failed to appear in court on the broken tail light charge. Sarkis said her son simply forgot to go to court and has since had his license restored. Sarkis also said they were only recently notified that the license had been suspended. According to my father, the DMV report shows that Scott had been notified at the time of the October incident.

"The officer was within his right not to let anyone drive the vehicle because there was no licensed driver. However, the officer said he was also under the impression that they planned to call someone to pick them up. There was access to a phone at the store," he noted adding Scott was stopped in October because there was a complaint about reckless driving.

Concerning any other incidents, Dad said he hadn't found any documentation. The police chief also noted that an officer has to have cause to search a vehicle and a citizen can refuse to allow the vehicle to be searched. At that point, the officer will either obtain a search warrant or move on depending on the circumstances. Dad did say his department would be making some changes after the beginning of 1996. Plans were to go to two 12-hour shifts in the patrol division and shorten the chain of command which will allow Dad a greater opportunity for direct supervision of his officers.

\* \* \* \* \* \* \* \*

As for the holiday season in 1995, there were no traffic fatalities in Pulaski County that are alcohol related and local law enforcement officers hoped to keep it that way. While the Virginia State Police, as always, planned to step-up patrols over the New Year's Holiday, so did the local police and sheriff's departments.

Dad noted that his patrol would ring in the New Year by being out in full force.

Cooley has a grant for DUI enforcement that will pay for this year's extra patrols within the town.

"We urge you to please don't drink and drive," he advised citizens. "If you are caught, the experience is not a pleasant one. First, you have to go through a roadside test and be checked out by the alcohol sensor. If you flunk those tests, then you are carted off to the county jail for a breathalyzer test and where you may be locked up."

In 1994, 379 Virginians lost their lives as a result of alcohol-related crashes. In 1995, figures indicate there have been 156 alcohol-related crashes so far. Overall, 832 individuals have died so far this year in Virginia crashes. That is down from 871 who died last year. Seven drivers and one passenger died as the result of eight single-vehicle crashes over the Christmas holiday weekend in Virginia, according to the Virginia State Police. This was half the number of last year. Alcohol was listed as a factor in three of the crashes. Seven of the victims were not wearing safety belts and victims ranged in age from nine to 54. The 1994-95 New Year's holiday weekend brought 12 traffic fatalities on Virginia roads, according to state police statistics.

\* \* \* \* \* \* \* \*

Kicking in 1996, the Pulaski Police Department formed a new committee to bring together police, government, residents and community organizations to identify crime problems. According to Dad, the newly formed Crime Control Planning Committee would not only identify community crime problems, but also devise strategies to address those problems and then have those strategies implemented. He explained that the committee consisted of representatives from agencies and organizations that had an interest in, and some influence over, crime, drugs, violence and disorder in the community.

It would now be up to the police department's Crime Prevention Unit to provide data collection and crime analysis to be used by the committee when targeting problem areas within tile town. The Crime Prevention Secretary, who has been hired through the Crime Control Planning Grant, would serve as staff to the committee. Officials intended for the planning committee to meet the second Tuesday morning of each month. In February, the committee organized and selected a chairperson and vice chair.

According to Councilman Eddie Hale, some police officers were concerned that an experimental 12-hour shift for patrolmen will be dangerous and believe it may be a safety concern for the town. However, Dad argued that he had worked such shifts for about 15 years and there has never been a safety problem. He implemented the plan in mid-January to better utilize manpower and vehicles. In a committee meeting a couple of weeks later, Hale said a concern had been brought to him about the prospect. Dad said he was initially told of a few concerns by officers, but most were worked out and no one mentioned a safety concern.

"I suspect some officer that may be used to a cushy eight-hour shift may be the one complaining," he told reporters "I only wish if they were truly concerned about the department's safety, they would have brought the concern to my attention."

Hale suggested the formation of a safety committee, but was reminded that safety was already assigned to Public

Operations. There is also an employee safety committee. Ultimately, the Public Operations Committee decided not to act on Hale's suggestion.

"If these folks were working monotonous jobs or were even dispatching, I wouldn't even attempt a 12-hour shift. But these guys are out there doing diverse work. Besides, they don't work a full 12 hours. It basically works out to 10 and 11 hours," he offered in defense of the decision. "We have a day and night shift. They work their 12 hour shift through a week and then have four days off. The four days off can only relieve stress, not enhance it."

"In the case of an emergency," Dad added. "We have half the department to pull from reserve, instead of having a third of the department sleeping." Dad also noted that cars were only run for a maximum of 12 hours a day instead of 24 hours, which allowed for greater efficiency in their use and hopefully resulted in more durable vehicles. While Dad said the shifts were experimental for the time being, he fully expected the shifts to be permanent by July 1996.

Chapter 16
Getting Flack from Politicians

Dad reported to the press on February 22, 1996 that the majority of calls that came in to the Pulaski Police departments were related to domestic violence, noting that he didn't believe the town was alone in the problem.

"Domestic violence was a problem everywhere," he said.

A new law had just been placed into effect that required all statewide law enforcement officers to make immediate arrests in violent situations within the family environment. However, Dad was skeptical that the new legislation would make that much of a difference.

"Most of our officers are already doing what the new law calls for, which is to use good judgment," he said.

In April, Dad presented a budget for 1996-1997 to the town council that was 24 percent lower than in the previous fiscal year. The proposed Police Department budget is $1,222,147. In 1995, Dad's department received $307,500 in grants and anticipated getting at least $222,000 more in grant money in 1996. That provided the department a two-year total in grant money in excess of $500,000. One way Dad intended to save money is by permanently adopting the 12-hour work schedule. This resulted in a savings of $9,000. Dad said the schedule provides increased coverage in the community and more training opportunities while reducing overtime by 67 percent. The increased community coverage came by spreading the patrol division members over two shifts instead of three. The new shift schedule would not require any new positions. However, there would be promotional opportunities for two additional commanders and one additional sergeant. The number on payroll was decreased by two over the previous year with the elimination of the

Juvenile Intervention Specialist and a part-time position of mentor/leader.

Both were grant positions. In the previous two years, the number of personnel within the department had decreased by four. Objectives for the upcoming fiscal year include the installation of computer-aided dispatch, which is an incident based reporting system and computerizing personnel record and administrative record paid for through grant funds. The department wanted to improve crime prevention efforts through neighborhood watch and its citizens committee. There would be specialized enforcement concentrating on those driving under the influence stressing seat belt usage, drug interdiction and bike patrol. A wellness program also offered as well as increased training for all departmental employees with an emphasis on scenario-based training, all thanks to dad's hard work to fund the department through grants as opposed to tax dollars. The department would also seek accreditation through the Virginia Department of Criminal Justice Services and continued to pursue grants in order to meet essential needs.

There was a slight spark of tension at the Town Council election forum that year concerning the fact that Dad had yet to move to Pulaski. Incumbent members of council, Mayor Graham, Holston and D'Ardenne stated that the chief has only recently sold his home in Wythe County and is actively seeking a residence in the town. Council members also defended letting the chief have a vehicle to take home with him, saying it is important for him to have radio contact with the department at all times as chief. Former council member and contender Polly Mitchell challenged that, saying she is concerned with the town hiring people from out of town. "When they never move here," she said. "I don't feel we owe him transportation to Wytheville. I don't think any of our administrative staff should live out of town."

Each candidate was allowed to make an opening presentation.

It was clear that Dad was initially hired because he was the right man for the job regardless of where he lived. It was a half-hour drive and selling our home to find adequate living in Pulaski was more difficult than people realized. Thankfully, there were members of council who understood that and I appreciate them. One would think he would have been given a bit more consideration. Given all the money he had saved Pulaski, letting him drive 25 mile home shouldn't have been that big of a deal, especially since he would drive 166 miles roundtrip for his first year in Vinton, but I suppose I shouldn't be qualified to judge impartially. Still, as much as needed to be done in Pulaski, the fact that this was even an issue is pretty ridiculous. Nevertheless, we were all in a house in Pulaski by Halloween, no matter how much we all hated it. I have to say that I was very proud of my dad's response in the April 26, 1996 newspaper.

Town Council rejected dad's offer to remove from the political table the issues of his taking a town police car home and where he resides.

"I am dismayed to learn that one of the candidates is attempting to use, as a campaign issue against the incumbent council, the fact that I have not yet moved from Wythe County and that I am using a town-owned police car," he wrote in a memo to the town council. "I am, at my expense, installing a cellular phone and a police scanner in my personal vehicle. As soon as this is completed, I will use my personal vehicle in lieu of a town-owned vehicle until such time that my residence is established here."

"As you know, the delayed closing of my property in Wytheville, as well as some special housing needs of my family, have prolonged my move here," he wrote on the subject of moving to Pulaski. "My family and I are now negotiating on a home in Pulaski and hope to finalize some plans in the next couple of weeks."

Dad said he appreciated the response of the mayor and council members Alma Holston, Roy D'Ardenne and John Johnston. All defended him in a recent political forum when asked about where Cooley lived and the fact he took a town car home. At the forum, it was noted that it is vital for continuous communications and immediate response to emergencies. At a finance committee meeting, it was agreed Dad should continue to drive the town car, and it was noted council hired him with the understanding he could use a town-owned car. Councilman E.G. Black summed up the feelings of council regarding the memo and my own feelings quite frankly.

"Tell him to forget this crap," he said.

"The chief's done a superb job," Councilman Rocky Schrader responded, citing one area in which he said the chief has been especially helpful in is the removal of junk cars. "Police have pulled in 133 junk cars."

\* \* \* \* \* \* \* \*

On May 17, 1996, the Pulaski Police department sponsored a golf tournament open to any current or retired members of law enforcement, corrections or the court system. At the conclusion of the tournament there will be a drawing held. Proceeds gained from the drawing will be used by the department to assist in funding several projects including Peace Officer Memorial Day, Chiefs Challenge and Operation HEATWAVE. The week of May 13-19 was designated as National Peace Officer Memorial Week in honor of the men and women who hold the powers of enforcement of federal, state and local laws. May 15 has been declared Peace Officer Memorial Day by Congress.

"This is one of the most important days of the year for those men and women in law enforcement because it is a day set by law to honor those individuals in law enforcement who have died in the line of duty," Dad said. "To express our appreciation for the men and women in our locality who have dedicated their lives to protecting and serving our community the Pulaski Police Department will once again be hosting its annual Peace Officer Memorial Reception for all law enforcement agencies operating within Pulaski County."

The Chiefs Challenge was a program designed to increase public awareness of safety belt and child safety seat laws and to promote correct usage of safety belts. The overall goal of the program was to reach 70 percent safety belt usage within the town by the end of 1996.

"Our department has participated in the Chiefs Challenge program for the past five years," Dad commended his officers. "Untold numbers of lives have been spared and many serious injuries prevented by promoting special activities and programs designed to remind citizens of the importance of buckling up."

"Buckle-up America, a special week designated to traditionally mark the start of summer vacation travel in the United States, will also be promoted in conjunction with the Chiefs Challenge," he added.

Operation HEATWAVE is a statewide effort designed to increase public awareness of the Help Eliminate Auto Theft program. This program is sponsored by the Virginia Department of State Police in cooperation with the Virginia Association of Chiefs of Police. The goal of participants in this program was to familiarize citizens with the toll-free auto theft telephone number and to encourage citizen participation.

\* \* \* \* \* \* \* \*

Empowering police, fire and engineering department members with the authority to cite property owners for yards full of trash and debris was just one change being considered by the Pulaski Town Council Ordinance Committee in a review of the town's Nuisance Abatement Ordinance. During a meeting on April 30, 1996 at 7 a.m., members of the committee discussed cross-training the police department. This would allow them to cite violations of the nuisance abatement ordinance as soon as time permitted. It was noted by Assistant Town Manager Rob Lyons that the Blacksburg Police Department is responsible for issuing the citation in that town.

"There may be an effective way to supplement the Engineering Department's efforts. It will give us more eyes and ears. We're currently talking with Pulaski Police Chief Herb Cooley to see if the officers can be cross-trained," said Lyons.

"It runs the spectrum from someone with a squirrel loose in their attic to children fighting and then to the more serious cases such as murder or other crimes of violence," Dad said of the 7,000 calls his department responded to in 1995. "When an officer goes to a scene where shots have been fired, he or she never knows what they're walking into. We have a way of doing things and we do it that way for a reason. Sometimes the public doesn't always understand our reasons. Officers are more than just men and women in a uniform. They're your neighbor, a church member, a little league coach. Some are parents. All are peace officers because they care about the community. Police officers are not one dimensional." "Our most visible unit is the Patrol Division. The uniformed officers and the marked cars are who and what the public sees most often. Their day runs from 6 a.m. until 6 p.m. Every day they're out there patrolling the streets of Pulaski. When you say police department the patrol unit is what most people will think of first. Their job is to maintain the peace and dignity of our town. They are the ones who are going to give you a ticket if you're speeding and they are the ones who will respond first when you call for help. The patrolman today is highly trained. We spend literally thousands of hours on training. We train them in everything from report writing to the use of deadly force when a situation calls for it. Most modern policemen have a college degree."

\* \* \* \* \* \* \* \*

Within the patrol division was the newly created bike patrol unit. Police Corporal Terry M. Smith, a member of the Bicycle Patrol Unit reported an excellent reception of the unit by the public.

"Never before during my nine years of working in law enforcement have I seen so many people who are eager to talk with the police. These citizens are not making complaints or in need of assistance, rather they simply want to talk about how impressed they are with how the town of Pulaski has taken this nontraditional approach with police patrol," asserted Smith.

"Several residents of Pulaski County and surrounding areas have told us how they wished they would see us patrolling their neighborhoods. On one occasion a visitor traveling via interstate, who stopped in Pulaski for lunch, followed Officer Rob Davis and I until we stopped. The person just wanted to talk about our activities on bicycle patrol, examine our equipment and tell us how he hoped his local police would begin such a program. This gentleman from South Carolina left Pulaski with a positive impression of both our town and the police department. Our activities have taken us to areas of the town where it would be impossible to patrol with a police car. In particular, the areas of the planned expansion of the New River Trail State Park and the existing portion of the park located inside the town of Pulaski. Citizens we have observed walking on the trail have stated how they feel better about the park knowing that it is now being actively patrolled by police. A father and his child playing in the Dora Highway Park approached me recently to explain how he felt our presence in this area had made a difference with the undesirable and intoxicated pedestrians who in the past have used this area to loiter, litter and consume alcoholic beverages in public."

"My girl loves to play here," the man told Smith. "I will bring her more often now that you guys have run off the drunks."

"That's a great response," said Smith. "Two other areas of concentration have been the downtown business area and the Memorial Square Shopping Plaza. These two areas seem to have most of the people most of the time. Citizens as well as business owners and operators have expressed their pleasure to see us constantly patrolling these areas.  Also, since we began this duty there have been no pocketbook larcenies reported from either area during our patrol tour of duty "This had been a problem for months prior to our patrol," reported Smith.

He said that they also encourage juvenile bicycle operators to wear helmets.

"Having suffered a severe head injury myself as the result of a bicycle accident several years ago, I can tell them first hand that it's not a pleasant experience.  This has had an effect on at least one juvenile I had occasion to speak with. Two day after I talked with him I saw him wearing his new bicycle helmet," said Smith.

"With the more serious crimes a citizen will most likely have contact with an investigator. The Investigation Unit deals with felony cases. Like the Patrol Division its members are also highly trained," Dad stated. "Investigators also have specialized training in investigations of such crimes as child sexual abuse, homicide, the collection and preservation of evidence, and arson investigations. This division has investigated over 500 felony cases last year."

Gayle Mitchell serves as support staff to investigations. "Recently, we have been inundated in the media with reports alleging misconduct and excessive use of force by police officers. Citizens have expressed outrage and it seems that a profession once held in high regard is now being viewed by many with contempt," Mitchell stated. "It's unfortunate that the public seems to be judging all law enforcement officers by the actions of a select few. As an employee of the Pulaski Police Department, I have been afforded an opportunity to view police officers from a somewhat different perspective than that being portrayed in media reports. It's a perspective which the ordinary citizen rarely has an opportunity to observe. Yes, police officers are human and they do sometimes err in judgment. However, I feel we, as citizens, are often times hasty in our judgments when incidents such as the much publicized Rodney King beating or the more recent incident in South Carolina occur. We sometimes tend to allow these negative incidents to overshadow the positive attributes of police officers as a whole. It seems as though we somehow, during these times, have a tendency to forget that the men and women who have chosen this profession risk their lives daily to make their communities a safer place in which to live. For the past five years, I have been privileged to work with a very special group of individuals, individuals for whom I have developed an immense amount of respect. I quickly discovered that while some might tend to view the law enforcement profession as exciting, the job is in reality far from glamorous. Police officers are subjected on a daily basis to an extremely high stress environment. Verbal abuse, lack of respect and close scrutiny by the public encompass an officer's life. The duties of those in law enforcement do not0 cease due to inclement weather. While we celebrate the holidays and birthdays with family and friends, the police officer must continue with his or her duties. Though they expect no praise, their efforts are often thankless and even in circumstances when policy and procedure are strictly adhered to their best endeavors never seem to be quite good enough. Still, these individuals diligently report for work each day and hope that in some small way their efforts will somehow make a positive-difference. Under the direction of

Chief Cooley, the Pulaski Police Department is composed of four primary, divisions: Investigations, Narcotics, Patrol and Support Services. Though the department functions together as a team, each division is assigned specific responsibilities and duties. Under the guidance and supervision of Commander E.A. Hogston, the investigation division is currently staffed with three full-time detectives whose primary responsibility is the investigation of felony cases.

Hogston monitors case investigations. He's also the liaison with the Commonwealth's Attorney.

"However, the actual investigation of each case is the responsibility of the assigned investigator," he explained. "At the conclusion of the investigation each detective is required to complete a case report, which is forwarded to the Commonwealth Attorney for review. Support staff is also important to the department."

"In an effort to meet the overall objectives of the department, employees of the Support Services Division have the responsibility of providing support to other divisions, noted Mitchell."

She added, "Support Services is comprised of the Records Department Crime Prevention Unit, Communications Division which includes dispatching and parking attendant and secretarial staff. The Records Department is under the supervision of Sandy Wilhoit, and is responsible for the preservation of police records and the storage and retrieval of police data and statistics. Tammy Boyers oversees the mentor program of 'We Love Our Kids.'"

Officer Vanessa J. Hill oversees the Crime Prevention Unit with a focus on educating citizens about safety, targeting specific areas such as home, and business security, safety restraints and drunk driving. The secretarial staff's primary duty is to provide administrative and clerical support to various divisions within the department.

"The public's perception of the Pulaski Police Department depends on the personal integrity and discipline of all department employees," Dad added. "To a large degree, the public image of this department is determined by the professional response of the department to allegations of misconduct against it or its employees. The Pulaski Police Department must have the capability to competently and professionally investigate all allegations of misconduct by employees as well as complaints impacting on the department's response to community needs. Recently, there have been some complaints against the department for harassment. There is a policy whereby citizens can complain. We investigate these complaints fully. When they complain to outside agencies, we cooperate fully in an investigation. If anyone wishes to make a complaint about the actions of a police officer, or about any aspect of our operations, there are several steps to follow. Then, a police command officer will assist you in filling out a report of complaint form. This form asks you to identify yourself and then to give specific details about your complaint. Your complaint will then be investigated. You may be contacted and asked additional questions about the complaint. A letter from me will be sent to the person filing the complaint acknowledging receipt of the complaint and that the investigation has been initiated. When the complaint has been investigated, I will review the investigation and will write to the person making the complaint explaining what has been found out about the matter. Depending on the complaint, punishment for an officer involved in some type of misconduct could range from a reprimand to dismissal from the force, to criminal charges being placed."

Technicalities allowed Christopher Shawn Wheeler, 16, to escape both the death penalty and a life sentence for the murder of Wythe County Deputy Cliff Dicker. In a court ruling on June 3, 1996, Circuit Court Judge Colin Campbell said Wheeler can be tried on no higher charge than second degree murder. Campbell had made a similar ruling in April, but agreed to hear new arguments based on recent Supreme Court rulings designed to boost the charge against Wheeler to capital murder. While second degree murder carries a maximum sentence of 40 years, prosecutors hadn't yet given up on a life sentence for Wheeler. New charges of robbery and the use of a firearm in the commission of a robbery were filed. The use of a firearm in the commission of a robbery carries a possible life sentence. However, the court had currently refused to hear any new charges related to the case. Options for the commonwealth's attorney office included trying to start over in Juvenile Court or wait until there is a conviction for second degree murder and then bring the robbery charges. Attorneys for Wheeler indicated a willingness on the part of the youth to enter a plea that doesn't admit guilt, but agreed there was enough evidence for a finding of guilt by the court. Problems arose for the prosecution when a statement by Wheeler about what happened the day Dicker was killed was thrown out because a parent or guardian wasn't present at the time the statement was taken. Without Wheeler's statement it was agreed that the evidence only supports a second degree murder conviction. Dad, who was previously chief deputy for the Wythe County Sheriff's Department, reacted to the ruling with dismay.

"Personally, my reaction is that it is a shame. It's obviously a coldblooded murder and a technicality will let the boy escape justice." Dad said, adding that he was the one who hired Dicker and worked with him for about 14 years.

According to reports at the time of Dicker's murder, the 58-year-old deputy was serving detention papers on the boy at his home when he was wounded by Wheeler. Wheeler allegedly told Dicker that he wanted to change clothes before going with the deputy. When Wheeler returned he allegedly shot Picker with a .22 caliber rifle. Then Wheeler was said to have killed Dicker using Dicker's own gun, shooting him in the back of the head. Wheeler was 15 at the time of the shooting and it was ruled that he should stand trial as an adult.

\* \* \* \* \* \* \* \*

In 1994, Pulaski had no murders or manslaughter crimes, but there were eight reported rapes, three robberies, 54 aggravated assaults, 144 burglaries, 535 larcenies, 39 motor vehicle thefts and again there were no arson charges. Part I Offenses in Pulaski County totaled 783 in 1994. Local law enforcement officials attribute the drop in the number of serious crimes to better training of police officers and more community involvement. "Violent crime is down," commended Pulaski County Sheriff Ralph Dobbins. "Part of that is due to increased patrolling. Part can be attributed to a more aware public. Through programs like Community Crime Watch citizens have learned what to watch out for and to report suspicious behavior by a stranger in a neighborhood before something happens.

"Community awareness is a major factor with the drop we're seeing in serious crime rates," said Dobbins.

Dad echoed those sentiments and also attributed efforts to involve all segments of society in preventing crime as another reason the violent crime rate was dropping. He believed that such groups as the Community Crime Awareness Committee that has formed in the Town of Pulaski under the direction of the Pulaski Police Department will also lessen crime.

"The purpose of the committee is to create a climate in which crime is less likely to occur," said my father. "This committee works with all age groups and all segments of the community. We want to make everyone aware of the shared responsibilities toward creating a crime-free Pulaski."

## Chapter 17
### Hard Times in Pulaski

In August 1996, a new statewide program requiring able inmates to do laborious works within jail campuses was established by Governor George Allen. Dad described the work the inmates are doing as "outstanding."

"They have totally landscaped, raked and seeded the area behind the National Guard Armory. They've cleaned up a former town shop building. There have been no problems," Dad noted. "The inmates seem to be very hard workers and it has worked out fine for the town."It's a great program. The inmates are mostly short-timers looking for a way to spend their time constructively.

The following month, a major drug bust occurred. Dad, Dublin Chief Russ Gwaltney, Sheriff Ralph Dobbins and Commonwealth Attorney Everett Shockley held a press conference at 11 a.m. on September 11, 1996 to announce the investigation and reveal charges.

"The excellent level of cooperation between the agencies of this task force has led to the arrests and charges," Dad stated. "The advice and cooperation the Commonwealth's Attorney provides for the Task Force while the cases are being worked and the excellent prosecution record we have on drug cases is documented in such undertakings." "The drug problem is a primary concern in the community in that not only are drugs being sold and used, but other criminal problems arise out of the drug trade. This is why the departments place such emphasis on working drug cases," he added.

The Pulaski Chief said the benefits received by law enforcement on these types of operations are not just in the number of dealers arrested and drugs removed from the streets, but also in the form of information received on drug trends in dealing, usage, street costs and other individuals involved that allows the departments and task force to continue the vigorous enforcement of drug laws in the towns and county. Dad also stressed that this was not a single effort, but was the combined efforts of the various departments involved in the task force.

Dad was busy making some changes in his department that he hopes would provide renewed vigor for his staff. With these staff changes, Dad also set for his department to strive toward. He named E.R. Barr and W. G. Davis patrol commanders. They joined B.D. Buckner and E.L. Taylor in this capacity. E.A. Hogston remained commander of investigations.

Davis had been an acting commander along with R.J. VohUchtrup.

"Sgt. VonUchtrup was promoted out of patrol to investigations. More importantly, he will be made the accreditation manager for the department which is seeking accreditation through the Department of Criminal Justice Services," said Cooley.

"We will have concise regulations that will tell us what to do and how to do it. It will keep us from litigation," VonUchtrup remarked. "We will be doing things properly."

VonUchtrup would also handle citizen complaints and internal affairs investigations in conjunction with Hogston. VonUchtrup will report directly to Dad. His assignment was for an undetermined period of time, but would continue through the completion of Accreditation by the Virginia Department of Criminal Justice Services. V.J. Hill, Crime Prevention Specialist, would also become the Youth and Family Services Advocate. Due to the high volume of cases involving child abuse, child sexual abuse and domestic violence, my father felt that this was vital that a concentrated and specialized effort be made in the prevention, enforcement and successful prosecution of these cases. Hill was to be involved in any investigation concerning these issues.

"We want to work on 'community building' through the police department. We now have the leaders in place to take this police department into the 21st Century," Dad remarked.

With that objective in mind, the police chief listed four goals he hopes to see are being sought by his four commanders as well as the patrolman on the beat.

"The number one goal is the improved delivery of services. We are a service to the town. I want the officers to work hard, but work smart. Sometimes you can work hard, but not work smart. "We need to make the public better aware that we care. Sometimes this message is lost on the public because of the nature of our business," said my father. "The second goal is team work. That starts with us working with each other. This is where we drop the ball sometimes. We also have to work on being a team with the community," Cooley's third goal was self improvement for all members of the department.

"We need to improve our self image. We can't downgrade the agency without hurting ourselves. I'm currently looking into programs available that will allow those working on a degree to further that degree. "Also, physical fitness is important. I've been talking for two years, about this aspect of the job. If we allow a man or woman on the street as a police officer who isn't physically fit, I'm liable. We have an obligation to see that each officer is in condition for the job.  After the first of the year, I plan to set some standards regarding physical conditioning," Dad told his command staff before presenting his final goal for improved public relations.

"I want us to treat people like we'd like to be treated. Tone down your demeanor and treat everyone with respect. "I get more complaints about rudeness than "anything else. Don't let some of these folks bring you to their level," said Dad, telling his staff that he believes the 12 hour shift plan was working. "It also helps us control overtime and allows time for training. We also now have command staff here 24-hours a day. "The four days on and four days off is also working. This is a stressful job and we need to get it put of our system before coming back to work and the four days on and four days off allows that."

With staff now back at full strength, Police Chief Herb Cooley has added one additional responsibility for his force, which was nuisance abatement. Officer on patrol were look for trash, junk vehicles and tall grass. There would be a master list compiled by the town's Building Department that will show addresses which have previously been served with a warning. Officers would also have a form to fill out and leave with either the landowner or the renter regarding any type of nuisance. A follow up would then be done by the building department. Dad noted that failing to comply with the town ordinance on nuisance abatement was a Class Four misdemeanor.

A proposed K-9 unit for the Town of Pulaski Police Department was discussed prior to the November 19, 1996 council session when the Public Operations Committee meets at 6 p.m. Mayor Andrew Graham raised some concerns at the Oct. 15 council meeting, asking about liability, costs associated with upkeep for the dog. Town Manager Tom Combiths said there was no such plan or program in place, but did say he would gather information on this matter for council's review. Town Attorney Frank Terwilliger said in October that as far as he knew there was no such program or plan in place. There was mention of one policeman having a dog which he was training or has already trained, but officials said a month prior that it was not being used by the police department.

The committee reviewed a report prepared by the town attorney on the proposed K-9 unit at the November meeting while Dad had prepared proposed policies, procedures and an agreement with the officer handling the dog, which addressed issues identified by the town attorney.

Staff also provided information on costs and training associated with a K-9 unit. During a Public Operations Committee meeting the previous week, it was mentioned that the Pulaski County Sheriff's Department has two dogs, a drug dog and a tracking dog and State Police also have a drug dog locally. The dog the Pulaski Police Department has been considering for use was trained for multiple tasks including, drugs, tracking and crowd control.

The Town of Pulaski Police Department would use a drug dog for six months and at the end of that time a report on the results and costs was to be given to Town Council. Council gave Dad approval to use the dog owned by Cpl. M.D. Dowdy in his department's fight against drugs.

"We are having an increase in drugs. There's no question we are getting a lot of drugs in town. There's no question we are missing a lot of drugs. We have gotten over 100 incidents off the street," the chief told the committee," he said. "A K-9 program pays for itself. It is 'worth its salt' and will sustain itself."

It wasn't long, however, before Soldat, the German shepherd being used for the program, bit someone.

"Any use of a canine unit by the Pulaski Police Department is on hold indefinitely," Dad informed Town Manager Thomas Combiths, via memo. "Soldat, a canine owned by Officer Dowdy, is no longer being considered for use by the department and is being housed at Augusta Kennels in Bland County."

"Any future plans to establish a canine unit will be presented to the appropriate committee of council for consideration before any formal action is taken," he concluded. "I still feel that a canine unit is an essential element of an effective drug enforcement program and should not be ruled out for future consideration."

\* \* \* \* \* \* \* \* \* \*

Speculation of a rift between officers of the Pulaski County Sheriff's Department and the Pulaski Police Department was unfounded, according to both Sheriff Ralph Dobbins and my father. While both admitted that there were occasional personality clashes between officers, they stressed that it was the type of situation you would find in any work environment. Both Dobbins and Dad believed that the rumor mill was cranked up when they mutually agreed to form separate tactical squads. Up until shortly before this decision was made, Pulaski, Dublin and Pulaski County had a joint tact team. A tact team handles high-risk situations.

"It had just gotten too big," said Sheriff Ralph Dobbins during a joint interview with Dad on November 22, 1996.

"Some people are just trying to make more of this than exists," Dad told reporters. "The best thing to do was break it apart."

Both agreed there was one incident between two officers that may have been blown out of proportion.

"The sheriff and I were talking about it within an hour of it happening," Dad stressed.

"We did what you would do with any situation like that," Dobbins stated. "We separated them for a cooling off period."

Then the fire was fueled further by a letter from the property owner where the joint drug task force meets. In that letter, it was reported the Town of Pulaski was no longer a member of the task force and should collect its property at the site. However, the writer of that letter had since admitted he was given wrong information and the task force remains in place with Pulaski, Dublin, Pulaski County, Virginia State Police, Alcohol Beverage Control and the Alcohol, Tobacco and Firearms agencies all represented.

Both Dad and Dobbins reported the task force was now in the process of formalizing its structure and policy.

Both agreed that, while the mission of the task force hasn't changed, the structure needed improvement.

"For years, it has operated on just a handshake, but it, too, has grown to the point that a formal structure with written policies is needed," said Dobbins.

Dad agreed. It was also noted that due to various time constraints related to November and December that the changes to the drug task force would not be developed until after the first of the calendar year.

"I was one of the founders of the task force," said Dobbins. "I'm not about to see it lost."

As for the tact team, both men agree that having two separate teams was a good idea in that one team could provide backup to the other when needed.

"We can be more effective and more efficient if we each have our own tact team," said my father. "It gives us more people trained in high risk situations and better risk management. A tactical team is trained at a higher level than regular officers. They're trained to go into hostage situations or any high risk situation. The officers are usually more experienced. I expect our tact teams will still do some training together. The split on the tact team is actually a way to get more officers trained at a higher level and make the town and county safer places,"

Dad also noted that the town and county are still working together on several projects including the TRIAD, which is an organization that promotes safety among senior citizens.

**Pulaski's Herb Cooley (left) and Pulaski County's Ralph Dobbins say all is well between departments**

Members of the Pulaski Police Department played Santa to 65 children in the town delivering about $2,500 in toys, clothing and other gift items over the 1996 Christmas holiday.

"Throughout the holiday season officers and staff volunteered their time to help the area's under privileged children, Dad said of his department. "Working with the Bunt's Memorial Fund, the officers went to local schools to gather names of children. The response was so overwhelming, we quickly found that the available funds would not allow all the children to be included in the program."

Being faced with the dilemma of having to exclude names from the Christmas list, the police department and other town employees rallied together with local businesses and citizens to collect funds and gifts to include all the children.

"The police department, together with Wal-Mart, set up an Angel Tree to collect gifts," Dad said. "We also arranged for the Pulaski County Melodies, a children's choir composed of students from the county's elementary schools, to perform in concert."

The admission to the concert was an unwrapped toy.

"Police department's personnel, volunteering their off duty time, collected, organized and wrapped the gifts," Dad said thanking all who participated and made the event a success. "Then officers and volunteers accompanied by Santa and his elves delivered the gifts directly to the children."

Concert Toy-Raiser A Success

Staff photo by Mile Williams

Pulaski Police Chief Herb Cooley welcomes the audience to Claremont Elementary School Thursday night for a concert by the Pulaski County Melodies. Admission to the police department-sponsored concert was one new, unwrapped toy. The toys will be distributed by the police department to the Salvation Army to benefit needy children. Three large boxes full of toys were collected at the concert.

* * * * * * * *

Bicycle safety, vandalism, closed roads, drive-up mail boxes, highway matters and inoperable vehicles were disclosed Monday afternoon by Town Council's Public Operations Committee. Mayor Andrew Graham had told council several weeks ago that he had received several complaints about bicycle riders and vandalism.

"Members of the Police Department say they know of no serious problems with bicycles, except for riding on the sidewalks in spring and summer," Dad said in a January 16 memo. "State code prohibits bicycles on sidewalks or public walkways and requires helmets for riders 14 years old and under."

He said localities may pass an ordinance requiring the safety helmet, but he was unable to find in town ordinances any local controls where bicycles may be ridden.

"There is no evidence that some reports of vandalism involved a bicycle but is usually done by someone walking by vehicles using a sharp object," he added. "I only know of only one documented incident where bicycles have caused damage to a vehicle. It occurred in Wade's parking lot a few weeks ago."

Staff looked at placing an island or median in First Street, SW, where drive-by mail boxes would sit in the middle of the street. Town Engineer John Hawley told the committee that the street width was 40-feet from curb to curb with a four-foot median not leaving sufficient space along each side for traffic and parking. He also said postal trucks use the entire street width to back into loading docks at the Pulaski Post Office, thus a median near Washington Avenue would pose a problem.

One suggestion was to locate the boxes on the First Street parking lot which would reduce congestion around the post office. Another was to enlarge the no parking zone around the existing boxes for easier access to and from the mail boxes. The town asked the Virginia Department of Transportation to include a request for relocating the Dora Highway-Route 99 intersection, west from its present location. This, said Hawley, would entail bridge work as the Route 99 four-lane project is undertaken. He also said a new route would eliminate traffic past the cliffs on Dora Highway and could help enhance the work on the extension of the New River Trail into town. VDOT officials indicated this was a workable idea. A letter was sent to the Urban Division of VDOT requesting consideration during the design phase of the road project. Projected costs range between $500,000 and $600,000, Hawley said.

My father had assigned Corp. C.V. Paschal as a full-time inoperable vehicle officer to oversee nuisance abatement and code enforcement in reference to business licenses, adding that his department was now at a point when it is necessary to deal with inoperable vehicles by towing and working more closely with the problem. Dad noted over 200 such vehicles had been removed the past year. Two were removed prior to the committee meeting. Paschal will also work with Finance Director Wade Bartlett on enforcing town laws pertaining to business licenses. The closing of the road to below Gatewood Dam was discussed. Hawley said he had been in contact with the National Forest Service reference to the road leading to front side of the dam. He said he was surprised to learn Friday that the road had been closed. He said dumping of trash, debris and other items was the main reason the road was closed. The town has an agreement with the Forest Service to maintain access across their land to the dam. The creek below the dam is the only stream in Pulaski County stocked by the state for trout fishing. The forest service has said it will open the road at certain times for fishing and hunting. Committee members felt there was no interest in a small lot on West Main Street as they could not see any definitive use for the land.

* * * * * * * * *

Leaders of the Pulaski County Drug Task Force failed to work out an agreement satisfactory to all members regarding task force rules and regulations. Pulaski County Sheriff Ralph Dobbins reported in February 1997 that the task force will proceed without the Town of Pulaski Police Department as a member at this time.

"The task force is not disbanding," Dobbins said. "Chief Herb Cooley has indicated he intends to do his work in the town and we'll continue to do our work in the county, working with Dublin, Virginia State Police and Alcohol Beverage Control officers.

The supposed peace treaty between Dad and Sheriff Dobbins was apparently downplayed in the press or was simply no longer in existence by February 1997. An incident of a town officer making an arrest in Pulaski County while driving through the Fairlawn area only heighten tension between the two departments and their respective leaders. The driver was eventually charged with reckless driving, driving on a suspended operator's license and attempting to elude a police officer. Dobbins maintained that the town officer should have contacted his department when he noticed the reckless driving pattern. Instead, the town officer made the stop. The officer has maintained that there was an immediate danger to the public.

Dad complained that Dobbins' officers wouldn't transport the accused. Dobbins said he believed that the way the stop was handled was illegal and he advised his officers to let the town officer wrap it up. At one point in time, some town officers did have county authority through their work with the task force. However, Dobbins said that authority has expired. Dad said he felt that his man was left hanging. Dobbins responded that one of his officers provided handcuffs for the town officer who was in an unmarked car to use and also saw that the suspect was secured in the town car. My Dad also maintained his officer was just doing good police work and doesn't understand the conflict. Dobbins noted that my father provided Pulaski Town Council with a three page report on the incident, but he didn't bother to get back to him about the matter. "If I went into Montgomery County and started working, Sheriff Marrs would go through the ceiling and the citizens of Pulaski County would be asking what I was doing over there when I should be working my own jurisdiction," said Dobbins.

Dad was left baffled by the situation. Dobbins said he didn't feel Cooley is a "team player."

"I don't feel that I've been invited to play on the team," Dad responded. "We are working with the State

Police and ABC. I'm not sure there is a problem. It's just a matter of sitting down and looking at our priorities and how we can best serve the area and best serve our citizens in the most effective way to fight drugs. I see us as having to step back and look at the situation and then it will naturally flow back together. As for not being on the task force, it hasn't slowed our drug investigations. There's been no disruption of service to the citizens. There's no question that a task force is good to have, but we can cooperate without a formal task force. It's happening now. There's no breakdown in communication and no loss of drug enforcement. I see the drug task force as taking on the big picture. But, sometimes it can distract from what localities are doing op an ongoing basis. I think I've been a team player in communicating and cooperation. I didn't disband the task force. The individual goal is enforcement of drug laws. We need to be cooperative and effective and I'm willing to do that in whatever capacity. I'm not doing anything to hinder law enforcement in the town. The lines of communication are open. If the task force or sheriff needs us we're going to be there. Sometimes people make too much out of a task force. It's nothing more than people working together."

"We can do that," Dad said assuredly. "I've been in the business 30 years and I've never had a problem working with others. I want good, effective drug enforcement. I believe the work of the task force is good and we need to keep the doors open regarding it. Chief Russ Gwaltney said that he felt that Dad wanted to do a lot on his own.

"It's a similar situation to the nine-man SWAT team we had. Cooley wanted to pull away. I'm not putting him down. He just seemed to want to go in that direction," Gwaltney commented. "I've assured Cooley that whatever equipment or manpower he might need that we're ready to help in any situation," "We're not at each other's throats. We're just going separate ways for awhile."

By February 18, 1997, a petition is circulating through the Town of Pulaski calling on Town Council to conduct its own investigation of the Pulaski Police Department. At that point, 120 signatures had been collected and Carl Allison intended to collect more signatures if needed.

Dad believed the petition to be unfounded.

"I believe it is totally false," he stated.

"The signers of this petition are concerned about the behavior of members of the Town of Pulaski Police Department," read the petitions. "We believe that Pulaski Police Officers often violate the constitutional rights of citizens, use excessive and illegal force and exhibit a lack of respect for the citizens they serve. The many complaints made to the Pulaski Police Department often do not appear to be investigated. We ask the Pulaski Town Council to conduct its own investigation of the Pulaski Department and the chief of police."

Dad had known about the petition for about a year.

"It's really nothing new," he stated.

Allison admitted that his action was prompted by the arrests of two of his sons last year, but says the behavior of the police was not right. Dad said the incidents were investigated.

"At least one of the sons pleaded guilty to the charges," he recalled. "All complaints are investigated. Some people feel they are above the law. I want to stress that no rights were violated. We put this in to policy and teach it to our officers and it is strictly enforced."

Allison maintains his son had no choice in the court master. He claimed that the trial was put off numerous times and that his son had to do something to get on with his life. In this instance, the son received 18 months probation.

"The matter was handled in court and the court has spoken," Dad responded. Allison said he had been working on the petition for about a year, brut felt it was time to go public.

"We're getting more petitions out now," he said.

Dad remarked that his department gets complaints, though the serious ones were very few in number.

"All complaints are investigated. All complaint information is forwarded to me. We've done articles telling people how to file complaints," he noted. "I consider it a complaint if someone calls and says it took too long for an officer to respond to a call or that an officer is needed at a particular intersection."

Dad also reported that there had been dismissals from the police department since he took command. "I won't go into details because it's something we don't publicize."

Chapter 18
Addressing the State

 With all the useless pressure my dad had been under by Pulaski citizens and Council Member Polly Mitchell, I was especially glad to see an editorial letter of support for Dad from his former boss and longtime friend, Wythe County Sheriff G. Wayne Pike. The letter appeared in Pulaski's *Southwest Times* on March 9, 1997.

 "Recently, I read articles in the *Roanoke Times* in reference to complaints about the Pulaski Police Department. I also got a copy of the *Southwest Times* and read information about the same topic," Pike wrote. "First, let me say that I have known Chief Herb Cooley for 30 years and have worked closely with him. Of all the people I know, Herb Cooley is one of the most non-violent people I have ever met and is one who would never condone the unlawful or' unnecessary use of force. As a well educated and well trained professional, Chief Cooley would be an asset to any agency. The F.B.I does not invite just anyone to attend their academy nor do colleges graduate people with honor who are stupid. I have seen these kinds of complaints all my law enforcement career. Violators, jealousy, and family of people who are in constant conflict with society norms, laws and are trouble makers in general, are the usual complainers. I have seen them all!! These kinds of people want one thing: to be able to do what they want, when they want, and to answer to no one. Often they are abusers or victims of abuse. If you look at police records, you will find that these types of complainers call the police often and/or are often arrested and may often have police records. When people or their families often have conflict with the police, time after time, who do they blame? The police of course! Of course, I realize that some people do have legitimate complaints about law enforcement officers, but in general, these are people who have never, or very seldom, have reasons to come in contact with police officers. The citizens' concerns or questions are often derived from misunderstandings about the situation and most of the time the problem can be resolved by well trained and concerned law enforcement officers and officials such as Chief Herb Cooley. I believe that the other 9,980 citizens of Pulaski want good law enforcement. Of course, violators, drunks, and others who support them do not, until they themselves are threatened by the one they like to protect. Then they want the police there quickly. In a recent case, I dealt with a father who was living in fear of his son, a constant trouble maker and inmate at our jail. His court record is varied and long. Finally, he gets a sentence of more than a year. You guessed it!! The father wants him out. I certainly did not help in this request. Then what? I became the adversary. The family shows up at the Board of Supervisors meeting to complain about my no smoking policy and inmates having to pay for phone calls. Law abiding citizens are tired of listening to and paying the bills for these people. Tax payers who work hard every day and obey the law do not deserve, nor should be subjected to seeing their hard earned money going for taxes to keep up a few criminals and misfits in our society. Yes, violators and supporters do not want good law enforcement, but you, the hard working tax payer, who obeys our laws, want, need, and should work hard to keep good law officers who keep our homes, businesses and streets safe."

\* \* \* \* \* \* \* \* \*

"We as the police have the highest divorce rates, the highest suicide rates and we receive little recognition, but why do we do this?" Dad asked in his opening speech at the 1ª Annual Police Recognition and Awards Dinner, held Thursday, May 15, 1997 at 6 P.M. at Pulaski's First United Methodist Church. "Because there is a special bond between police officers."

I attended this banquet in which many special awards were given in recognition of May being Peace Officer Awareness Month. Special memorial tributes were given in memory of Terry L. Griffith and his friend Cliff Dicker, both of whom were killed in the line of duty in 1994. In remembrance of these officers, the Wythe County Sheriff's Office Color Guard made an appearance and included Sam Viars, Chad Trivett, Jerry Turpin, Wes Billings, and Forest Carter. Statistics say that every 60 hours a police officer dies, and according to the Sheriff of Wythe County, Wayne Pike, guest speaker, police officers were often murdered by citizens who are not a part 'of the community.

"People who murder police officers only succeed in removing them physically. Their spirits are still here. They're with us. Let's rededicate ourselves to those, who have dedicated themselves...with their lives," said Pike. "Let's always support our men and women in uniform, who keep our streets safe."

Numerous awards were given to those officers who performed in an outstanding way. Strict criteria are met in determining who will be awarded. A panel is formed and nominations are taken to the panel, where they make the decision to accept or reject the nomination. The following awards are listed below.

The Chiefs Medal of Achievement is presented to a member of the force in recognition of an example of professionalism and dedication which resulted in the performance of an outstanding accomplishment. This award went to Sgt. Tony Meredith. The Chief s Exceptional Service Medal is presented to an officer that most personifies the professional police officer by their exemplary demeanor, personal appearance and level of physical fitness. This award went to Commander Wes Davis. The Mayor's Medal of Achievement is given to a member of the force in recognition of actions or accomplishments, which personify the highest ideals of professional police work performed in conjunction with service to the community. This was presented to Sgt. Jim Gregory. The Triumphant medal is awarded, one medal per category to those who have risen above the best in the spirit of competition.

In the first category, M.P.O. Rob Davis took the award for the highest overall score in 1995 for physical fitness assessment. In the second category for interdepartmental competition, the medal was presented to Sgt. Sheldon Ainsworth Three Letters of Exceptional service was presented to Cmdr. Ed Hogston, Chief Dispatcher Liz Moore, and Officer Vanessa Hill. The Combat Cross medal was presented to members of the force who enter a combative situation with an opponent who is dangerously armed. These medals were awarded to Sgt. Tony Meredith (2 medals), Det. John Goad, Sgt. E.T. Montgomery, Det. Terry Smith, and Cmdr. Ervin Barr. The Gallantry Star Medal is presented to the member of the force by who performed under calculated risk of injury, prevented or brought to a halt a serious crime. This medal was presented to Officer Amy Prescott (two medals), Cmdr. Barry Buckner, Sgt. Jim Gregory, Sgt, Bob Von Uchtrup, Sgt. Sheldon Ainsworth, Cpl. John Leeper, Narcotics Investigator, Monroe Blevins, and Special Agent, Thomas "Scott" Fairburn. The Purple Heart Medal was presented to Det. John Goad, and the Legion of Honor Medal was presented to Cmdr. Ernie Taylor and Cpl. Marty Dowdy. The Unit Citation Award was presented to the members of the force who played an active role in a team effort relating to a difficult and dangerous police action. This award was given to Sgt. Sheldon Ainsworth (two awards), Cpl. John Leeper (two awards), Cmdr. Ervin Barr, Sgt. E.T. Montgomery, Det. John Goad, M.P.O. Rob Davis, Officer Kirk Hendricks, Officer Amy Prescott, and Deputy Terry Smith.

The Meritorious Service Award is presented to a member of the force who has either performed some

outstanding accomplishment relating to the saving of some
person from serious injury or death, or has solved a difficult
and serious criminal case, or apprehends a dangerous felon
who poses a threat to the community. This award was given
to Sgt. Jim Gregory (2 awards), Sgt. Bob Von Uchtrup (2
awards), and Officer Andy Anderson. The Lifesaving Award
was presented to Officer Andy Anderson. The Honorable
Service Award was presented to Det. John Goad (three
awards), Commander Wes Davis, Sergeant E.T.
Montgomery, Sgt. Jim Gregory, Sgt. Tony Meredith, Cpl.
John Leeper, Det. Mike Hudson, Officer Kirk Hendricks,
and Deputy Terry Smith. The Exceptional community
Service Award was given to those whose efforts have
enriched the lives of the citizens of Pulaski and was given to
Sgt. Jim Gregory (three awards), Officer Amy Prescott (two
awards), Cmdr. Ervin Barr, Sgt. E.T. Montgomery, MPO
Rob Davis, Officer Kirk Hendricks, Officer Andy
Anderson, Officer Todd Lytton, and Mary Ellen "Cricket"
Cregger. The Military Recognition Award was presented to
Cmdr. Wes Davis who served in the Vietnam War, Cpl.
John Leeper who served in the Gulf War, Sgt. David Moye,
Officer "Mitch" Mitchell, Sgt. Tony Meredith, Officer Rusty
David, Det. Mike Hudson, Det. John Goad, and Sgt.
Sheldon Ainsworth. The Police Department Instructors
award which was awarded to members of the force who have
met the standards of the Dept. of Criminal Justice services
and have become certified instructors. This award was
presented to Sgt. Jim Gregory, Cmdr. Wes Davis, Sgt. Tony
Meredith, Cpl. John Leeper, Chief Disp. Liz Moore, Cmdr.
Ervin Barr, Dispatcher Angie Viars, Officer Vanessa Hill,
and Cpl. Marty Dowdy. The Educational Achievement
Award which is presented to members in recognition of their
effort of continuing their education. This award went to
Chief H.G. Cooley, for obtaining a Masters, Bachelors, and
Associates degree. The following were awarded for
Bachelor's Degrees: Officer Todd Clayton,, Officer Rusty

David, Officer Vickie Raines, and Dispatcher Hoback, The following have obtained Associates Degrees: Sandy Wilhoit, Officer Todd Lytton, Cmdr. Ervin Barr, Officer Amy Prescott, Cmdr. Wes Davis, Sgt. Tony Meredith, Officer Stacey Dixon, Disp. Angie Viers, Disp. Barbara Owens, and Officer Vanessa Hill. Sgt. Sheldon Ainsworth and Sgt. Tony Meredith both received the Police Academy Honors Graduate Award. Also honored for academic grade average were Chief H.G. Cooley, Sgt. Bob Von Uchtrup, and Officer Stacey Dixon. The Letters of Commendation Awards are given in recognition of praiseworthy performance and were given to Sgt. Tony Meredith (three letters), Cpl. Marty Dowdy (three letters), Sgt. Jim Gregory (two letters), Officer Vanessa Hill (two letters), M.P.O. Rob Davis (two letters), Debbie Bivens, Sandy Wilhoit, Officer Kirk Hendricks, Gayle Mitchell, Sgt. E.T. Montgomery, Officer Andy Anderson, Cmdr. Wes Davis, Det. John Goad, Chief Disp. Liz Moore, Ronda Dalton, Barbara Owens, and Mary Ellen "Cricket" Crigger.

Photo by Stacey Howard

**Officer M.D. Dowdy is recognized by Police Chief Herb Cooley during ceremony**

Since Dad's arrival in Pulaski in 1994, his department had received over $1.3 million in grant dollars, which was just about equal to one year's budget for the department. For 1997-98, not counting grant funds, the police department's budget was projected to be $1,343,000. Grant funds pushed that to about $1.5 million. The department has 41 employees. Dad reviewed his budget with Pulaski Town Council during a Tuesday afternoon budget session prior to the regular council meeting on May 21, 1997. He was questioned by Councilman Charles Stewart about why salaries in his department are up 4.8 percent when the town plan only calls for an average four percent increase. He explained that one secretarial position is feeing reclassified and upgraded to that of an administrative secretary and the pay adjustment is more than four percent. Dad was questioned by Mayor John Johnston about grant positions being absorbed into the regular police budget. He explained there are six employees in his department funded through grants and none have been placed in the regular police budget, except for the matching funds needed for the grants. He explained that the grants allow his department to do more in the community.

"Without the grants we just respond to calls. For about $1.3 million, the local match has been $207,000. That's a good dollar use," said Dad. "The grants have enabled us to move into the 1990s."

Dad was also questioned about the number of vehicles in his department. The police chief reported that he has a fleet of 21 vehicles. Eleven are patrol units. There are two cars that are 1991 models, two that were built in 1989 and three that are 1993 models. Dad emphasized that having a larger fleet actually reduces maintenance costs.

"I also have accountability with fewer people using the cars and that cuts maintenance and increases the useful life of the vehicle. When I worked in High Point, they had about 20 vehicles and the cars lasted maybe three or four years. Now, High Point has something like 200 cars and they run them as long as 10 years."

The 11 patrol units are operated by 20 patrol officers. However, Dad said some units are used by only certain officers due to the different equipment needed by different police officers. Dad also told council he wanted to get more into community policing.

"We want to do more bike patrolling and more foot patrols. We're getting good feedback from the public on the bike patrols. "People will talk to a bicycle officer more easily than they will a cop in a cruiser," stated my father. "With community policing, we increase public confidence in the police force while at the same time reducing crime."

Dad had also recently met with local heads of industry and talked about how the department can better work with them.

"Then we're going into businesses. Often, the only time a business person sees a police officer is when there is a crime. I want to build a better relationship with industry and business," he added.

Police Chief Herb Cooley is the "victim" of "foul play" as he is drenched in the dunking booth during Depot Day on Saturday. Sany Wilhoit, the chief's secretary missed as she tossed three balls to try and dunk the chief, but an alleged co-conspirator "accidentally" hit the water release control

The Pulaski Police Department received a grant which would allow officers to become more involved in community policing, Pulaski Town Council learned Tuesday, July 15, 1997. The grant for $55,281 requires a five percent match on the part of the town, or $2,910. Chief Herb Cooley said earlier Tuesday that the grant will pay officers overtime to spend more timeout of the patrol cars, have closer proactive relationships with the public arid for additional utilization of the bike patrol officers. "This proactive relation would involve citizens' input in describing what issues are important to them," the chief said.

Town council and staff would create a climate in the community in which crime was less likely to occur. Dad said that due to limited resources and a lack of manpower, town officers perform the normal functions required in police work and respond to calls for service. This, he said, puts officers interacting primarily with people in crisis or with career criminals. In the community policing, the chief said part of the program involved educating officers in their response to sensitive issues which created a partnership within the communities. Educating citizens in the importance of becoming involved to help ensure that minor conflicts did not escalate into serious criminal actions and improving the overall quality of life in their neighborhoods is also a goal of the program. Dad stressed the fact that no new officers or employees will be required or hired under the grant. He said the bicycle patrol unit, consisting of six trained officers, would be expanded so that at least one officer will be assigned to each shift.

"The equipment and training needed would greatly aid in our community policing efforts," noted Dad, saying that bike patrol officers are more accessible to citizens on a one-on-one basis which allows officers to share information and enhance communications with the public.

The police chief noted in the narrative for the grant, that budget restraints will not allow the department to expand the bike patrol unit any further, although several officers have expressed interest in the unit. With Southwest Virginia being rural, communities are "tight knit" where individuals grow up together, go to school, get married, work and play together. Although there is nothing wrong with these "tight knit" cliques, it does pose problems for law enforcement agencies when people in these groups sell drugs.

Motorists traveling to the area of Claremont School during the last week of August 1997 learned quickly that the traffic pattern had changed for the sake of the safety of students. The previous school year, a student was injured when he ran across the street in the path of a vehicle passing a line of traffic headed toward the school. Signs have been placed on Newbern Road informing motorists that all traffic, except for school buses, was prohibited on Ward Lane between 7:30 and 8:30 a.m. and 2:30 and 3:30 p.m., Monday through Friday. Other traffic going to Claremont School during these morning and afternoon hours were directed to use Craig Street, Short Street, Baywood Street and Ridge Avenue, instead of Ward Lane.

"The main focus is the safety of students," Dad told public. "There continues to be a dangerous situation of vehicles passing stopped school buses.

"We realize this is an inconvenience to motorists, but it is for safety. We are sorry for the inconvenience, but not for promoting safety," he added. "Getting vehicles off Newbern Road has been a problem. I have been in a line of traffic in that area and observed cars pulling out of line passing stopped cars and trucks heading toward oncoming traffic on the two-lane street. What has been done is to make a longer, winding path to the school which can accommodate more vehicles. This is the best solution we could come up with. We have worked with town engineering, police officers, school personnel and school transportation officials."

"If anyone has a better solution to this problem, we would like to hear from them," the chief said.

Police reminded motorists that passing vehicles or buses on Ward Lane was not allowed. It is also against state law to pass school buses loading or unloading children. Police said once these route changes became familiar with all those involved, everyone should see a great improvement in traffic and pedestrian safety in the surrounding school area. To help implement this rerouting, the Pulaski Police Department would have officers stationed at certain points throughout the new routes. Dad said four officers had been working in this area, which put a strain on the department. Within the next couple of weeks, police would begin writing tickets to those violating the new directions and not following directional signs.

\* \* \* \* \* \* \* \*

Two Pulaski police officers were injured and four people charged in an incident early on the morning of October 2, 1997. The incident also resulted in the destruction a deputy's cruiser and injuries to the officer who was responding to help town police. Cpl. M.D. Dowdy and Sgt. A.C. Meredith were injured when assaulted after responding to 24 Highland Terrace about an earlier assault about 12:18 a.m. Dowdy responded to this address and Meredith was flagged clown by a man on Randolph Avenue who said he had been with Kim Brown earlier when a fight ensued and he tried to put her and her belongings out of his vehicle. Curt Jones said, according to police, that she hit and scratched him and poured beer on him and his possessions. When officers attempted to talk to Kim (Kimberly) Brown she said she had been assaulted, but did not want to press charges. Jones has said he did not want to press charges either.

Officers detected an odor of alcohol, after which the confrontation grew until the two officers were being cursed and attacked by at least four people, two brothers and two sisters. Dad said both officers were being examined at Columbia Pulaski Community Hospital the same morning. Meredith was out of work until Oct. 7 and Dowdy, who has a cracked or broken nose, was off for an undetermined length of time as of October 2.

"Our officers are lucky that they were not hurt worse," Dad told reporters. "I am appalled that the officers were attacked in such an outrageous manner. They were only going to summons one person, but with this type of behavior four people have been charged and three officers hurt. It is just outrageous. I am sorry about the deputy who was trying to come help our officers. These injuries and loss of the deputy's cruiser are the byproduct of these people's behavior."

Deputy J. A. Radcliffe received about 10 stitches for a. head injury when his county cruiser crashed on the south side of Draper Mountain about 12:41 a.m. while responding to radio traffic about the town incident. Sheriff Jim Davis said Radcliffe told investigators that the 1997 Ford's rear end came around as he entered a curve with a dip in the road. He was running with his emergency lights on as he headed north on Route 11 at the foot of the mountain. Davis said Radcliffe was taken to Carilion Radford Community Hospital for treatment. The sheriff said this is a lesson in safety for everyone.

"The use of safety equipment and training prevented more serious injuries," Davis said.

The accident involved only the deputy's vehicle. Radcliffe was able to escape from the demolished vehicle through a narrow opening and walk to a nearby residence to call in about the single-vehicle accident. Davis said Radcliffe might return to work Friday. Charged by town police are: Kimberly Brown, 22, with felony assault of a police officer, resisting arrest, curse and abuse, and destruction of property; Veronica Brown, 32, with felony assault on a police officer and obstruction of justice; Holland Brown, 43, felony assault on a police officer and resisting arrest, and Stephanie Brown, a 38-year-old male, with felony assault on a police officer, resisting arrest and escape from custody. All four reside at 624 Highland Terrace.

The three local law enforcement departments in Pulaski County have received a total of $14,000 in grants from the Virginia Department of Motor Vehicles for specific transportation safety projects as of October 27, 1997. The Pulaski Police Department received $6,500, Pulaski County Sheriff's Department, $1,500, and Dublin Police Department, $1,000, as part of the 1997 mini-grant program in which the six DMV districts distributed $530,000. The most recent allotment from DMV shows the Town of Pulaski receiving a total of $5,000 for two programs, pedestrian and bike safety, and occupant protection. Dad said these two grants, for $2,500 each, would help the department continue stressing safety in the two specific areas.

"The annual grants program enables communities to customize local solutions to their specific transportation safety issues. In addition, the grants assisted in reducing the number of fatalities and serious injuries in their communities, thereby reducing accident costs to all Virginians," said DMV Commissioner Richard D. Holcomb. "The program allows localities and local safety organizations to apply for and receive up to $1,500 in mini-grants for special projects during the year. These funds are used for community safety activities such as bicycle and pedestrian education programs, occupant protection awareness, alcohol awareness and selective enforcement initiatives."

"Localities can apply for funds anytime during the year versus the one-time annual grants program," Holcomb added. "This provides the community the ability to react to safety issues that suddenly arise during the year and eliminates the bureaucracy normally associated with grant award programs," he said. Grants are available from federal funds provided by the National Highway Traffic Safety Administration and the Federal Highway Administration, and approved through DMV. The county sheriff's department used the grant for radar equipment to help enforce speed laws and to improve safety throughout the county. Focus of the radar use was in areas and communities where complaints of speeding were reported. Pulaski Pp used the funds for bike safety and bike patrol and buckle up emphasis. Some equipment, brochures, pamphlets and other materials were also purchased. Localities throughout the Old Dominion will receive $1.9 million in transportation safety funds through DMV. About $1.4 million includes annual grants and the remaining $590,000 includes the mini-grants."

The story of the Town of Pulaski's approach to public safety has been told to local government leaders from across Virginia. My dad presented "Community Approaches to Public Safety: Town Track" during the recent Virginia Municipal League (VML) conference in Hampton.

"Police officers can't do the job by themselves. The community and police have to work together to curb crime," said Pulaski Town Manager Thomas Combiths in the opening session.

He praised Dad, who became Pulaski's chief in 1994, for leading his department and the town in bringing this partnership together. Assisting the chief in his presentation was Sgt. Bob VonUchtrup, a veteran of the New York City Police Department, who is the Pulaski department's accreditation manager. The two officers have almost a century of experience in law enforcement, with both men beginning their careers in the early 1960s. Dad said about 170 persons attended this session of the VML program with numerous questions asked at the end of the presentation and interest shown after the session.

"When we travel back to our original home departments, Bob to New York and myself to High Point, N.C., we see departments that have changed drastically over the years. They are much more into building community relationships and forming lasting community partnerships," Dad told the group. "We will discuss and hopefully outline a course of action to better guard the safety and welfare of our citizens and to preserve our good quality of life."

The chief briefly described the town in rural Southwest Virginia, nestled cozily in the New River Valley and surrounded by the Blue Ridge Mountains. The town of about 10,000 covers about seven square miles and was established in 1896 along the railroad which eventually became the Norfolk Southern Railway. He mentioned nature trails, hunting, fishing, arts and crafts, back to nature and invited his listeners to come visit this area.

"We believe we have a unique quality of life in Pulaski and one that is well worth preserving. We want our citizens to have certain expectations," Cooley remarked. "We want them to expect to have secure businesses, not be broken into or robbed; to be secure at home, whether at home or away; to walk our streets or trail and not be mugged, molested or harassed and for our senior citizens to be protected. Search against abuse and scams, for our children not to be abused and to be safe in their daily activities."

Dad added that in order to provide the type of police services and live up to these expectations, officials must forecast or look at future trends in crime, and plan survival skills for the 21st century by becoming proactive, forming community partnerships, include all ages and all cultures, and have a diverse police force.

"If you think these principles only apply to larger departments, I would like to share with you a few points of research conducted by the National Center for Rural Law Enforcement Division of the University of Arkansas." He continued before listing a number of points. "A majority of hostage and barricade situations occur in rural areas and small towns. Rural and small town officers' chance of vehicle pursuit is 200-300 percent greater. Rural and small town community officers deal with a higher level of stress than urban officers. Motor vehicle deaths per 100,000,000 vehicle miles are 2.5 times higher in rural and small town areas. One-third of all Americans live in rural areas and small towns. 90 percent of all police agencies serve populations with less than 25,000 residents. 75 percent of all police agencies serve a population of fewer than 10,000 residents. Rural and small town violent crime has increased over 35 percent in the last 10 years. Rate of police officers killed in rural counties and small towns-cities was greater than in large urban areas during the last five years. The average starting salaries in rural police and sheriff's departments is $15,000 per year, compared with $26,000 in urban police and sheriff departments. With this research in mind we can no longer say, 'that only happens in the big city,' or 'this is just little ol' Pulaski, Va. We don't have to be concerned with that.' This is outdated thinking and can lead us down the road to disaster. In today's highly mobile society, New York City's criminals can be our criminals in a short amount of time."

"Small town departments must plan proactive police strategy and form those community partnerships to be effective. He said there are two prerequisites to consider future trends in crime and to prepare our organizations by getting our own house in order," Dad remarked.

He then listed four future trends which were older citizens, violent and unskilled citizens, diverse population and economic uncertainty.

"We are no longer a nation of youth, and we are rapidly becoming a nation of middle aged and elderly. What does this mean to law enforcement?" asked my Dad. "Quite simply: older citizens, older victims," he said, pointing out additional factors including geriatric offenders and an aging workforce.

Some points about the older population the chief mentioned were that they average household over 60 years of age is worth $250,000, people often pay cash and that we are in a different era of trust.

"It used to be a man's word was his bond and a handshake was a contract," he explained. "Tempting prey for con-artists and marketing scams. Only five to seven percent of crimes against elderly are reported because of embarrassment, helplessness or just not knowing what to do. The aging workforce means elderly drivers, fewer violations, slower reaction times and missing signals and signs and the sadness of taking an elderly citizen's driving privilege away."

He told the local government leaders that the Town of Pulaski has a number of senior support programs in place. He also mentioned another aspect of the elderly population which doesn't sound too bad for law enforcement's officers. That was a report of no brawls and less violence. He then went to another trend, which is the unskilled and violent society, mentioning several aspects of the socially unskilled:

"We are graduating kids from high school that are illiterate," he said in terms of education, explaining that the new generating was receiving less education than parents. "An estimated two-thirds of this generation cheated their way through high school, concerned only with self and immediate gratification. Missing is the work ethic, the 'don't lie' ethic, unlike the 'word is bond' of the past. Seniors growing up with a dream need a vision and commitment to attain it. Today's juniors see what the seniors have and want it now, short cutting the 'working to achieve' pact."

"The emotionally unskilled are elf centered, wanting immediate gratification and become totally frustrated if they don't get it," he pointed out before elaborating on addiction. "We are a nation of addicts, consuming 65 percent of the world's drugs. No society in the history of the world has used drugs like we do to slow down, to speed up and to get high for recreation."

"An estimated 16 percent of our young people suffer from some form of mental illness, many are on Prozac or other anti-depressants," he mentioned, noting the youth of today are angry and not sure why. "We are a violent and angry nation where youth are killing youth, parents and toddlers; gangs and gang violence; senseless random violence; lower offender ages; adolescent homicides and suicides are rising rapidly."

"Stranger-perpetrated murders are now a major problem and are difficult to solve. There is no motive." He mentioned policing a diverse society where gender issues are confronted with female victims, female offenders who are more violent and are incarcerated in larger numbers," Dad said. "The changing face of America means that Hispanics/Latinos will be the largest minority in the U.S. at 15 percent and the Asian population is growing rapidly and will soon be at least 10 percent.. The problem is we are not saying 'Let's work on this together, but instead we are retreating into our own racial culture."

The chief said police are being caught in the middle of hate crimes-racial crimes and gang wars. He then mentioned the economic uncertainty, asking if the American dream was still alive. "There are computer crimes and a litigious society where people are ready to sue," he noted.

"Now we have at least a prediction of what we are facing in the next quarter century and we can begin our proactive strategy planning. "What do you feel is the biggest barrier to community partnerships?" he asked the town, city and county leaders. "Unfortunately it is the police themselves."

"It's hard to break old habits," Pulaski Police Chief
Herb Cooley said in ending "Community Approaches to
Public Safety" in the town track at the Virginia Municipal
League (VML) meeting in Hampton. He discussed the idea

of law enforcement community cooperative efforts and partnership that will be necessary for the safety of public in the changing society. Dad explained what the Pulaski Police Department was doing in the area of police community relations and law enforcement. Saying that it is hard to break old habits, he said officers are used to adversarial relationships and are reacting to calls. Officers are now being asked to be proactive and problem solvers and not be as "macho" as in the past.

"So, before you can venture forth, your own house must be in order. Restore organization," he told the city, town and county officials. "Leadership begins with the mastery of self. You cannot manage others until you manage yourself."

"The most powerful tool is at your disposal," he stated offering several aspects of achieving individuality. "Be accountable to someone. Grow and learn. Don't let the problem employee ruin your perspective. Be a person of character."

"We trust who we know, and distrust those we do not know," the Pulaski Police Chief said in talking about responding to the challenges and discussing leadership skills needed by law enforcement officers for the future. "Leaders must aggressively and continuously maintain an environment of open communication to combat fear of the unknown. We should attend to those around us in work; good thoughts are worthless."

"Diffuse the power of problem employee(s) by dealing with misunderstandings. Fight rumors, talk with supervisors. Too much time is spent with the group. They are the worst problems that we have today," he stressed offering tools to combat workplace fears. "The key to survival is what the middle group decides." An evil man flees when no one pursues, but the righteous are bold as lions. I urge the elected local government leaders to study great corporations. Spend time with people when there isn't a problem. Rules without relationship don't work. Talk with those who aren't a problem (usually 70 to 90 percent of the staff). Ask for feedback. Don't allow workers to fight against each other. Kill rumors."

Dad told the town managers, mayors and council members in closing that accreditation, available from the Virginia Department of Criminal Justice Services, "is an excellent way of getting 'our house' in order."

## Chapter 19
## Wrapping it Up in Pulaski

Town council's Public Operations Committee heard Dad explain his request for the use of a narcotics detector dog (K-9) on a six-month trial period. On January 6, 1998, the committee gave its approval of using the dog, owned and handled by Cpl. M.D. Dowdy. The chief said the program would include a written contract with the dog owner, with provisions to cover the Fair Labor Standards Act, Workman's Compensation, veterinary bills and the injury or loss of the dog. He also said written verification would be obtained of the department's liability insurance coverage for use of the dog, both on and off duty.

Written policies and procedures covered care and feeding of the dog, ongoing training, use of the dog for drug and tracking purposes, use for apprehension purposes, and the use of controlled substances for tracking. Dowdy had acquired a pharmacy license for the handling of drugs. Dad said his research with the Roanoke Police Department and other departments with K-9 units, as well as his own projections, put the estimated cost of the project for a year at $1,200. This, he noted, included food, insurance and vet bills which should be minimal barring duty related injuries.

"No cost is figured for the officer because all K-9 operations are within his normal schedule," Dad informed the council. "The K-9 officer will continue to do all other normal duties of a police officer."

Training of the officer and dog will be constantly updated. Dad said that at this time no salary increase was planned. Call out time and time maintaining the K-9 would be built into the officer's 28-day schedule, thus there is no added cost to the town. • An older patrol car has been converted to a K-9 vehicle.

"Special equipment was donated by local businesses that are K-9 supporters or paid for from drug grant funds," said Dad. "If I didn't feel the dog was needed, I would not be here. When you need a dog, you need it within 20 minutes."

He said Sheriff Jim Davis has retired the county's K-9 unit due to the cost. The State Police does have two drug dogs located within the county, which were now available, Dad noted. Sheldon Ainsworth, of the town police department, told the committee about a recent incident in which two men from Roanoke were apprehended. One had been convicted for selling crack cocaine and the other was wanted by police.

Officers had to wait an hour after calling for one of the State Police dogs. He said the men were cooperative, but a lengthy wait could jeopardize an investigation.

"People who deal drugs don't like drug dogs. If a call is made for a dog, many people will tell you what they are doing," he said. "Drug smugglers and dealers are becoming more sophisticated, using hidden compartments with secret ways to get into them or get them opened and hiding drugs in tires and in plastic."

Dowdy said the dog can be trained in about a day with a new scent.

"We want to try the dog for six months. If it is not cost effective, I don't want it used," Dad told the committee. "The dog will be available for use by other departments. "

"There's no question drugs are out there. We want to give the drug task force support and back them up," the chief said.

A question about the seizure or forfeiture law was raised. Through legal procedures and the court, assets seized are divided by the state and local departments.

"Having the dog in town, much of the work will be done in town. If there is a joint operation, assets are divided," Ainsworth said. On another front, the police chief also told the committee about a recent opportunity to purchase a step van to convert into tactical van and/or mobile command center. He said the department had an opportunity to

purchase such a van for $1,200. He also said town garage
workers inspected the vehicle and said this was a good buy.
Dad said no budget amendments are necessary for this. The
van would be equipped with lockers for members of the tact
team to store their equipment and supplies, with a table or
desk and a generator.

"We feel sooner or later there will be a train
derailment which will force the evacuation of the Municipal
Building. The van, with the generator and mobile phones
and radio equipment would provide communications and a
base for emergency operations," said my dad. "We are
talking free or a minimum cost for the vehicle. Tact team
members will work on and prepare the vehicle for its special
use. Committee members were provided copies of a
proposal for restructuring the New River Regional Police
Academy to bring it into line with state code."

The town pays $163 per police department
employee to the academy, located in New River. Dad noted
that he sent many officers to the Cardinal Academy in Salem
for special training. He added that with the number of
persons certified as instructors, the department can have its
own training program.

Nobody lost their job because of the consultants'
study of the Town of Pulaski operations, Pulaski Town
Council said Tuesday, January 13th during a work session on
the report. They said attrition should take care of reduction
in numbers as recommended in the "Organization Master
Plan, and Financial Plan for Pulaski," prepared by Municipal
Advisors Inc. of Virginia Beach. The session centered on
the fire and police departments, with other matters added,
including two executive sessions. Fire Chief Jeff Hall and
Police Chief Herb Cooley discussed their departments. Dad
presented a plan of changes in the police department
because of the loss of grant positions and others to be lost in
the near future.

"This, coupled with an ever- tightening budget, forces us to explore, ways to maximize our efficiency in the use of people power, equipment and operational function," he said in a prepared presentation. "By taking a few simple measures, I feel that we can continue effectively and efficiently without any demotions or loss of present personnel. I am, however, putting in place some lateral transfers and changes in duty assignments and other responsibilities. Job descriptions will be modified accordingly," he said. "This will be the first step of several in what will be a period of adjustment and customizing our operation to achieve maximum efficiency. Future moves will include civilian personnel taking on more administrative duties." Some of the changes of duty assignments included eliminating the detective commander position and a transfer laterally to patrol, transferring a sergeant position to detective division to supervise the unit, as well as carry a full case load, transferring one narcotics position to patrol, reassigning the Domestic Violence Officer temporarily to assist with accreditation, due to loss of VSTOP grant, establishing a temporary position of administrative commander to oversee maintenance and upgrading of all department equipment and logistics during the accreditation process

Dad said the department had received six grants over time and hopes to retain or have two renewed.

"In order not to have all our eggs in one basket, each specialty will have a primary person in charge with one or two secondary persons who can handle the same function," he said providing an outline of the new duties, listing persons in the primary and secondary roles.

The detective division, which had been led by Commander E. A. Hogston saw Sgt. D.A. Moye moving into the department and be in charge of crime scene, property and evidence room and liaison with the state forensic lab. Hogston was assigned as a patrol commander, a change in duties from commanding the detective division,

301

handling payroll functions, serving as liaison with the Commonwealth's Attorney, in charge of the evidence room, taking items to and bringing them back from the lab in Roanoke, being involved in purchases, seeing speedometers and radar units were maintained and calibrated, being in charge of equipment, such as leather wear, guns, ammo, flashlights, etc., for officers, and other duties. Detective Master Police Officer Mike Hudson will serve as liaison with k the Commonwealth's Attorney and supervise case packet preparation. Secretary for the detectives, Gayle Mitchell, will assist Hudson and Moye, as well as helping Mary Ellen Cregger with payroll. She would be the primary person working with grants, assisted by Vanessa Hill, who has worked in investigations and with sex crimes, and abuse cases. Hill will also be working with Robert VonUchtrup on the accreditation. Sandy Wilhoit, administrative secretary to the chief, would serve as the primary person on all equipment inventories and the secondary person working with VonUchtrup on general training. She would also maintain training records and be assisted by Cregger.

Dad's changes included having dispatchers work 12-hour shifts, beginning Feb. 2, as an experiment.

"This will be re-evaluated after two months, he said. "Shifts will correspond to public and work-load demand. The narcotics K-9 will be on the road as soon as a few administrative details can be worked out.

Council member Charles Stewart distributed comparative reports of fire and rescue service expenditures and law enforcement and traffic control 'expenditures. Figures from the Comparative Report of Local government Revenues and Expenditures for L the year ending June 30, 1996 showed the Town of Pulaski numbers compared with those of several area localities. For law enforcement the chart showed Pulaski spending $138.94 per person, just behind Wytheville's $145.27 and ahead of the $115.30

average for Southwest Virginia localities. Bluefield spent
$101.37 per capita for the services.

Stewart showed a potential savings of $235,987 if the
expenditure for the town was the average $115.30 for the
town with 9,985 residents. The consultants said the town
police department's response time to calls of 2.4 minutes is
well below the national average of five minutes and that the
department has 3.10 sworn officers per 1,000 population
which is above the national average. With grant funded
positions excluded, the ratio is closer to the national average.
The consultants recommended council not appropriate
funds to pay for grant-funded positions when grants expire.

They said the department should continue to seek
grants for equipment and other onetime expenditures and
for personnel that do not require a local cash match from
the town. The consultants also recommended consolidating
communications with the county which could save the town
an estimated $50,000 annually. Currently, the county
handles communications for the Town of Dublin. Dad, in
reference to the consolidated dispatching services, that it can
be looked at, but not to expect less people working in that
area. He also said it might take about $1 million for
equipment up front to make equipment compatible. A
location would also be needed. He said he was not speaking
in favor of or against the consolidation, but said it must be
looked at carefully.

the above photo, Chief Herb Cooley presents Robert Whetsel, manager, a certificate of appreciation with, left to right, Commander Wes Davis, Lori Johnson, and Sgt. Tony Meredith present. Below, Chief Cooley presents a similar certificate to Shannon Clyburn, Tracy Spencer and Thresa Kennedy, Sonic servers, for their help and support.

### Crime Stopper Recognized

Pulaski Police Chief Herb Cooley (left) and Sgt. J.W. Gregory present Jamie Viars with the department's Crime Stopper Award. According to Cooley, the Claremont Elementary School fifth grader observed a hit-and-run accident. The next day, the boy saw the vehicle involved, took down the license plate number, and reported it to police. The report resulted in charges being placed against the individual involved.

Pulaski Police Dept. photo

\* \* \* \* \* \* \* \*

On March 6, 1998, Tonya Hall Harrison, 26, and Charles David Harrison, also 26, of 429 Second St., SW, Pulaski were found dead both from gunshot wounds to the head. Dad said the call was received about 7:17 p.m. at which time officers responded to the Harrison's upstairs apartment. He said the couple has two children, one about four months old and a nine year old, who were not in the apartment when the shooting occurred. He said the children were with other family members in the downstairs apartment at the time. Cooley said the man was dead at the scene from a gunshot' wound to the temple. His wife had a gunshot in the head, but was taken to Columbia Pulaski Community Hospital and then to Carilion Roanoke Memorial Hospital where she died just before midnight. The chief said the investigation was continuing and autopsies were performed on the bodies Saturday. He said all reports would be submitted to Commonwealth's Attorney Everett Shockley for his review. The bodies were found on the kitchen floor where a .25-caliber semiautomatic handgun was recovered. Dad said investigators interviewed several witnesses who were in the immediate area at the time of the shooting who said that Tonya Harrison was apparently moving out of the apartment. Sgt. David Moye and Investigator John Goad of the, Pulaski Police Department are handling the investigation. Police said one witness told them he had taken David Harrison home from work. He asked the man to return later and take him to the store. Upon going to his apartment, David Harrison was unable to get in because his wife had locked the door and he broke out a window to get in. Tonya Harrison returned home to an apparently angry husband, reported police. She reportedly called her mother and advised her that she and David were fighting again and that he had broken out a window. Her mother then called David's mother to ask her to check on the couple when she got a chance. When his mother arrived at the apartment, she found Tonya packing her possessions to leave. Police were informed that Tonya told David she was leaving the next day, to which he replied that he didn't care if she left that night. At this time, police said, David left the apartment with two other persons, who said they went to a nearby store. The man who had taken David home from work told police that he made no threats or gave any hints of what was to come.

When they arrived back at the apartment, David's mother pulled in behind them and attempted to talk to him about the situation, but he went back upstairs to the apartment without talking. While the three persons were still there, they told police they heard three to five shots fired. This was at the time Tonya's mother was arriving to get some more of her daughter's belongings. The witnesses found David in the kitchen floor on his back with a gunshot wound to the right temple. Tonya was also in the kitchen floor with a head wound. Calls to 911 were made and the two victims checked at which time emergency personnel and police arrived. Dad said the couple was known to police, who have responded to the apartment in the past for domestic disputes. One of the most recent incidents resulted in assault charges against David Harrison for assault on his wife, assault on a police officer, impeding a police officer and curse and abuse.

* * * * * * * *

Traditional law enforcement is becoming a thing of the past due to technology and speed, the speed with which information is transmitted and speed with which people travel, Dad told Pulaski Rotary members later in March 1998. Focusing on the theme of community policing, Cooley and three members of the town department discussed crime prevention, bike patrolling and accreditation.

"We are going door-to-door, forming neighborhood advisory groups, working more closely with citizens and neighborhoods," said the chief. "The 'I can't help you' response has been removed from the police vocabulary. There is a misconception that community policing is soft on crime. It is not soft on crime. There is more awareness and feeling and touching with officers more accessible to people instead of just riding around in patrol cars."

He added that the department is involved in aggressive traffic enforcement in efforts to make streets safer by removing drunk drivers and habitual offenders from, the highways. He also mentioned that the quality and education of people hired today as officers.

"I don't hire anyone with less than a two-year degree," said Dad.

Rotary members learned that the department's bike patrol officers, who must attend a weeklong school, logged 810 hours while riding 1,300 miles during 1997.

"I would estimate that we dealt with between 175-200 vehicles and at least double that on vehicle occupants," Sgt. S.W. Ainsworth reported to Dad adding that there were no real problems. The traffic checks were part of the Intensified Drug Enforcement Assistance (IDEA) grant the department received in mid-March.

The chief also reported that the department's efforts to rid the town of inoperable vehicles were continuing. Special emphasis has been placed on inoperable vehicles and as of March 12, 1998 the department had targeted 28 such vehicles for some type of action. Eleven of the vehicles were covered, according to town code regulations, eight were enclosed by privacy fence, five were removed and, as of the date of the report, four owners had not complied. A new list of inoperable vehicles was being compiled for special attention for the enforcement of the town code which states the number and manner of keeping such vehicles in town.

At the May 7, 1998 Town Council meeting in Pulaski, Dad told council he was not asking for anything new in his portion of the budget, noting that the department had received some $900,000 in grants during the past three years. The town manager noted that the proposed budget includes 12 grants for the police department totaling $293,202 with the town match of $53,977. "For every dollar the town spends, it gets $4.97 in federal and state aid in return," Combiths said.

He said that since 1995, the town has received $945,000 in grants, costing the town a match of $169,000. In discussing the police department budget, the chief distributed a chart showing the department's vehicles, listed with mileage, year, make and model. The department has five vehicles with over 100,000 miles. The mileage ranges from 110,000 to 144,000. The remaining 13 vehicles have mileage ranging from 90,000 down to 16,600.

Dad said the schedule for purchasing new vehicles in previous years was two in one year and three the next. He said his budget for next year includes two vehicles. The chief noted that each officer did not have his or her own vehicle, that two officers share a car. There were vehicles for the chief, K-9, narcotics, commanders, crime prevention and investigations.

Questions were raised in regards to the number of personnel in the department and the possibility of not filling vacancies when they occur. Dad said officers and staff in the department didn't understand the Municipal Advisors, Inc. management study which recommended some cuts.

"There was not enough time spent by the consultants in the police department. With five officers on a shift, it does not mean that all five are working every shift," said the chief. "Something will take officers away from the job. Vacation, comp time, maternity leave and other circumstances all must be considered. The town is growing in such a way that we will need more officers. The addition of the town industrial park will require patrols. If an officer is involved with a drunk driver it takes another officer to operate the breathalyzer and it usually takes at least two hours each."

He then mentioned involvement with a juvenile which could take two to four hours and an emergency commitment order takes several hours, adding that one fourth of an officer's time is spent with paperwork.

'They must document what' they've done for everyone's safety, and then there's court time," he said. "During summer months, town police must patrol and respond to calls to Gatewood Park, an eight-mile trip one way."

In-car camcorders were mentioned by council with members noting that with circumstances now growing more dangerous and critical and that their use would be good for officers and the town. Dad said the cameras would probably cost about $3,000 each once installed. He noted that the system was a closed system which prevents any tampering.

Council expressed interest in further information on the cameras in light of news reports from across the country.

I briefly got my hopes up that Dad would return to Wythe County after I heard that Wayne Pike was resigning as sheriff to accept a position with the state parole board.

Dad, who worked with Pike for a number of years in North Carolina and Wythe County, had been mentioned as a contender for the post.

"I have not talked with Wayne for five or six weeks. I have not, been contacted by any Wythe County officials, any Republican people or anyone else concerning the position," Dad said on June 19, 1998. "If anyone contacted me, I would talk with them. My brother, Doug, would probably have a good chance, better than me," he said.

My uncle, Doug Cooley, a lieutenant colonel working under Pike, resigned from that position to take a job with the state Department of Criminal Justice Services. The top three officers now working under Pike were Col. Kermit Osborne, Capt. Keith Dunagan and Capt. Sam Viars. All three were expected to be possible candidates for the job. Dunagan and Viars were promoted in 1997 after Doug left the department.

My hopes didn't last long. A 23-year veteran of the Wythe County Sheriff's Department was sworn in as sheriff on Friday, July 10, 1998, filling a vacancy created when Wayne Pike, Wythe County Sheriff for almost 20 years, stepped down following his appointment to the Virginia Parole Board. Kermit Osborne, a Grayson County native, settled in Wythe County in 1971 following his military service and joined the sheriff's department in 1975 as a road officer. Osborne was appointed by the circuit court to finish out Pike's unexpired term.

"I am relieved with the decision by the judges, so the department can move on and continue the excellent law enforcement and safety programs instituted by Sheriff Pike," Osborne said from his office. "I hope to continue the efforts to keep the public informed of what is going on in the department and the county. I look forward to working with the press. This is very important in our work," he said.

Kermit would go on to serve as sheriff until his retirement in 2005, elected twice after finishing out Pike's term, which ended in 1999. His name was one of two submitted to the circuit court judge.

The other was my uncle Doug Cooley, a lieutenant colonel with the department, who left the Wythe County department in 1997 to accept a position with the Virginia Department of Criminal Justice Services. The Cooley name was mentioned often in discussions about Sheriff Pike's replacement with Dad and Doug both listed as top contenders. Unfortunately, neither of them won out.

Dad served as one of Pike's top officers, having worked with him a number of years in North Carolina and Wythe County. They also attended Guilford together and served as motorcycle officers together in North Carolina. Gov. Jim Gilmore announced Pike's appointment June 4 to the parole board which issues final discharge of parole for inmates incarcerated prior to the "no parole" law and sets regulations governing granting of paroles and release of individuals under indeterminate commitment.

That same month, the Pulaski police force was host to a special target training event on Draper Mountain.

"The course objectives are designed to enhance the quality of training and increase weapon proficiency and safety," Dad explained. "Often, military and law enforcement training tactics are quite different in nature. "This course will serve to integrate the operations of military and law enforcement objectives."

"It's much different now. There's no more standing and shooting at a target. There's much more to training than the public is aware of," Dad noted as the visiting officers went through one drill.

The visiting officers were divided into two groups, one using 9 MM handguns and the other using long-range, high-powered rifles in sniper training. The trainees arrived in Pulaski around noon on Wednesday, July 21 and spent little time settling in before heading for the firing range. Dressed in camouflage clothing with regulation body armor and weapon, additional clips and other equipment, the men were given little opportunity to relax and talk during several hours on the firing range Wednesday.

Dad said they finished the live fire and limited visibility exercise around midnight.

The course of study included intelligence gathering operations, mission objectives and planning, special weapons deployment, live fire exercise including special weapons and chemical munitions and hostage and officer rescue techniques. Tactics in the sessions included entries, vehicle assaults, officer rescue, a raid briefing and a student raid. The training concluded Friday, July 23rd before noon. Training officers from the Pulaski department were Commander Barr, Sgt. Sheldon Ainsworth, Cpl. John Leeper, Sgt. E.T. Montgomery, Officer A.K. Anderson and Detective John Goad.

Dad said the department was contacted by Fort Lee personnel about their personnel training here after Ainsworth had participated in training exercises there.

"I'm glad we have arrived at a point to do training and have instructors teaching other law enforcement personnel," he said.

Capt. Mike McCormick, of the Fort Lee contingent, who has served in Korea and elsewhere overseas, told Dad that his department's firing range layout was very good and they loved this area.

The Pulaski Police Department lost 10 officers the between December 1997 and January 1999, mainly due to better benefits, including a state retirement plan, offered by other police agencies. Dad said on Tuesday, January 12,

1999 that the town and department had $75,000 invested in each of these officers over the first two years. This meant a loss of $750,000 as well as trained and experienced officers.

"Everybody in our area is taking my officers. We are a sitting duck here," he said during a meeting of the Safety committee, appointed by Mayor John Johnston.

The four-member committee of council members Lane Penn and Jim Neblett, Robbie Gardner and Claude Yelton was appointed by Johnston following an "Organization Master Plan and Financial Plan" for the town by Municipal Advisors Inc., of Virginia Beach in mid-1997.

J.R. Schrader/SWT

**Pulaski Police Chief Herb Cooley (left) presents Sgt. John Leeper the Chief's Exceptional Service Medal.**

**Pulaski Police Chief Herb Cooley congratulates Sgt. Jimmie Gregory on his efforts to fight drunk driving as recognized recently by MADD (Mothers Against Drunk Driving).**

The Pulaski Police Department is using eight bikes as part of its total patrolling program. "It is cost effective and gives us the benefit of foot patrol, better contact with the citizens, and we can get to almost anywhere in town that we could access by car. It is great public relations, too," Dad said, adding that Pulaski officers using the bikes are specially trained on how to use the bikes, fitness, making arrests, even shooting and hitting a target after a vigorous ride or chase. "It keeps officers in shape," he said.

"Bikes are the most effective and efficient way to reach people in most instances."

Dad noted that the bikes would be in use more if the department were at full strength. As of June 1999, they were used at festivals, in good weather, in shopping centers and when possible to patrol downtown areas.

"We have even considered bike tracks on some of the patrol cars so an officer can drive to an outlying area or shopping center, park, and then ride the bike to do closer patrolling," Dad said. "You can get places you can't cover in a car and to be more covert and quiet, too. Basically, it works!"

The Department received a grant from the Department of Criminal Justice to implement a Citizens Police Academy which would begin in September.

"The goal of this academy is to enhance the relationship between the police department and the community, resulting in a better understanding of what the community can expect from the officers who serve them and the service they can provide," stated Dad.

The academy met on Thursdays from 6:30 to 9 p.m. for 12 weeks, beginning Sept. 16. An application process was followed in selecting participants who must be at least 18 years of age, live or work in the town and have no felony or Class One Misdemeanor convictions.

"The Citizens Academy is designed to give citizens an overview of the police department's function and operational procedures," the chief continued. "The curriculum and teaching methods are similar to the traditional police academy. However, the weekly sessions are not designed to train the participant as a police officer. Citizens will have the opportunity to ask questions, discuss issues and participate in some of the things officers do as part of their job."

Department personnel, other law enforcement personnel and representatives from the Commonwealth's Attorney's office brought a wide variety of skills, training and experience as instructors for the classes.

On Friday, August 20, 1999, American Electric Power donated an electric ZAP Smith & Wesson "tactical" bicycle to the department's bike patrol. The $2,000 vehicle is a durable mountain bike that has been modified to provide the performance and reliability necessary for police work, according to Joe Weddle, AEP's Pulaski District manager, who presented the bike to my dad. The bicycle was equipped with halogen lights, a siren and a two-speed electric motor which was powered by a recyclable 12-volt lead acid battery.

"I believe this contribution is particularly fitting for AEP, since the bike features a useful electric technology," said Weddle, also a member of Pulaski Town Council.

"This is a great opportunity for us to play an active, positive role in our community," Dad said. "This is a welcome addition to our bike patrol unit. It is the nicest bike we have. It is top of the line."

"There are positive things going on in the police department," Dad told Pulaski Town Council on September 7, 1999, mentioning the recent grant received from the Community Oriented Policing Services (COPS) School Based Partnership Program (SBP).

Pulaski received a federal grant of $121,512, the highest amount throughout the state. The grant will help law enforcement agencies to curb school violence. Dad also introduced new officers to council. They include Betty East, Heath Haug, Kirk Hendricks, Ryan Hite, Lori Hughes, Barbara Owens, Michael Rose, Mark Russo and Mike Weiss.

The Transportation Safety Commission met with the Town of Pulaski Police Department yesterday to discuss issues ranging from the growing incidents relating to the drug called Oxycotin to the need for police cars. Dad represented the police department along with Lt. Barry Buckner, Lt. E.R. Barr and Sgt. J.F. Leeper. Lt. Barr said the department is in need of newer cars. There are a total of 25 cars in the current fleet, but some cars have over 100,000 miles. There is only enough money for one new car in the budget. Lt. Barr told the committee they are looking into options including, a leasing program which will provide the "same cars for the same money."

Cooley informed the committee that the department is undergoing a burden of taking suspects to the regional jail in Dublin. He said it was eight miles out of the town's jurisdiction which often caused these officers to be tied up from 30 minutes to two hours in Dublin. The department considered using "video magistrate." The officers could bring a suspect to a designated room in the municipal building and speak to the magistrate over the phone rather than driving to Dublin. Officers will then only need to go to Dublin to take those suspects who are to be incarcerated. Dad said it would save a lot of time.

Sgt. Leeper was the head of drug enforcement, but Dad spoke on his behalf stating that drug trafficking has increased. He said crack cocaine had arrived strongly, but a drug known as Oxycotin was becoming a bigger problem as well. Oxycotin is a pain killer that was used for serious cancer patients. He said it is very addictive and that the narcotics department has 40 to 50 targets, but it takes time.

Dad said the state and sheriff's offices were working closely with them to fight the drug problems. The police department was also interested in enforcing a contract for new officers who were trained by the town. He added that it was often that a new officer will be trained by the town, but will leave soon after.

"The problem with this is the town's money is spent on these officers' training. If a contract is installed, an officer will be obligated to serve the town for three years," Dad explained. "It will protect the town and ourselves,"

Town attorney Randy Eley researched the details of such a contract. The police department and the town discussed using part of the School Base Partnership Grant to purchase Geographic Information Systems. It is a Q&A computer program that includes street maps, water mains, crime areas and much more. Dad said the police department would use it to track assaults, but it can be used for maintenance, fire hydrants and can even tell the grade of a kind of hill.

"It's use is basically unlimited," he said. "The school resource officer program is for teachers and students to create an environment conducive to learning."

The program received excellent comments from students and teachers alike. Although Dad did not suspect Y2K to be a problem, he assured the committee the entire department would be on call from Dec. 28 through Jan. 4. He suggested that residents not withdraw all their money and keep it at home. They do suspect robberies will take place due to the talk of such actions. The police department suggests improving the condition of the municipal building with minor remodeling. Dad said the department was looking into renting some space at Meadowview Apartments for office space, community policing and a way to bring more security to the area. The police department agreed to meet with the safety committee quarterly, but requested additional meetings when needed.

"I'd like to confess my appreciation for being the guinea pigs and being the charter members of the Pulaski Citizens' Police Academy," Dad said to the graduates of the town's first Citizens' Police Academy on December 15, 1999. "There were 11 citizens total who participated in this 12-week academy where they learned the hows and whys of the police department. I'd like to thank these folks for taking an interest in their town and the police department."

\* \* \* \* \* \* \* \*

Acting on information that proved to be false, Pulaski Police Department raided a southwest town residence on May 22, 2000.

"We acted on information we felt was true and had a search warrant when the 4 a.m. raid was made. After finding nothing the informant told them about, police questioned the individual who confessed he had lied. There is a separate investigation underway," Dad said. "Information received previously from this person had proved correct and beneficial to investigators. We have apologized to the couple and will replace or repair the door damaged when the raid occurred. Officers were not at a wrong address. We were at the address given. The information was erroneous."

On August 22, 2000, Dad announced that he was resigning his position as the Chief of Police for the Town of Pulaski and accepted the same position with the Town of Vinton after six years. In that time, many changes had taken place. Equipment in the police department had been upgraded, the department has been completely computerized, a physical assessment program that had recently been implemented for officers and the accreditation process, which was close to being complete.

Although he would be supervising fewer officers, Dad felt that the move is an important stepping stone in his career.

"I only have about six more years to work before I retire," he said. "I think this is a great career move because I will be able to spend these next six years supervising a smaller department but making more money."

When Dad came to Pulaski Police Department in 1994, there was only one computer in the entire department located in the dispatch office. By his departure, there was at least one computer in every office along with five computers at the dispatch station. This allows every officer at the department to have access to inter-departmental e-mail, internet services, and the incident based reporting system. Dad had implemented community policing programs and initiated neighborhood watch and advisory groups throughout the town. He encouraged his officers to attend extensive training seminars and now has a total of 19 officers at the department who are general instructors for Virginia's Department of Criminal Justice Services. Dad also acquired at least nine positions through state grants. These positions have added many new programs to the department. Under his command, a regulated physical assessment program for new officers had been established, the pistol range had been rebuilt by officers and members of the National Guard and

Marines, and the state accreditation process was near completion. One of the programs that Dad was proudest of implementing during his career is the Citizens Police Academy. The citizen's academy allows local citizens, who are chosen by application, to participate in training similar to classes received by recruits at the Police Academy. This course, which continues for 12 weeks, provides an opportunity for citizens to study radar and traffic enforcement laws and train on a firearms simulator. The first Citizens Academy was conducted in the spring of 1999 and was a great success, graduating 12 local residents.

Lori Meredith/SWT

**Pulaski Police Chief Herb Cooley assists Officer Chad Davis with a report. Cooley's last day is Sept. 1.**

*The Southwest Times* saluted Dad on September 3, 2000 in an editorial.

"Another one of our community's leaders has bid us goodbye," it read. "After six years as chief of police for the Town of Pulaski, Herb Cooley left last week to take on that same title for the Town of Vinton. It's a smaller department with fewer people to manage, a situation Cooley said was too attractive for him to pass up. His departure comes as somewhat of a surprise. The Vinton Town Council had already hired him before he ever said a word publicly that he was thinking about leaving. That is his right and we can't fault him for that. Decisions such as this are best made swiftly, and we wish him well at his newest challenge. Though his tenure here was relatively short, much of his work will be long remembered. For example, he helped bring our police department into the "cyber" age by procuring more computers for officer and staff use. Cooley has also been instrumental in helping the department pursue various grants, such as the one which will pay for new officers to specifically patrol two area apartment complexes. He's also found enough grant money to create at least nine officer positions within his department. The program of many Cooley is most proud are those he implemented with regard to community policing. He helped organize the Citizens Police Academy, which allows residents to apply to participate in training similar to classes attended by recruits at the Police Academy. Along this same thread, Cooley also helped organize police advisory groups and neighborhood watch programs throughout town. There are other, more physical accomplishments: the new shooting range, new physical assessment program, but the intangible relationships Cooley worked to build between officers and the people they serve will be the legacy he leaves behind. Our town has its share of crime and troublemakers, but for some time we have been blessed to live without major tragedies or confrontations. The shootout involving officers last month was an aberration, not the rule, amidst the peace we now enjoy. Cooley can take credit for that, too. He obviously did not create the peace, but he worked and managed his department in a way which arguably inspired it and fed its growth. Our town council is now busy at work to find someone to fill Cooley's shoes. Capt. E.T. Montgomery, a career officer, has been chosen to fill as interim chief until a new chief is hired. We thank Chief Cooley for the work he has done for the community and wish him well in his new endeavor. He will be missed."

## Chapter 20
## A New Tenacious Leader

Andy Corbin came to work at the Vinton Police Department in 1979, having established a long tenure there before Dad arrived on the scene. His first day on the job was a bit troublesome. On September 5, 2000, Town Council had called a meeting to introduce the new police chief. Dad was on the way and had a flat tire or some other vehicle problem. He called to explain his delay and the Town Manager went and provided transportation to the meeting. While some might view this as an omen, Dad just laughed it off.

Andy said that if he had to use one word to describe Dad as a supervisor, that word would be "fair". He was clear to clarify that he meant the term not be used not in the sense of being mediocre. By giving employees the benefit of the doubt and working with them to resolve a problem rather than using supervisory intimidation as a corrective tool, Dad was anything but mediocre.

The veteran cop said he learned a lot from Dad including tenacity as well as the constant desire to strive for improvement for the department as well as an individual.

"Most problems do not arise overnight, nor are they resolved overnight," Andy stated. "One of the things he implemented early on was sending his senior supervisors to higher level advanced management training such as the Institute for Leadership in Changing Times, an intense week of training at Virginia Tech which involved a team project and an individual project at the end."

As fair as Dad may have been, he had zero tolerance for lying, maintaining a constant sense of honesty and integrity.

"I have quipped in the past you could probably get away with murder and still keep your job as long as you didn't lie about it to him," he jested. "That was a bit extreme, but in reality, you could do something really stupid and still keep your job."

"We can forgive mistakes of the head," he would always say to his employees. "We cannot forgive mistakes of the heart."

"If you just did something stupid but were honest, you were OK," Andy said of Dad's tactics as a supervisor. "If you did something you knew was wrong deliberately and then tried to cover it up, you were gone."

On one occasion, Andy recalls working on a car in the Sally Bay, a garage type part of the police department building where cars could pull in to bring prisoners. As he finished with the car, Andy was backing it out and got too close to the door edge and put a small dent and scrape on the paint.

"Well I just did something stupid," he admitted to Dad immediately afterwards.

"Don't worry about it," he said after coming out to review the damage, never bringing up the issue again. "These things happen."

On another occasion, Andy was walking past Dad's office one day and he called him in.

"Andrew," Dad inquired as he read a name from his computer. "Do you know this fellow?"

"Yes, sir, I gave him a Fast Driving Award the other day," he said referring to a speeding ticket.

"Well, he sent me an email and complained that you were gruff," Dad informed him.

"Yes sir, I probably was gruff," admitted Andy. "He started off with an attitude with me and I let him know in no uncertain terms I wasn't going to put up with it. I didn't use any profanity or conduct myself inappropriately, but I wasn't going to put up with his attitude."

Dad paused for a moment, raised his trademark eyebrow and looked at him.

"You know," he said. "Sometimes I expect an old master sergeant to be gruff".

Andy never heard any more from that complaint.

Another time, Dad was walking down the hall outside an office Andy shared with Lt. Jimmy Houff.

"Houff and I have known each other from the beginning and I do mean the beginning," he explained. "Jimmy and I went through the Academy together. After we graduated, we never worked together on a shift but we shared the same patrol car. Often times I would get the keys from him as he was getting off duty or vice versa. Jimmy would always move the seat up to reach the gas and brake pedals. I would move it back so I didn't bang my knees on the steering wheel getting in and out. This ritual evolved into a quasi contentious relationship where we would release a verbal diatribe against the other. This 'ritual' continues, even to this day in our retirement and ride motorcycles."

Dad heard the ruckus and poked his head in the door.

"Is there a problem in here?" he asked.

"No Chief," the both replied. "We have been going at it like this for 20 years."

He paused for a moment, didn't say anything and continued walking down the hallway.

"I think I saw him just shaking his head back and forth," Andy recalled.

"Well, if these guys have been going at it like this for 20 years, there's probably some things a Chief should just leave alone," he suspected Dad of thinking.

"Herb Cooley was never content with the status quo," Andy said of my father. "He was constantly striving for better.

When Dad arrived on the scene at the Vinton Police Department, they only had four marked cars used by patrol and two unmarked cars used by the Investigators. These cars pretty much stayed on the road and operating

24/7/365. The life expectancy was about two years for a patrol car and at the end of that two years, that car was pretty worn out.

"I presume after his flat tire was fixed," Andy joked. "Chief started building up the fleet, gradually, which really relieved a lot of the pressure when a car needed to be in the shop for repairs. It also made it easier during events such as parades in covering intersections."

Andy explained that the life expectancy of a patrol car went from 2 years to about 10 years or more after my father began leading the force.

As cars eventually became individually assigned, the officers were also individually accountable for its condition, cleanliness, maintenance, and equipment.

"The Chief didn't simply go to Town Council and say that we needed more cars," he added. "He researched it, documented it, and made a case that a vehicle program of cars assigned to individuals was cheaper in the long run than a pool of cars where no one knew who was responsible for something missing or wrong with the car."

He also credited Dad with raising the bar for the department.

"Pay was woefully behind other agencies in the area and the Vinton Police Department was pretty much a stepping stone to other departments in the area," Andy told me. "Again, he did his homework and showed council how much it costs to train a new officer, and when that officer can actually start producing. It was just not cost effective to send a new recruit through the academy, complete field training and at the point where they were starting to become proficient would leave for another agency."

"Previous pay studies were based on comparison of the Vinton Police Department with other agencies of similar size," he added. "These comparisons were not accurate because employees were not leaving the Vinton Police

Department to work there. Our competition was other local agencies that were paying more."

Andy said with certainty that Dad departed with a legacy of honor and respect from other police agencies, public he served, and internally of fellow employees.

"There is no tolerance for any racial, ethnic or religious bigotry," Andy recalls Dad saying at the very beginning of his tenure in Vinton.

This was not a problem that needed to be fixed at the Vinton Police Department, but Dad drew that line in the sand and there was no doubt that anyone who crossed it would be dismissed.

"When he walked out of the Police Department for the last time, he left a neat, tidy, well run professional law enforcement agency," Andy said. "When the replacement Chief was selected, I was not part of his department plan and thus, lost touch with the internal dynamics. I have not heard anything negative or derogatory about the department since then. We now have a new Chief who took command when Herb Cooley's replacement moved on to another position."

One of the things Dad started, just as he had in Pulaski, was the Vinton Citizens Police Academy. It was a big hit with those who attended. One local businessman attended at least two of them and maybe more. He became a staunch ally of the police department.

"I remember at one Academy graduation, this fellow was speaking about his experience and was talking about your Dad," Andy recalled. "He recounted your Dad's past with the Coast Guard, High Point Police, Wythe County Sheriff's Office, Pulaski Police, and finally Vinton.

"Seems like Chief Cooley just can't hold on to a job," he commented finally.

"This, of course, brought lots of laughs, especially from your Dad," Andy told me. "As far as I know, the Citizens Academy is still going on."

One of the elements of Dad's persona that was most endeared him to his Vinton officer was his sense of humor.

He loved a good laugh. One day, Andy was patrolling when an officer received a call on two intoxicated males going into businesses pan handling for money. An officer, Jimmy Roberts, located the two nearby. Roberts, who now is a Captain in Manassas Park, Virginia Police Department, is a slightly tall, skinny fellow with a lank build characterized as pretty laid back in his demeanor.

"I was close and went to back him up," Andy recalled. "When I arrived, I activated my in car camera just out of habit. The weather was fairly comfortable, not too cold or hot, but the wind was very blustery. I recognized both of the males as frequent fliers with us."

Roberts started checking them for intoxication having on walk a straight line. As the guy was walking, a gust of wind caught his hat, blew it in the air in a perfect arch towards Officer Roberts who never flinched, moved or removed his gaze from the guy. He simply lifted his hand into the air, caught the hat and gave it back to the guy.

"My words don't do the situation justice but the video was hilarious to watch. I got back to the station, removed the tape and played it back for others to watch," Andy told me.

Dad was in his office working on something. Perhaps it was a budget or some other type of report when Andy went into to his office and asked him if he wanted to see something funny.

"When I played the tape for him he started laughing so hard I thought I was going to have to call EMS for him," Andy told me.

Dad was always looking out for the troops to bolster morale of his Vinton crew. One of his efforts in the direction was the annual awards banquet, a program he also founded in Pulaski. It is unknown they still exist in either place. Another thing he did was to initiate incentive pay, which based your grade of pay by your level of education via a point system. For example, if an employee had an associate's degree he/she got a certain number of points. More points were warranted for a bachelors degree and more still for a masters degree. An employee could also get points for certain skills and certifications such as Breathalyzer Operator, Bicycle officer, academy instructor as well as completion of ILCT, Forensic Academy programs.

 "In other words, the more valuable you were to the department, the more you got paid," Andy explained in closing. "There was direct palpable incentive to grow and learn."

 "It was a pleasure and honor to serve for your dad, Chief Cooley," Jimmy Houff told me. "He was a great Chief to work for. He treated me with respect and professionalism. I am very proud to have Herb Cooley as my Chief and honored to have him as a friend."

 Jimmy first met Dad when he was hired to be Chief of Police for the Town of Vinton in late August of 2000. The Vinton Police Department had been through some trying times with a Virginia State Police Investigation. According to Jimmy, Dad took over a department that had begun its recovery under Interim Chief Dave Edwards.

 "I was a Master Sergeant in charge of 2 platoons," he explained. "I was immediately impressed by his demeanor and professionalism. Chief Cooley's wisdom and experience

had an immediate effect on the department."

 At that time, department morale was low and officers were leaving for other jobs. Dad assessed the department's needs and formed a master plan of goals and objectives.

 "He was not a micro manager as he allowed supervisors to do their jobs which had not always been the case," Jimmy explained. "Chief Cooley improved communications within the department and would allow officer and supervisor input in department activities. I learned to be a leader and not just a supervisor. Chief Cooley led by example. I also learned that Chief Cooley loved law enforcement work as he dedicated his whole life to serve the community."

Jimmy had pickup truck and helped Dad move a couple of times. In all of his wisdom and knowledge, he noted that Dad had cheap taste in beer.

"Natural Light," Jimmy quibbled. "Really, Chief?"

Jimmy was also acquainted with Dad's less than masterful driving skills.

"If you rode with the Chief, you did so at your own risk," he said.

"Chief Cooley strongly believed in Accreditation and pushed hard for the department maintain and achieved State Accreditation," Jimmy added on a more serious note. "This contributed to the advancement of the department's standards, professionalism, and training."

Dad also believed in community policing and was involved in several community organizations. He was instrumental in creating the Vinton Citizens Police Academy, a partnership developed with the Vinton Area Chamber of Commerce.

"To be honest, the Chief that succeeded Chief Cooley was not of the same quality as Chief Cooley and the department is not what it once was," Jimmy admitted in closing. "Chief Cooley's legacy will always exist with the men and women that had the opportunity to work for him."

Sharon Poff was Dad's secretary for much of his Vinton tenure. She was Dad's right arm and through her sense of humor and gregarious personality, became part of our extended family. She was also a great maker of éclair cake, a dessert she would always send home to us on our birthdays. To my dad, there was no one like Sharon. No one could do what she did. She set the bar in terms of secretaries.

Already maintaining a long history with the department, Sharon knew the department needed maturity and was glad to hear that Dad, 57, was coming to lead it.

In name alone, Sharon was reminded of the jingle for Coolie fruit drinks, which were popular in the 1970s.

"We were a young department and needed guidance," she told me. "Your dad gave us that in abundance."

"He was a great thinker," she added. "I imagined his face on that famous sculpture."

Probably Dad's greatest achievement while in Vinton was his acquiring state accreditation for the department, an achievement succeeded by very few police agencies within the state of Virginia.

"It is a very hard thing to achieve and at times, it was painful because it required so much work," Sharon recalled with a laugh. "Basically, just because you had a set of rules and regulations in print didn't mean you were good enough. You had to be abiding by those rules and your Dad made sure that was true of the Vinton Police Department."

"He should have been a professor," Sharon said in retrospect. "He loved stuff like that."

She recalled one particular incident regarding the administrative rules and regulations, in which Sharon and Jimmy Houff and snuck in the declaration that staff members should get a 15-minute nap during the work day, an idea they had gotten from a recent *Parade* magazine article.

"He was going through and signing all these papers and when he signed that one, we got the biggest charge out of it," she said. "Of course, we let him in on the joke and though he probably could have killed us, he had a good laugh about it."

"He commanded obedience and respect and we gave that to him," she added on a serious note. "He trusted us to do our job correctly and we trusted him to lead us."

Sharon noted that Dad was a perfectionist when it came to his job and that, under his leadership, the department acquired benefits that would have never been attained otherwise.

"He knew what he wanted and how he liked things and I tried to stay a step ahead of him and have things ready before he got there," she told me. "I was there to keep the boys calm, but he ran the department and did a super job."

She also mentioned Dad's getting a fleet of vehicles for the department as well as new uniforms and many other improvements for the department.

"He knew what was good for us and had a great knowledge of grants that were out there to help us get these things," she added. "We were happy to do whatever he asked of because we were simply excited to know that improvements were out there."

Sharon also added that Dad worked well with organizations such as the Vinton Town Council in explaining why certain improvements for the police department would also prove to be of equal benefit to the town.

"It's takes a certain kind of verbiage to get the money flowing, but he knew that and he did the walk and talk that they wanted," she told me. "He could hit my grammar with a hammer!"

"He liked to be fed and liked sweets whether he admits it or not," Sharon said in closing. "He also has a great appetite for life."

Dad and Kip Vickers worked together for a number of years. As brother of current Wythe County Sheriff Keith Dunagan, Kip and Dad go way back.

"I first met Herb at the Wythe County Sheriff's Office," he explained to me. "I was applying for a job soon after my end of tour in the military at the sheriff's office that would require me to do a one year undercover narcotics operation and Herb interviewed me. He soon left to take the job as Chief in Pulaski and I actually interviewed for an opening there but was not hired. I reminded him of that often at our years in Vinton."

Dad was at Vinton as the newly hired Chief when he created the position of Captain and Kip ultimately applied and was hired to be his Assistant Chief of Police.

"Herb was a very laid back supervisor who allowed you to express and implement your ideas, but when I say 'laid back,' you also knew who was in charge when the situated dictated," he recalled. "I think he truly believed he was only as good as the people around him as he often said and was very discerning on who he hired and retained."

Kip said he learned a great deal from Dad as an administrator, too many things to mention, in fact. However, he recalling two mottos that he often used. When Kip eventually left the Vinton Police Department to head up the Cardinal Criminal Justice Academy in Salem, he abided by Dad's two most famous adages which were "We can forgive mistakes of the mind, but not the heart" and "Find a place for everyone where they can excel." That latter motto is one Kip says he implements in his own administrative tactics to this day.

"Not everyone is a great cop but most are good people and could be useful in some capacity," Kip said. "Herb was big on training."

One of the texts he used was book called *Good to Great.* The book researched numerous successful organizations and developed a list of common traits about the leaders in these organizations and one of the main conclusions was to get the right people on the bus and get them in the right seats.

"I thought Herb had been preaching that to me for years," Kip stated.

He also tragically recalled a terrible accident that involved a fellow on-duty officer, which resulted in the tragic death of two elderly females in the community.

"I just remember the way your dad took the whole situation head on and dealt with all sides involved," Kip noted somberly. "While there was outrage in the community, he had established a liaison to reach out to those families affected on the police and the civilian sides. There was so much that could have gone wrong in that scenario but by reaching out to all involved and the situation was squalled. The community as a whole was sort of held together by the actions of your father. I attended the funeral of these two women with your Dad and it was a very emotional hard time for us both."

According to Kip, some of Dad's greatest accomplishments while leading the Vinton police included acquiring the State Accreditation, creating a business blitz that assigned an officer to each business, K-9 unit, increasing patrol officers, providing cars for his officers to take home, raising to comparably levels as other agencies in the Roanoke Valley, and most importantly, creating a sense of professionalism throughout the department.

"Herb took not only a dying department but a struggling community and brought them together it was great to be a part of I will always look at those days in my career fondly," Kip said in closing. "His legacy will always be remembered."

While my Dad was missing holidays, birthdays and weekends, my Dad was busy being one of the most prominent figures in Virginia law enforcement with his groundbreaking achievements. During his 11-year Vinton tenure alone, my Dad led the department achieving accreditation through the Virginia Law Enforcement Standards Commission, $1.8 million of grant funds, and established business blitz and biking programs as well as the citizens police academy. He also oversaw the merger of the Vinton and Roanoke County Emergency Control Center and developed employee recognition through an annual awards banquet, an event he also initiated as Pulaski Police Chief. These were just a few of the accomplishments listed by Captain Ben Cook, who succeeded my father as interim police chief on July 1 and served as emcee for the banquet.

"Herb Cooley has not only been our chief, but a resource, mentor, father figure and close friend," Cook stated. "He has inspired us to be good officers and leaders and we will always try to maintain character, competence and commitment, the three characteristics he looks for in a police officer."

Fellow Chiefs of Police from Salem, Pulaski, Virginia Western Community College and Monroe, NC were on hand to honor my father as were officers from Roanoke City Police Department, Virginia State Police, High Point Police Department, Department of Criminal Justice Services, and US Attorney's Office. Several officers from the Vinton Police Department as well as Vinton Town Council also spoke, including Mayor Brad Grose and Town Manager Chris Lawrence.

"During his tenure, Chief Cooley elevated the level of professionalism in our police department, established respect for our department with other police agencies in the valley as well as with our citizens, and increased police department interaction within our community," said Grose.

Dad and Mayor Grose (right) presented an award to Karla Turman, daughter of Dad's late friend Cliff Dicker.
"

The level of professionalism Chief Cooley brings to the table is remarkable," said Lawrence. He has been a real asset to the town."

Chief Debra Duncan of Monroe, NC traveled more than four hours to pay tribute to my father. Having joined the High Point Police Department in 1980 just as my dad left for Wythe County, they became dear friends when she was named Virginia Tech police chief.

"Herb was a mentor who taught me that although you can't save the world, but you can never underestimate the impact you have as an officer in the lives of other," Duncan stated. "He also taught me to slow down and enjoy the most important elements of life, such as family, and not to be consumed by work."

It was my dad's lifelong friend and field training officer, Bill Collins, whose tearful speech choked us all up. Having got my dad his first police job as a beat cop in 1966 in High Point, NC, they have been friends for more than 60 years.

"I've known him longer than anyone here," he said. "I've followed his career all the way and consider him a great man, a fine officer and a good friend."

Blue Ridge Catering offered an excellent meal and my dad's wonderful secretary, April Alterio, did a great job of coordinating this surprisingly lavish affair. Sgt. Jimmy Testerman made an incredible slideshow, which featured pictures of my dad throughout his life that brought back wonderful memories. Many of them, however, I had never see before and was delighted to observe for the first time, such as photos of my dad in the U.S. Coast Guard and school pictures like the Galax Chapter of Future Farmers of America in 1957. This was a great showcase, so much so that I didn't take my eyes off the screen to enjoy my dinner until the first loop was complete.

Of all the agencies that came from far and wide to honor my father, I was sorely disappointed to see no representation from the Wythe County Sheriff's Office, where my father worked for a third of his career. He considers his Wythe County tenure among his most memorable. Some of my happiest memories with my dad are going to work with him there and being treated like family by the Wythe County Sheriff's Office. Considering his long dedication to the law enforcement and community organizations of Wythe County, I felt a disappointing letdown in my community that I've never experienced before.

After I published my thoughts, Dad came home a few days later, saying he had just come from the Wythe County Sheriff's Office where a pinto bean and cornbread dinner had been held in his honor. I was pleased to hear this.

"How about a Wythe County Sheriff's Office watch?" he said placing it on my wrist.

"But they gave it to you," I replied. "I don't want to take your gift."

"Why not?" he said. "You earned it."

I still have it among most treasured mementos.

That being said, I was overwhelmingly touched that, of the 92 attendees and 14 speakers, some came from as far away as Monroe, NC, to wish my father well. Everyone said remarkably kind things, all of which he undoubtedly deserves. I know it meant a great deal to him as it did to all of us. I want to personally thank the Vinton Police Department for giving my Dad such a lavish sendoff. Of course, most importantly, I want to say how proud I am of my father. My mother, sister, wife and I all love him very much and are proud to call him family.

Epilogue:
Life After Retirement

In March 2013, my uncle Mike Cooley was healthy. He celebrated his 63rd birthday on August 25th only to discover within days that he had inoperable, incurable and untreatable pancreatic cancer. Just like that, he knew his life would soon be over. Both of his parents died in the same way within two weeks of their diagnosis. Mike held on for three months, departing this world on November 18. This was a devastating blow for our entire family. To say that only the good die young is certainly the truth in Mike's case. He was certainly the most humble member of his family as well as the most jovial. His personality rubbed off on everyone he encountered. That was evident from the number of co-workers who travelled from as far as Gastonia, NC, just to honor Mike.

As a master's degree graduate of East Tennessee State University, Mike worked for nearly 30 years as manager of Parkdale Mills textile plants in Hillsville and Sparta, NC, where he was instrumental in turning a small corporation into one of the most successful distributers of textiles in the world. Shortly before his diagnosis, he sent me a petition he had worked up to be sent to the White House in an effort to help save jobs in his industry nationwide. He was a hard worker right up until the end, but more importantly, he was remembered by his employees as the most compassionate, witty, intelligent and fair boss they had ever known.

"When we found out Mike was sick, I went over to let Mike know that the company would take care of his needs and to encourage him," a Parkdale representative said at his funeral. "Instead, in talking about his faith and outlook on life, he encouraged me."

That was indeed the type of person my uncle Mike was.

"He was always worried about everybody else," my cousin Chase, Mike's only son, said to me in tears as we left the cemetery. "He never focused on himself."

My heart especially broke for him as well as my dad, who had seen his parents die the same way, followed by his younger brother.

I am proud to say that Mike and I were very close. He was my favorite uncle as well as a wonderful confidante and friend. I spent many weekends with him at his home in Galax, which had belonged to my grandparents during my teenage years. Those are the memories to which I cling now. He and my aunt Joy had a playhouse built over their cellar, where my sister would spend her visits. Joy would go up to play with my sister there, while Mike and I stayed in the main house. I can't tell you how many wonderful talks and laughs we would have over a bowl of Breyer's vanilla ice cream topped with Hershey's syrup, but I never eat ice cream when those times don't come to mind. Mike was very gentle, understanding and was always very easy to talk to about anything. No subject was too awkward or uncomfortable for him. He never imposed advice, but was always an intense listener. He was soft spoken, but had a wicked sense of humor that only those closest to him were privileged to know. He was always even-tempered. I might have seen him angry, but never heard him shout or use foul language. He was never afraid to express affection to those he loved or talk about his deep faith in God. He was not afraid to cry in front of you if something had upset him.

We stayed with them so often at one point that Mike compared his life to the sitcom, *Married with Children*.

"Instead of being married with children," he joked to his wife. "We're married with other people's children."

Mike also was known for looking exactly like my dad. Every time he visited us in Wytheville, someone would mistake him for my father. It had happened so many times that Mike eventually stopped correcting people. As he was

343

walking down the hall during my high school graduation, someone came up to him with a smile.

"Hey, Herb," they said. "How are you doing?"

"I'm doing fine," Mike replied, laughing to himself as he continued on his way.

I was blessed to get to speak with Mike for the last time over the phone about a month before he died. He had just returned home from the hospital and had called to congratulate Emily and me on the news of our first baby. He told me he was proud of me and loved me and I was able to return those sentiments wholeheartedly.

"I hope you already knew this," I told him. "But you've always been my favorite uncle."

"Well," he said with a chuckle. "I was hoping."

I can only pray now that time and distance hadn't made him ever doubt that.

During the entire process, I was so focused on trying to be there for my dad that I hadn't dealt with my own grief. His funeral was one of the toughest I've ever endured. While I sat through the heart-wrenching songs and video slideshow, I was overcome when I touched the casket as it went by. That was my brief personal moment to say goodbye to my favorite uncle and I could hardly bear it.

I don't typically like to talk about funeral homes, but Twin County Funerals in Galax has to be the nicest of such places I have ever encountered. Overall, they gave Mike the wonderful service he deserved and I was exceptionally impressed with the respect, courtesy, patience and organization offered by the staff. I have never been to a funeral home where the attendant personally brought you tissues. Small gestures such as this never go unnoticed or underappreciated with me, especially after Vaughn-Gwynn Funeral Home left me out of the procession to my great-aunt's graveside service, causing me to miss it back in January. Incidentally, that was the last time I saw Mike in person. At any rate, I am most appreciative and grateful to

Twin County Funerals for their first-rate service to our
family.

In closing, it is very hard to sum up my feelings about
Mike in just a couple of sentences. He was a rare kind of
good guy who left us much too suddenly and soon. His
battle with cancer was strong, courageous and selfless, just
like he was. He will be loved and miss every day.

\* \* \* \* \* \* \* \* \* \*

The moment Isabella Marie Cooley was born was
singularly the most frightening and purely happiest of her
parents' lives. After 14 hours of labor, Emily had only
dilated half way and Bella's heart rate was progressively
increasing. We had to move quickly. Emily was rushed into
the operating room for a Caesarian section. My mother
dressed me quickly in a set of scrubs so that I could join my
wife at the operating table.

The surgery began sharply at 9 p.m. Though I didn't dare look beyond the paper curtain that separated Emily's head from her stomach, I could feel the doctors tugging at her lower half as I held her hand in my best effort to comfort her.

Four mentions later, I heard a male voice in the room call out "21:04."

As I knew he was announcing the official time of my daughter's birth, I shouted it back with excitement to my wife. I knew she had made it. Then, in the same instant, we heard the faint cry of the beautiful human being our true love had created. We both cried with overwhelming joy and relief. May 27, 2014 at 9:04 p.m. was the single greatest moment of both our lives.

I saw her extracted from my wife's stomach, covered with her mother's blood, and I didn't even flinch. I had just caught the first glimpse of my daughter and reported to Emily what I saw.

"Honey," I said through joyful tears. "She has dark hair."

Mike, the nurse anesthetist, let me watch as they cleaned her up. He was a super nice guy whom I will never forget and I told him so. Later, after I was sent to the nursery with Bella, he stroked my wife's head and was so reassuring to her after she was sick during surgery.

Speaking of kind, the nurses at the Wythe County Community Hospital Women's Center were beyond awesome. Crystal, Misty, Jess, Tabitha, Nikki and Casey were unequivocally the best nurses I have ever seen. They were not only attentive and caring toward Emily and Bella, they were even superbly accommodating to me as well as our extended family.

As breastfeeding was important to Emily, Lou Ann, a lactation consultant was sent in to set her mind at ease, which she did brilliantly. It was a difficult task to master, but I was certain Emily and Bella would get there together.

Emily and I had a special rapport with Crystal in particular, so much so that she came to visit us of her day off just to meet Bella. Mike came to see us, too, which deeply touched us both.

Rhonda Charr, who was my nurse during a hospital stay in 1991 when I was six years old, serves as director of the Women's Center. She helped make us both comfortable and satisfied. They even provided us with a steak dinner while the baby went to the nursery. Given my cerebral palsy, I especially appreciated Misty who assisted me with my own personal needs in the middle of the night with the utmost grace and comfort.

Aside from these wonderful ladies, my caretaker, Jodi Shirk, went her usual extra mile to help us in every way. It is because of her that so many elements of this process were executed successfully. I literally don't think that I could have survived this process without her. She has been an ultimate godsend in our lives whose efficiency and selflessness are unparalleled. Her son, Zack Hatfield, who is like a brother to both Emily and me, was also present after Bella was born.

We have two wonderful sets of parents who have been an incredible sense of support for us. The same could be said for our siblings and their spouses, who are collectively the greatest family we could ever ask for. Emily's sister, Karen, was a particularly huge help to us, staying with us both in the hospital and the night before Emily was admitted.

At any rate, as I headed back to the nursery with Bella, I discovered she was seven pounds and fifteen and a half ounces and was twenty inches long. She was a perfectly healthy baby and the most beautiful little girl I had ever seen. I had asked the hospital pediatrician, Dr. Matthew Aney, if there was any chance she had cerebral palsy. Even though I knew my birth affliction was not genetic, it was something that worried me deeply. I prayed that my child would never have to endure the disability I have.

"Absolutely no brain damage," he reassured me. "She looks great."

There was a slight problem with the meconium, the product of the baby's firs stool, being ingested into her lungs. This would, thankfully, clear up within the next day. Otherwise, she was the picture of health. With that, the doctor opened the window to the nursery and both of our mothers were the first two up to the window. As sweet of a picture as I know it was for them, it couldn't have been sweeter from the other side. My heart melted as I saw both of Bella's grandmothers crying in the window with a beaming smile as they looked down at her. My mother then turned to Jodi as if the realization of her first grandchild has suddenly hit her like an epiphany.

"I'm a grandma," she said profoundly as tears poured down her face.

Seeing both of my parents hold her for the first time was one of the most gratifying experiences of my life. Seeing my sister hold her as she slept for over an hour was equally as amazing. My sister was the first experience I ever had with a baby and I've wanted one of my own ever since.

Bella and her Pop, Christmas Eve 2015

My dad and I have always shared a deep interest in our own family history. We have always enjoyed visiting Coal Creek Cemetery in Galax, which will likely be our resting place, where our family has been buried for generations. Just a year ago, we laid my Uncle Mike to rest there at the untimely age of 63. The earthly remains of my grandparents, Herbert and Irene Cooley, are also there. When my Granny died in 1992 when I was just seven, it was my first really big heartbreak in life. I often think about how she would have marveled over my daughter.

Being the newest Cooley, Bella and her mom accompanied my dad and me to the cemetery on October 17th as well as to an old family cemetery that houses the remains of Benjamin Cooley. Born to Englishman Abraham Cooley and Frenchwoman Sarah Reeder in New York, on August 3, 1774, Benjamin came to Grayson County at the age of twelve. His parents would live out the rest their lives in Grayson County and are unfortunately buried in unmarked graves nearby. When Carroll County was formed in 1842, 68-year old Benjamin was appointed as one of the first members of its court and elected its first-ever sheriff. That has obviously stayed in the genes, with my dad retiring in 2011 after 45 years in law enforcement, serving as Wythe County's chief deputy as well as Chief of Police in Pulaski and Vinton. Benjamin Cooley also served as the county's first commissioner of revenue before his death on March 24, 1847 at the age of 72.

Benjamin Cooley desired to travel to present-day Winston Salem, NC, where he could attain proper Moravian schooling to become a professional clockmaker. When this endeavor proved too expensive, he decided to hone his skills independently. As a result, he crafted the clock after the first one to ever exist in Grayson County, eventually inventing the wheel cutter, also known as the clockmaker's engine, which he crafted from self-wrought brass and iron. From his inventions, he crafted clocks and sold them nationwide. It is suggested through my research, although not confirmed, that the Smithsonian Institute may possess the original engine. If this is indeed the case, I'd love to make the trip to the nation's capitol to see it.

Three current generations of the Cooley family, that being my father, daughter, wife and I, travelled on October

17th to the Carroll County Museum, which is incorporated by the local historical society and stationed in the basement of the county courthouse. Nancy Morris of the Carroll County Historical Society was kind enough to let us take a generational photo with the clock, which none of us had ever seen. The magnificent 78"structure is encased in walnut and features a colorful cornucopia and harvest motif as a background. There is also a smiling moon landscape design as well as a similarly vibrant moon over a seascape background.

It was really something to think that something so majestic was crafted by one of my earliest ancestors. Such masterful craftsmanship must have stopped with my paternal grandfather who died in 1997. He could take a piece of wood and transform into a piece of art in record time. I used to love to "play school" with my Granny and he made me the most beautiful miniature teacher's desk, which I've always treasured and hope to pass on to Bella one day.

At any rate, it was a real treat to see the beautiful timepiece I had only heard about from my dad. Built in the early eighteenth century, estimated between 1810 and 1820, the clock travelled west to Missouri in a covered wagon and returned to Carroll County in the 1950s via station wagon. It was housed in the Carroll County Public Library until a couple of years ago, when the new museum opened up and it was placed among the exhibits there. Morris told me that the clock had recently been restored to working order. Unfortunately, the pendulum was being repaired on the day my family came into visit, so I didn't get to hear or see it in action.

That will just give us another reason to visit this incredibly fascinating museum. It has an incredible array of locally pertinent antiques and events. According to its website, construction for the building took place between 1872 and 1874. The facility presents the history of Carroll County and its various communities. Early Native American artifacts recovered from nearby archaeological are on display as well as a large Civil War collection including the drum used by the local unit. The courthouse was the scene of a tragic courtroom shooting in March 1912 where five were killed including the presiding judge and sheriff, making national headlines. The museum has extensive archive and reference materials in its resource section and offers tours by appointment. I was particularly gratified to see the colorful works retrieved from the lead mines in Austinville, which represents the maternal half of my ancestry, displayed directly across from the clock.

As soon as I entered the building, I noticed something very interesting about my family history. The desk at which Nancy Morris was seated belonged to my distant uncle, Alva Edison Cooley. Born in 1890 in the Coal Creek area, where our deceased relatives are laid to rest, he was Hillsville's first mayor. The 1917 University of Virginia graduate and World War I veteran practiced law in the area for 67 years and served as local VFW commander and fire chief. He also authored numerous books on religious subjects, which might explain some of my own vocational inclinations.

Zach Cooley with his wife Emily, daughter Bella, and father Herb (right) alongside the 19th century grandfather clock crafted by their ancestor, Benjamin F. Cooley, which is on display at the Carroll County Historical Society Museum.

It has always been a goal of mine to get my dad to Mt. Airy, NC to meet the sweet and beautiful Betty Lynn, known for her popular recurring role as Barney Fife on *The Andy Griffith Show*. My dad started me on all things Mayberry from a very young age. I used to go to work with my dad when he was Chief Deputy of the Wythe County Sheriff's Office and we would get home just in time to watch the rerun of *The Andy Griffith Show* at 5:30 every weekday evening on WDBJ7, which Dad always called his "training tapes."

She met my dad, who had watched her since her original debut on *The Andy Griffith Show* 55 years ago, but seemed at a loss for words for the most part. She said he was "darling."

Dad with TV star Betty Lynn (center), Emily and an unhappy Bella. Dad texted my mom to say he and Thelma Lou were headed to the county line and he would leave forwarding address for alimony. Mom still hasn't stopped laughing.

## Afterword

I have spent two years compiling the information in the preceding pages of this book. It has unquestionably been the most challenging and rewarding project of my career. To be able to research my father's exemplary career as police officer and law enforcement administrator over the past half century has been a revelation into a part of the life of my father that I never knew. I had wanted to know this aspect of my dad for a long time and now I feel that I do.

My dad was trained in leadership through working up the ranks of the High Point Police Department as well as in the public defender's office of the state of North Carolina. When he came to Wythe County, Virginia, he revamped the entire department along with Sheriff Wayne Pike. It makes me proud to know that the town in which I have chosen to raise my family was made to feel as safe as it does because of programs my dad spearheaded. Even now, he is helping keep his granddaughter safe.

As chief in Pulaski and Vinton, he worked those departments from the ground up, turning the latter into one of the few agencies in the state fully accredited by the Department of Criminal Justice. While many applaud his work, as you have read in this book, I felt he was significantly underappreciated in many cases. His 1991 loss for Clerk of Court in Wythe County and the pointless flack he received from Pulaski Town Council are prime examples of this.

While many law enforcement officers of today are on egocentric power trips, my dad was a master at getting grant money to help the communities he protected with top-notch programs at no expense to taxpayers. That's the element of Dad's career with which I was most impressed.

Presenting my father with a rough draft of the book, which came as a complete surprise to him, became the most gratifying moment of the whole process. If it never sells a copy, it will be a success in my mind for that reason alone.

356

It is my hope that those who didn't appreciate Dad as well as those who did will come to do so even more through the reading of this book. I know I have.

With sincere gratitude,

Zach Cooley
Wytheville, Virginia
November 2016